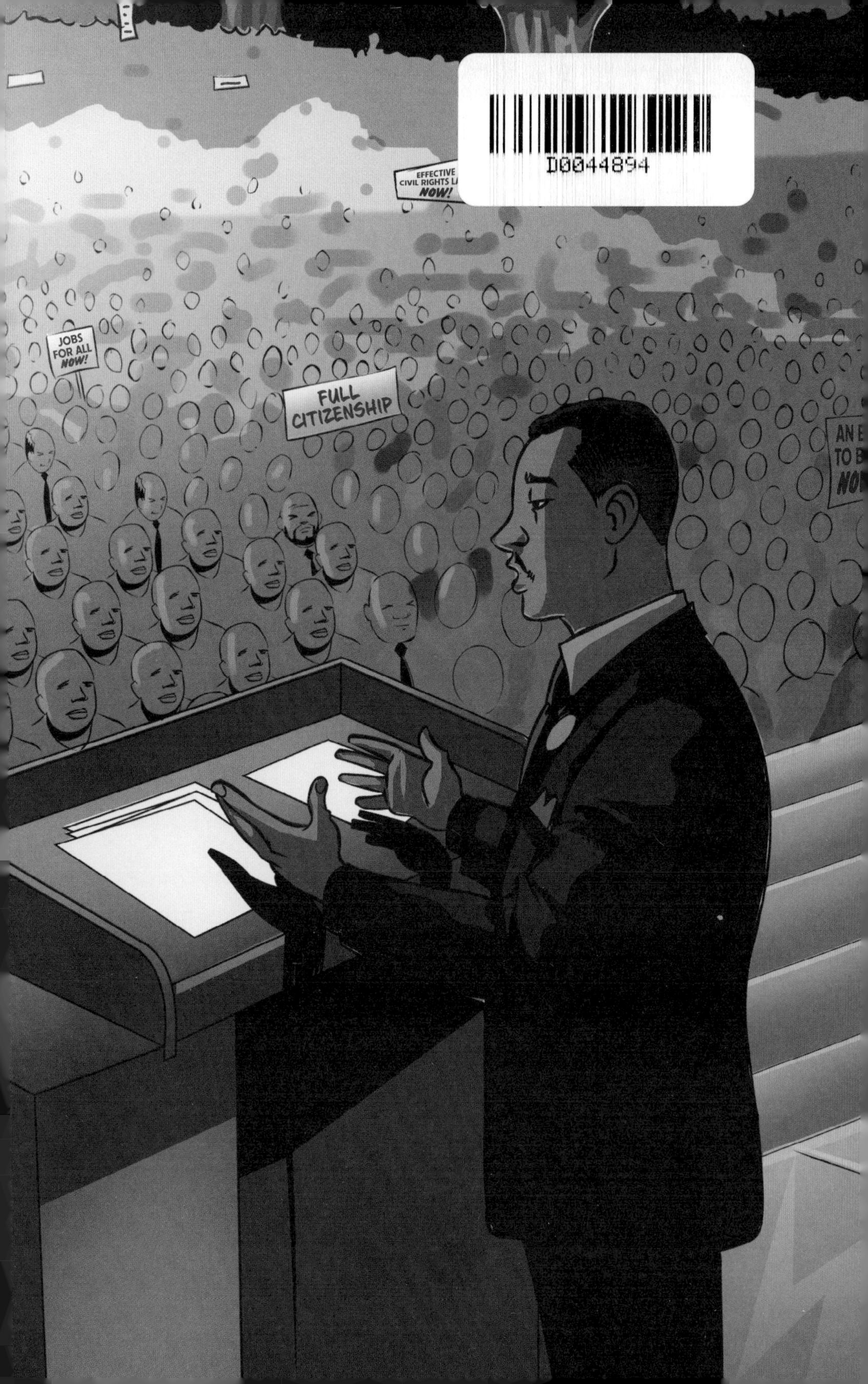
EFFECTIVE
NOW!
JOBS FOR ALL NOW!
FULL CITIZENSHIP

TORY!

UTHER KING Jr.

VOICE for EQUALITY!

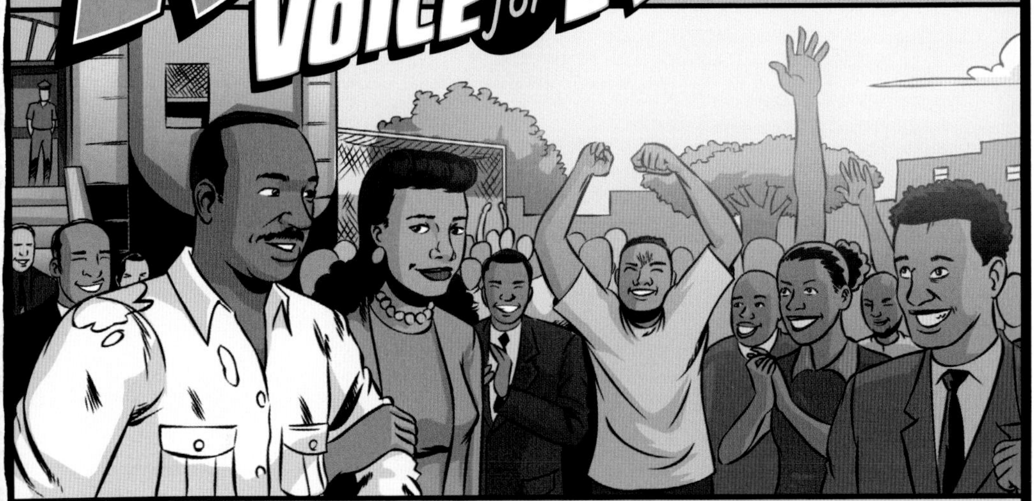

BY
JAMES BUCKLEY JR.

ILLUSTRATED BY
YOUNEEK STUDIOS

LETTERING & DESIGN BY
COMICRAFT

COVER ART BY
IAN CHURCHILL

PORTABLE PRESS
SAN DIEGO, CALIFORNIA

Portable Press
An imprint of Printers Row Publishing Group
10350 Barnes Canyon Road, Suite 100, San Diego, CA 92121
www.portablepress.com • e-mail: mail@portablepress.com

Printers Row Publishing Group is a division of Readerlink Distribution Services, LLC. Portable Press is a registered trademark of Readerlink Distribution Services, LLC.

Correspondence regarding the content of this book should be addressed to Portable Press, Editorial Department, at the above address. Author and illustration inquiries should be addressed to Oomf, Inc., www.oomf.com.

Publisher: Peter Norton
Associate Publisher: Ana Parker
Developmental Editor: Vicki Jaeger
Publishing Team: Kathryn C. Dalby, Lauren Taniguchi
Production Team: Jonathan Lopes, Rusty von Dyl

O•MF Created at Oomf, Inc., www.Oomf.com
Director: Mark Shulman
Producer: James Buckley Jr.

Written by James Buckley Jr.
Coloring by YouNeek Studios and Matt Harding
Lettering & design by Comicraft: John Roshell, Sarah Jacobs,
   Niklas Pousette Harger, Forest Dempsey, Tyler Smith
Cover illustration by Ian Churchill

Library of Congress Cataloging-in-Publication Data
Names: Buckley, James, Jr., 1963- author, illustrator. I Roshell, John,
   letterer. I YouNeek Studios, illustrator.
Title: Martin Luther King, Jr. : voice for equality! / author: James Buckley; interior
   illustration: YouNeek Studios ; interior lettering: John Roshell.
Description: San Diego, CA : Portable Press, 2019. I Series: Show me history!
Identifiers: LCCN 2018030623 I ISBN 9781684125463 (hardback)
Subjects: LCSH: King, Martin Luther, Jr., 1929-1968--Juvenile literature. I
   African Americans--Biography--Juvenile literature. I Civil rights
   workers--United States--Juvenile literature. I King, Martin Luther, Jr.,
   1929-1968--Comic books, strips, etc. I African Americans--Biography--Comic
   books, strips, etc. I Civil rights workers--United
   States--Biography--Comic books, strips, etc. I Graphic novels. I BISAC:
   JUVENILE NONFICTION / Biography & Autobiography / Historical. I JUVENILE
   NONFICTION / Biography & Autobiography / Social Activists. I JUVENILE
   NONFICTION / History / United States / 20th Century.
Classification: LCC E185.97.K5 B776 2019 I DDC 323.092 [B] --dc23 LC record
available at https://lccn.loc.gov/2018030623

Printed in China

22 21 20 19 18   1 2 3 4 5

I'M **LIBBY**. YOU MIGHT KNOW ME AS "**LADY LIBERTY**," THE STATUE THAT STANDS IN NEW YORK CITY'S HARBOR.

I'LL BE ONE OF YOUR GUIDES AS WE "**SHOW YOU HISTORY**"!

AND I'M **SAM**! I MIGHT NOT LOOK **OLD** ENOUGH, BUT SOON I'LL BE "**UNCLE SAM**," A LIVING SYMBOL OF THE UNITED STATES.

SAM, HAVE YOU EVER HAD A **DREAM**?

SURE, I HAVE THEM ALL THE TIME.

HAVE ANY OF YOUR DREAMS **CHANGED HISTORY**?

WELL, NOT **YET**. THOUGH MOST OF MY DREAMS INVOLVE **SPACESHIPS** AND **TIME TRAVEL**, SO YOU NEVER KNOW.

WELL, WE'RE GOING TO MEET A MAN WHOSE DREAMS **INSPIRED THE WORLD**.

THAT WOULD BE A DREAM COME TRUE!

MARTIN LUTHER KING JR. USED A POWERFUL WEAPON TO FIGHT THE FORCES OF RACISM AND POVERTY: **WORDS**.

IN A TIME WHEN MANY PEOPLE WERE **ANGRY**, HE PREACHED **LOVE** AND **PATIENCE**.

HIS POWERFUL WORDS, FORCEFUL **LEADERSHIP**, AND PERSONAL **COURAGE** HELPED CHANGE AMERICA.

WELL, HE HELPED GET THE PROCESS **STARTED**. WE STILL HAVE A LONG WAY TO **GO**.

BUT THANKS TO DR. KING, WE ARE **MOVING FORWARD** TO MAKE HIS DREAM COME TRUE.

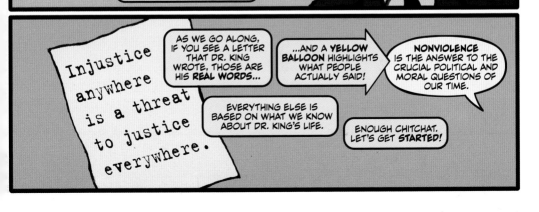

Injustice anywhere is a threat to justice everywhere.

AS WE GO ALONG, IF YOU SEE A LETTER THAT DR. KING WROTE, THOSE ARE HIS **REAL WORDS**...

...AND A **YELLOW BALLOON** HIGHLIGHTS WHAT PEOPLE ACTUALLY SAID!

NONVIOLENCE IS THE ANSWER TO THE CRUCIAL POLITICAL AND MORAL QUESTIONS OF OUR TIME.

EVERYTHING ELSE IS BASED ON WHAT WE KNOW ABOUT DR. KING'S LIFE.

ENOUGH CHITCHAT. LET'S GET **STARTED**!

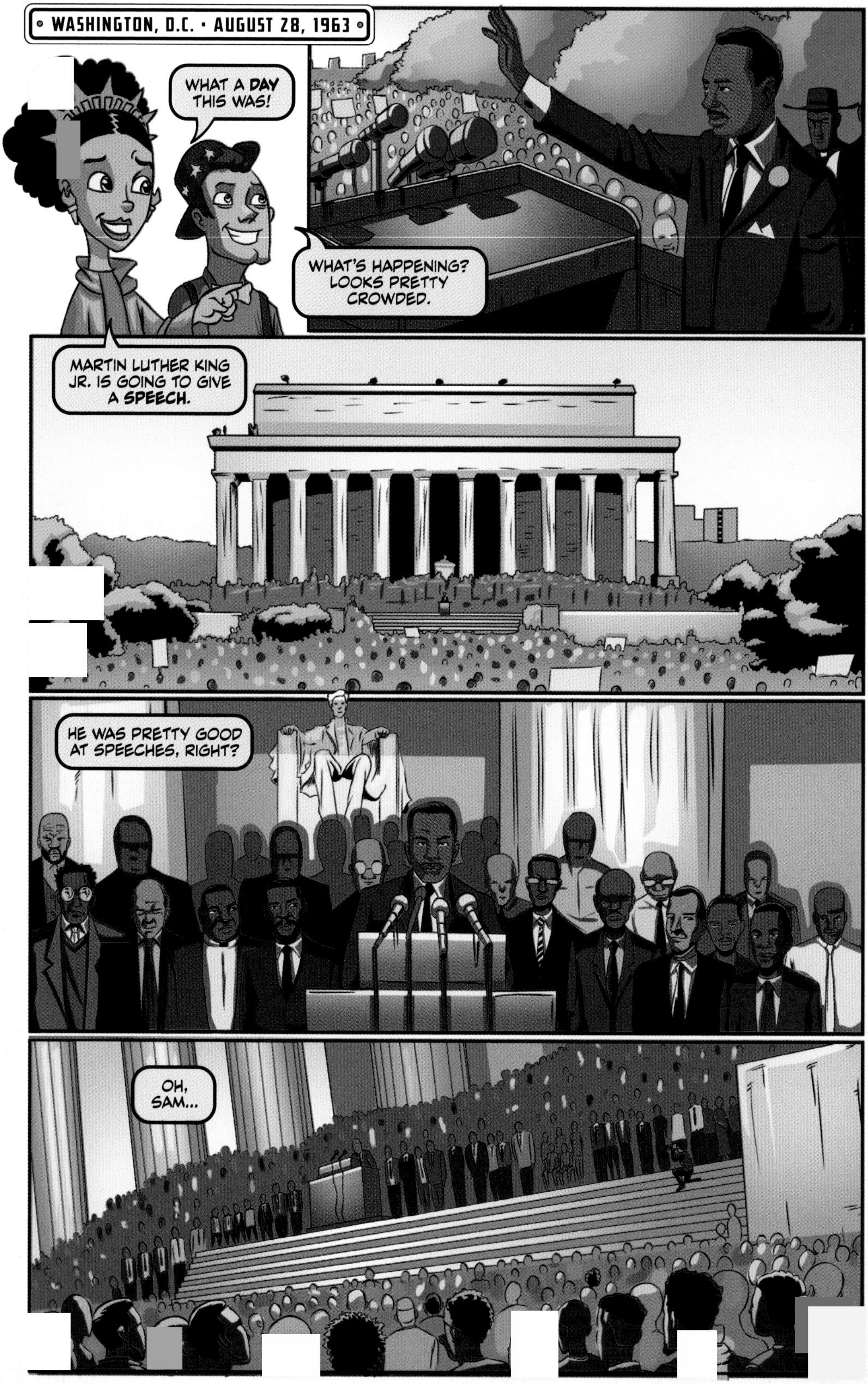
• WASHINGTON, D.C. • AUGUST 28, 1963 •
WHAT A DAY THIS WAS!
WHAT'S HAPPENING? LOOKS PRETTY CROWDED.
MARTIN LUTHER KING JR. IS GOING TO GIVE A SPEECH.
HE WAS PRETTY GOOD AT SPEECHES, RIGHT?
OH, SAM...

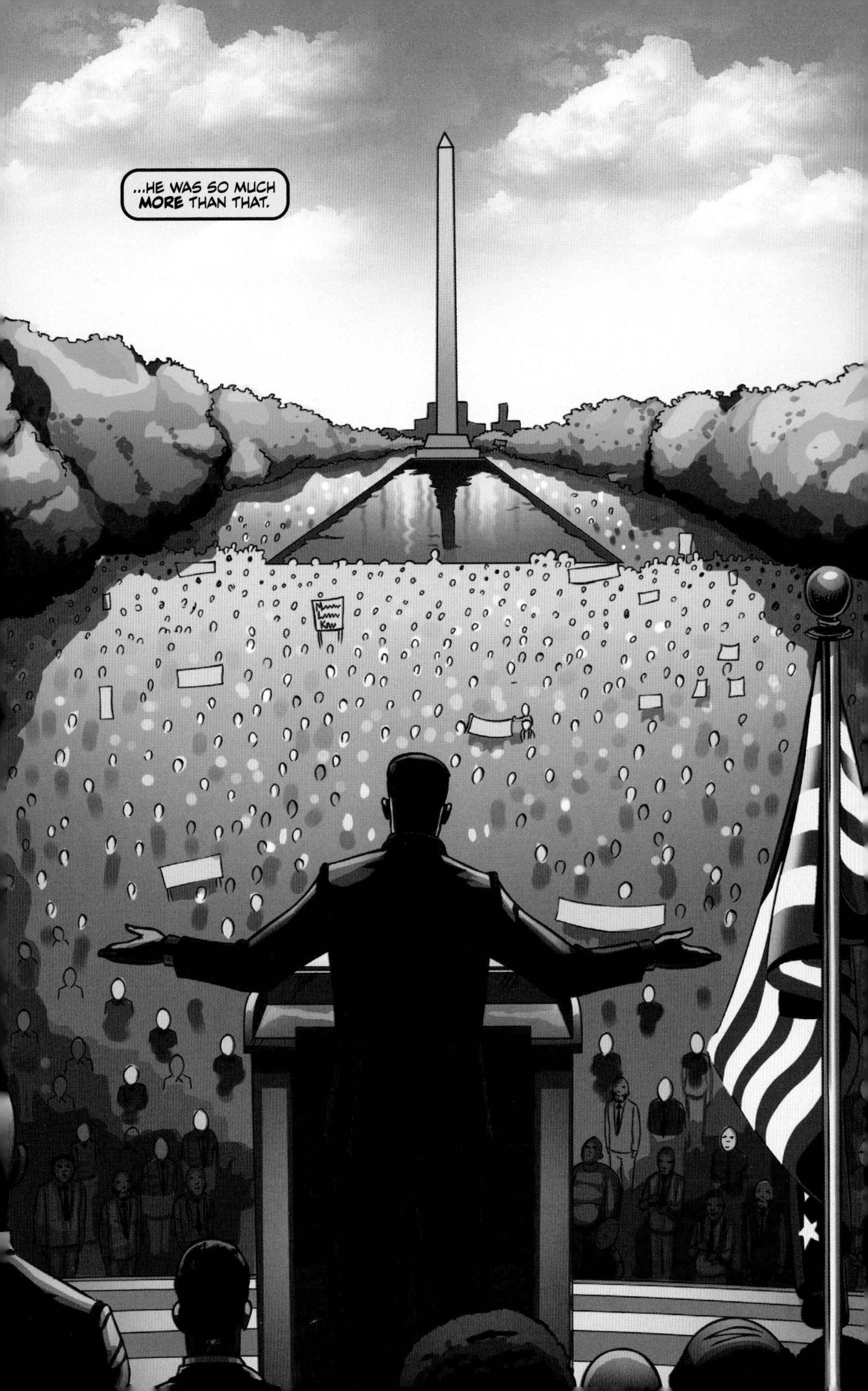
...HE WAS SO MUCH **MORE** THAN THAT.

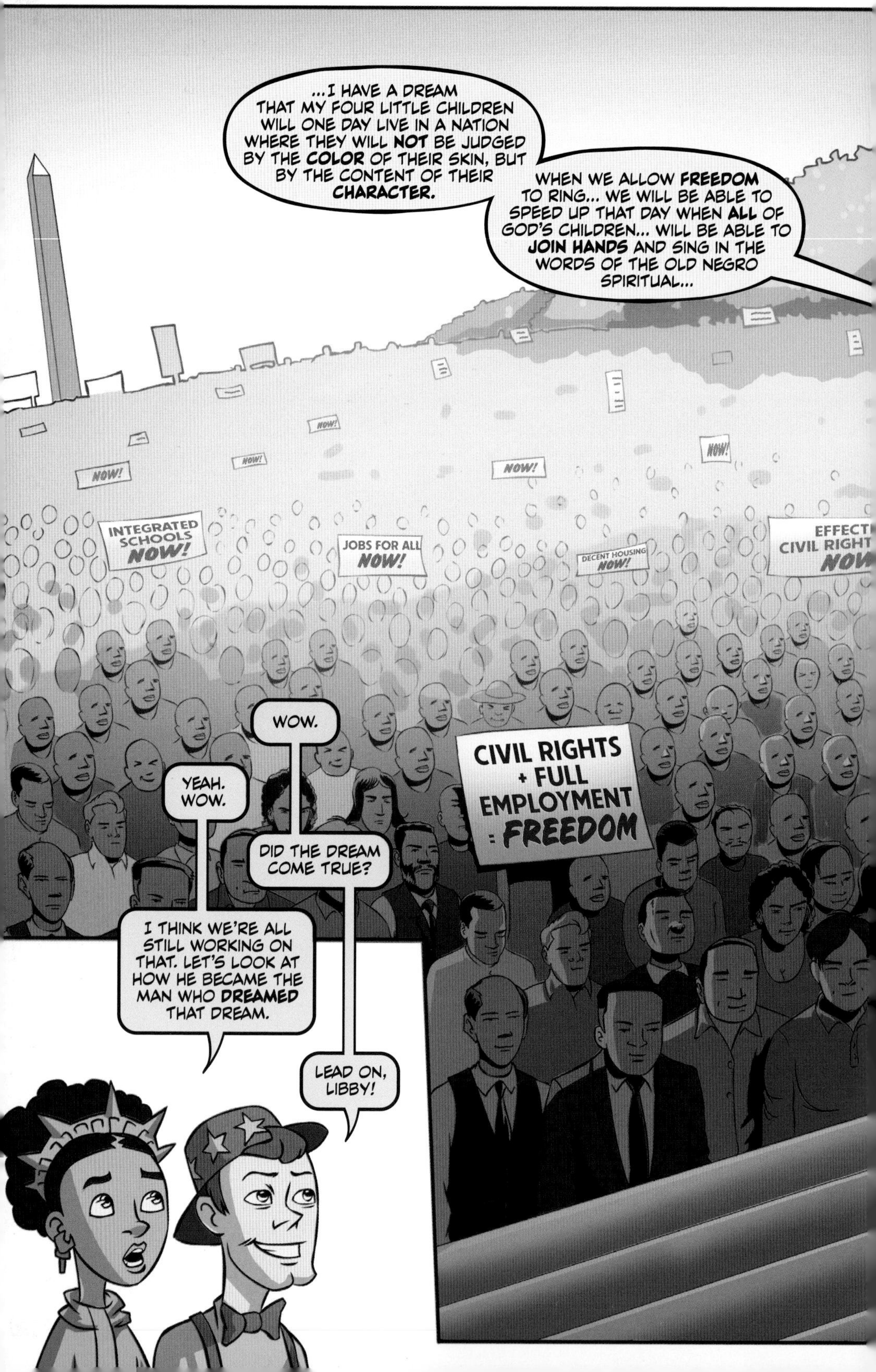
...I HAVE A DREAM THAT MY FOUR LITTLE CHILDREN WILL ONE DAY LIVE IN A NATION WHERE THEY WILL NOT BE JUDGED BY THE COLOR OF THEIR SKIN, BUT BY THE CONTENT OF THEIR CHARACTER.
WHEN WE ALLOW FREEDOM TO RING... WE WILL BE ABLE TO SPEED UP THAT DAY WHEN ALL OF GOD'S CHILDREN... WILL BE ABLE TO JOIN HANDS AND SING IN THE WORDS OF THE OLD NEGRO SPIRITUAL...
NOW!
INTEGRATED SCHOOLS NOW!
JOBS FOR ALL NOW!
DECENT HOUSING NOW!
CIVIL RIGHTS + FULL EMPLOYMENT = FREEDOM
WOW.
YEAH. WOW.
DID THE DREAM COME TRUE?
I THINK WE'RE ALL STILL WORKING ON THAT. LET'S LOOK AT HOW HE BECAME THE MAN WHO DREAMED THAT DREAM.
LEAD ON, LIBBY!

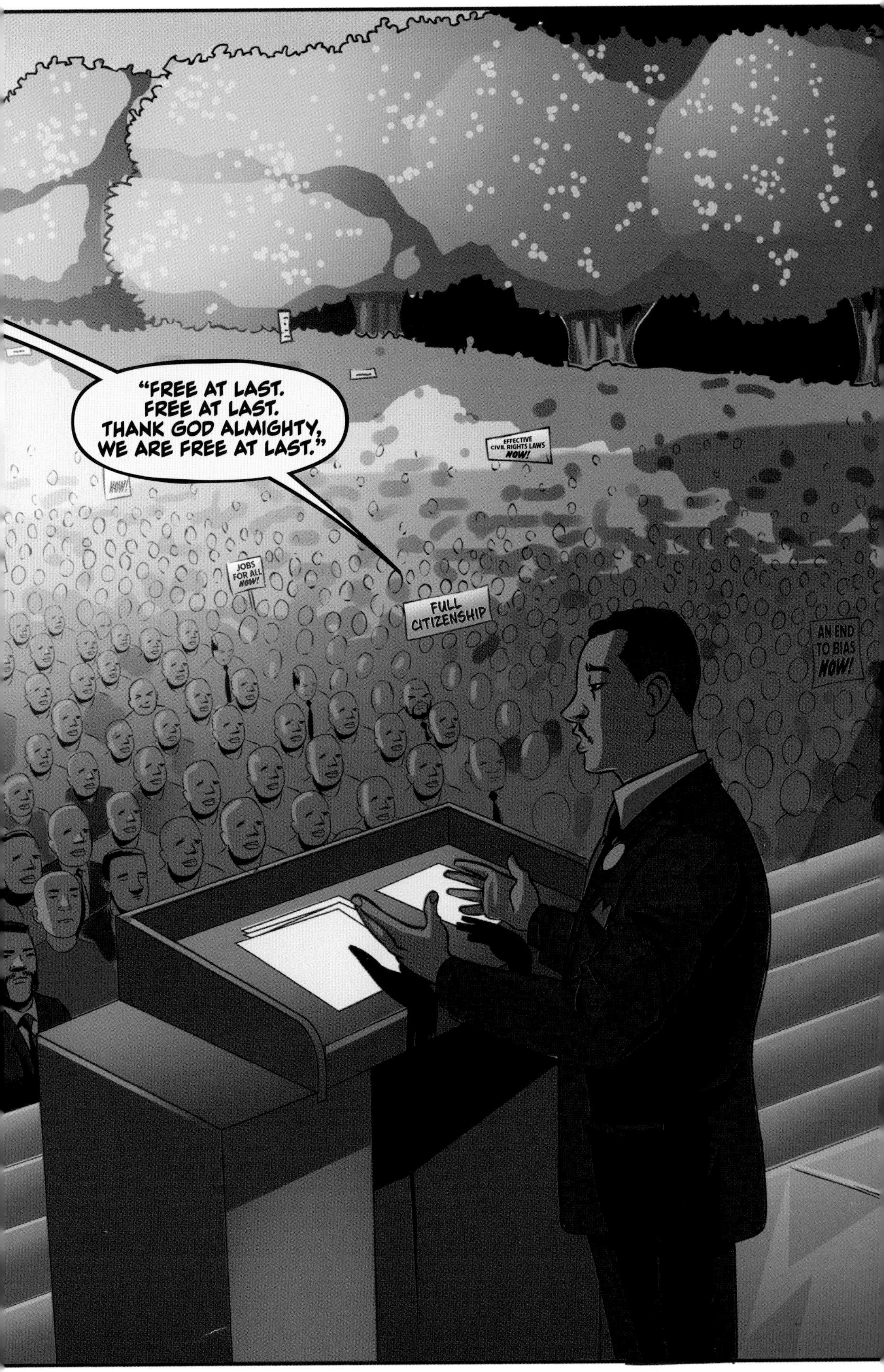
"FREE AT LAST. FREE AT LAST. THANK GOD ALMIGHTY, WE ARE FREE AT LAST."
NOW!
EFFECTIVE CIVIL RIGHTS LAWS NOW!
JOBS FOR ALL NOW!
FULL CITIZENSHIP
AN END TO BIAS NOW!

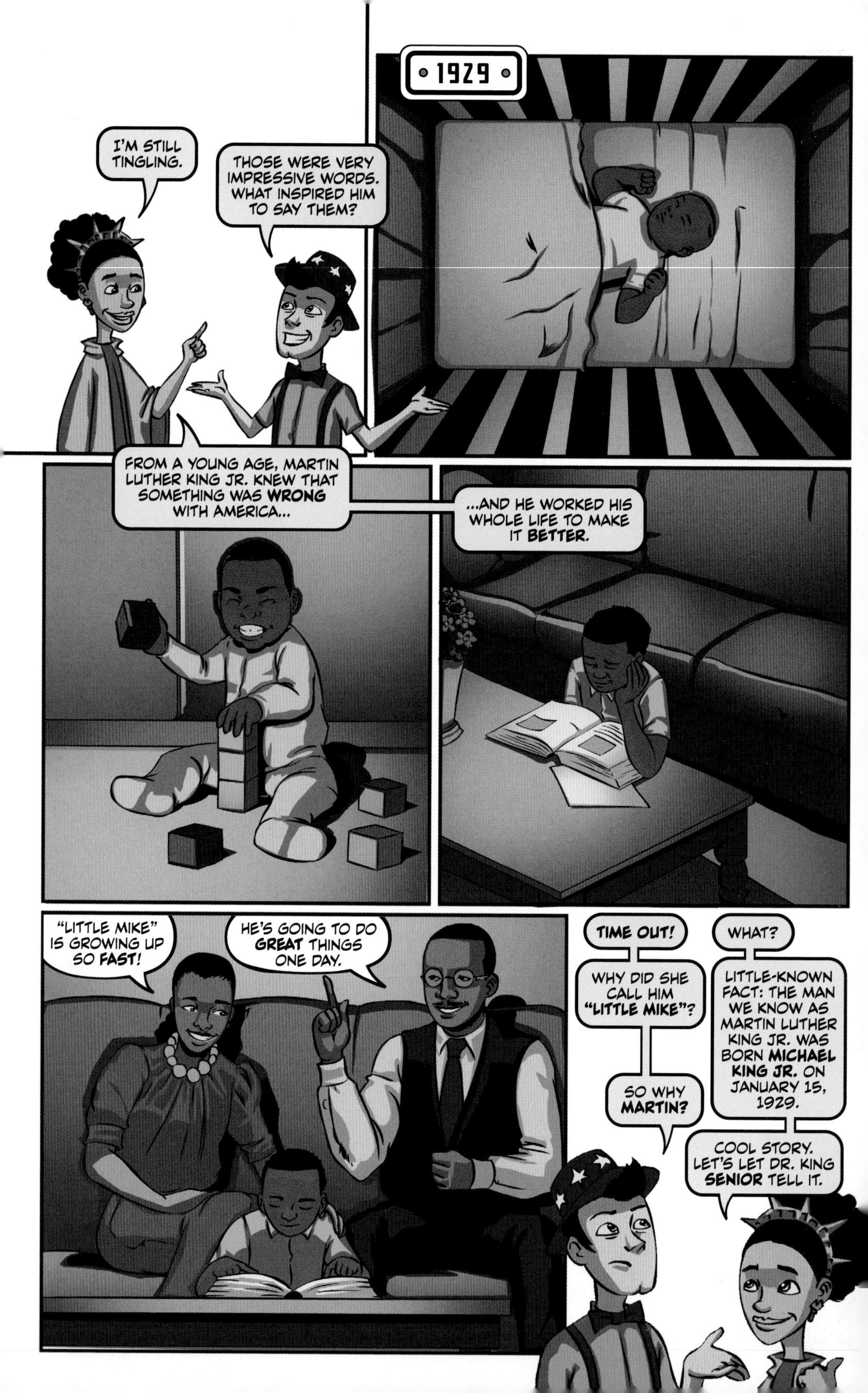
I'M STILL TINGLING.
THOSE WERE VERY IMPRESSIVE WORDS. WHAT INSPIRED HIM TO SAY THEM?
1929
FROM A YOUNG AGE, MARTIN LUTHER KING JR. KNEW THAT SOMETHING WAS WRONG WITH AMERICA...
...AND HE WORKED HIS WHOLE LIFE TO MAKE IT BETTER.
"LITTLE MIKE" IS GROWING UP SO FAST!
HE'S GOING TO DO GREAT THINGS ONE DAY.
TIME OUT!
WHY DID SHE CALL HIM "LITTLE MIKE"?
WHAT?
LITTLE-KNOWN FACT: THE MAN WE KNOW AS MARTIN LUTHER KING JR. WAS BORN MICHAEL KING JR. ON JANUARY 15, 1929.
SO WHY MARTIN?
COOL STORY. LET'S LET DR. KING SENIOR TELL IT.

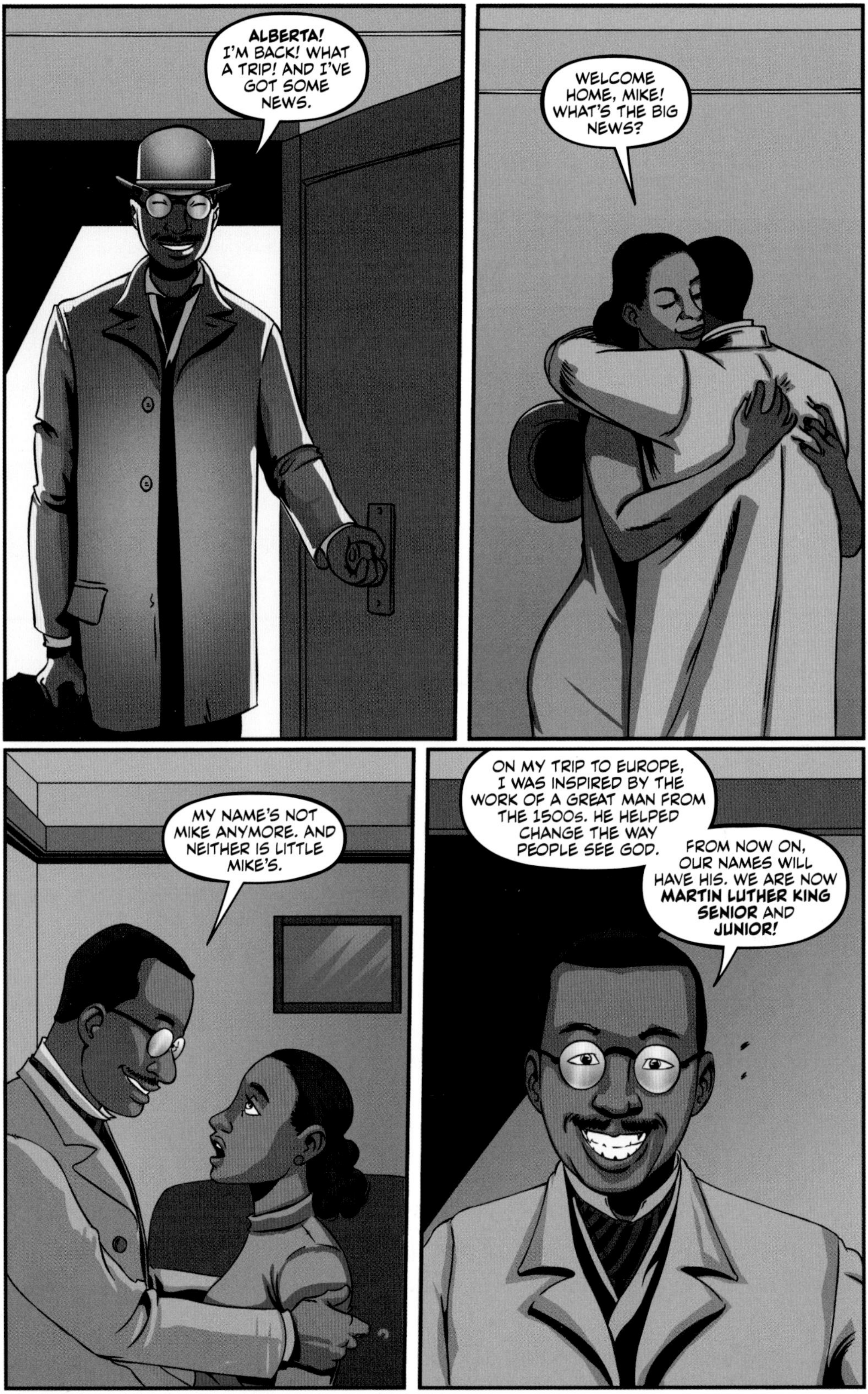
ALBERTA! I'M BACK! WHAT A TRIP! AND I'VE GOT SOME NEWS.
WELCOME HOME, MIKE! WHAT'S THE BIG NEWS?
MY NAME'S NOT MIKE ANYMORE. AND NEITHER IS LITTLE MIKE'S.
ON MY TRIP TO EUROPE, I WAS INSPIRED BY THE WORK OF A GREAT MAN FROM THE 1500s. HE HELPED CHANGE THE WAY PEOPLE SEE GOD.
FROM NOW ON, OUR NAMES WILL HAVE HIS. WE ARE NOW MARTIN LUTHER KING SENIOR AND JUNIOR!

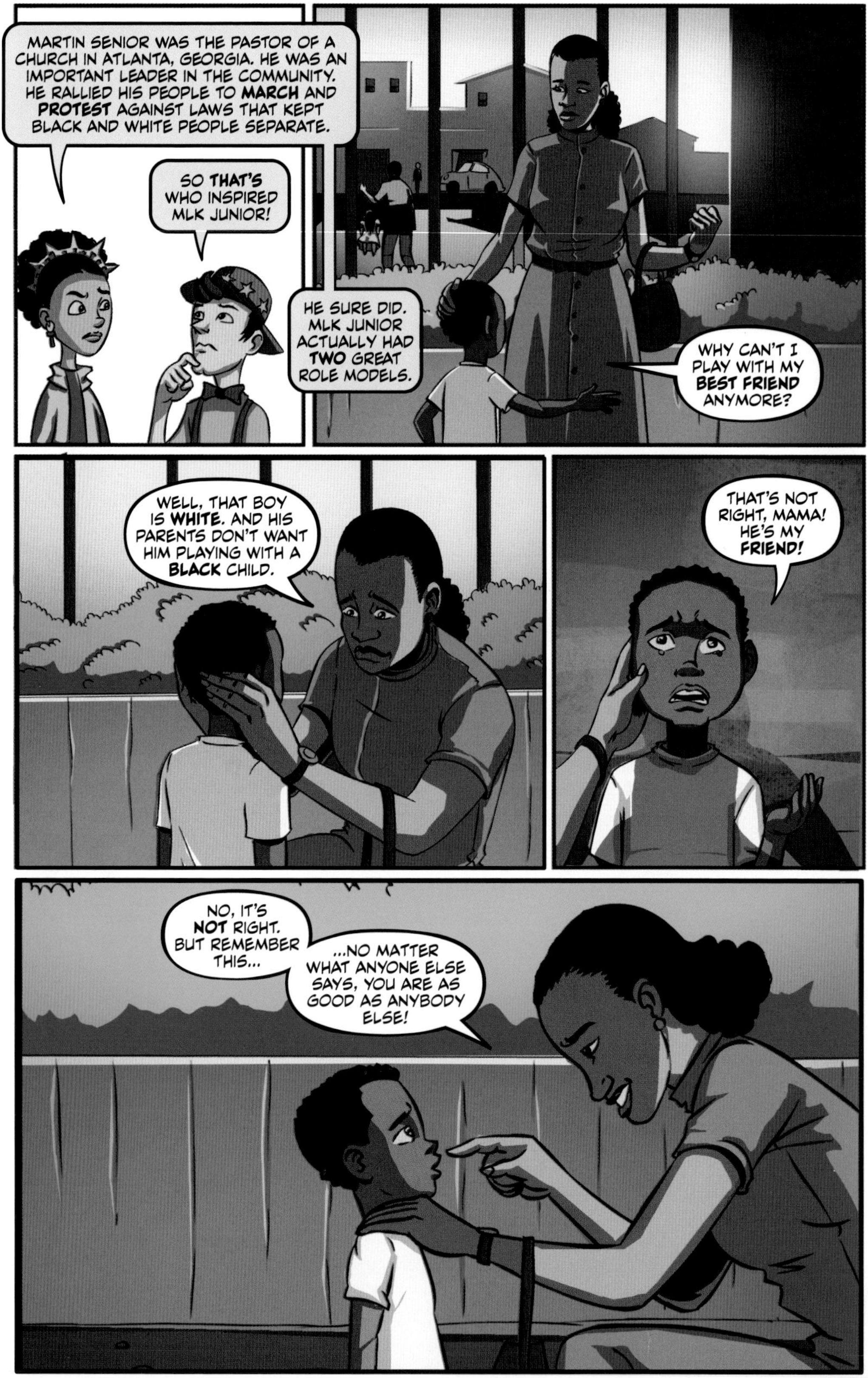
MARTIN SENIOR WAS THE PASTOR OF A CHURCH IN ATLANTA, GEORGIA. HE WAS AN IMPORTANT LEADER IN THE COMMUNITY. HE RALLIED HIS PEOPLE TO **MARCH** AND **PROTEST** AGAINST LAWS THAT KEPT BLACK AND WHITE PEOPLE SEPARATE.
SO **THAT'S** WHO INSPIRED MLK JUNIOR!
HE SURE DID. MLK JUNIOR ACTUALLY HAD **TWO** GREAT ROLE MODELS.
WHY CAN'T I PLAY WITH MY **BEST FRIEND** ANYMORE?
WELL, THAT BOY IS **WHITE**. AND HIS PARENTS DON'T WANT HIM PLAYING WITH A **BLACK** CHILD.
THAT'S NOT RIGHT, MAMA! HE'S MY **FRIEND**!
NO, IT'S **NOT** RIGHT. BUT REMEMBER THIS...
...NO MATTER WHAT ANYONE ELSE SAYS, YOU ARE AS GOOD AS ANYBODY ELSE!

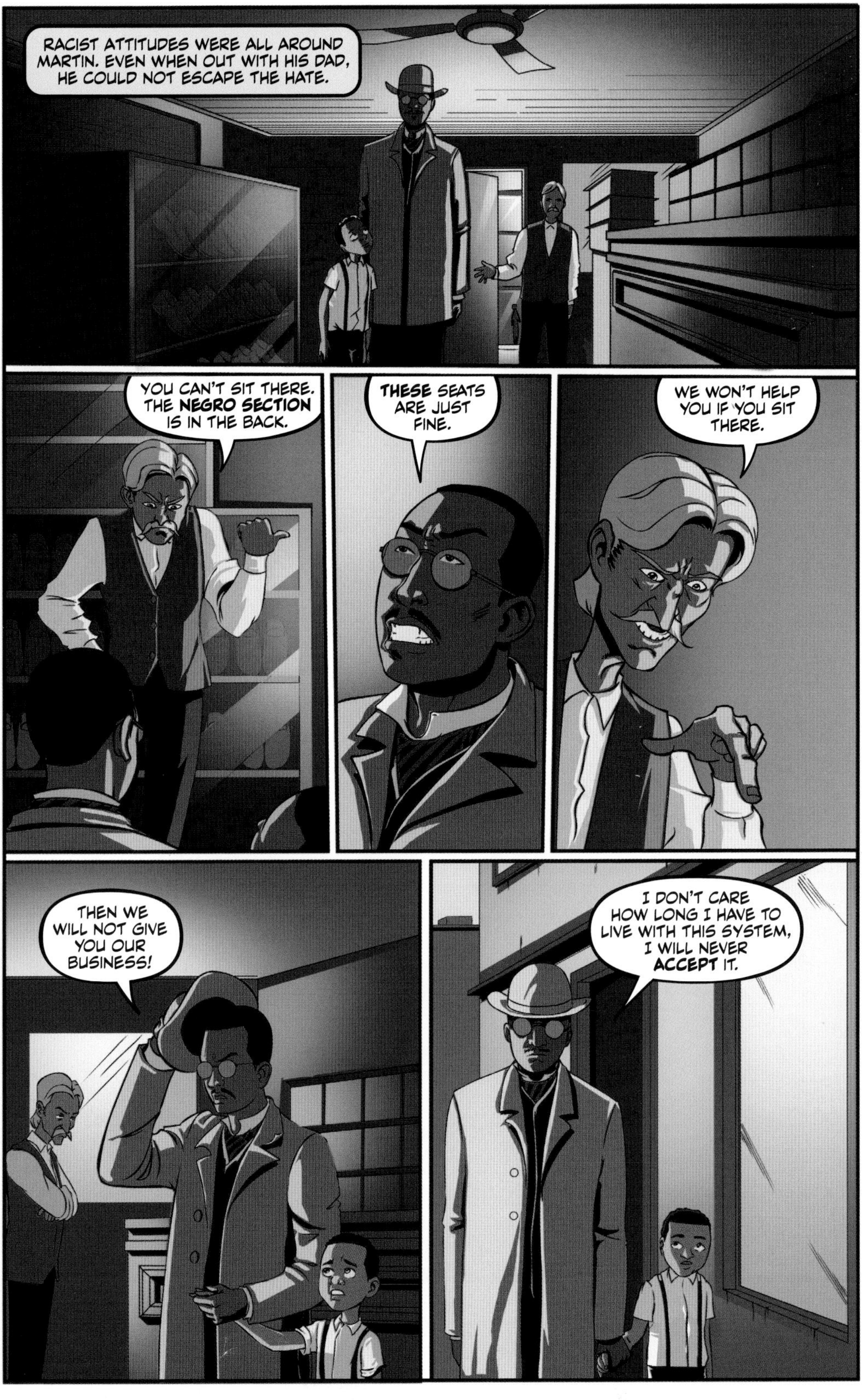
RACIST ATTITUDES WERE ALL AROUND MARTIN. EVEN WHEN OUT WITH HIS DAD, HE COULD NOT ESCAPE THE HATE.
YOU CAN'T SIT THERE. THE **NEGRO SECTION** IS IN THE BACK.
THESE SEATS ARE JUST FINE.
WE WON'T HELP YOU IF YOU SIT THERE.
THEN WE WILL NOT GIVE YOU OUR BUSINESS!
I DON'T CARE HOW LONG I HAVE TO LIVE WITH THIS SYSTEM, I WILL NEVER **ACCEPT** IT.

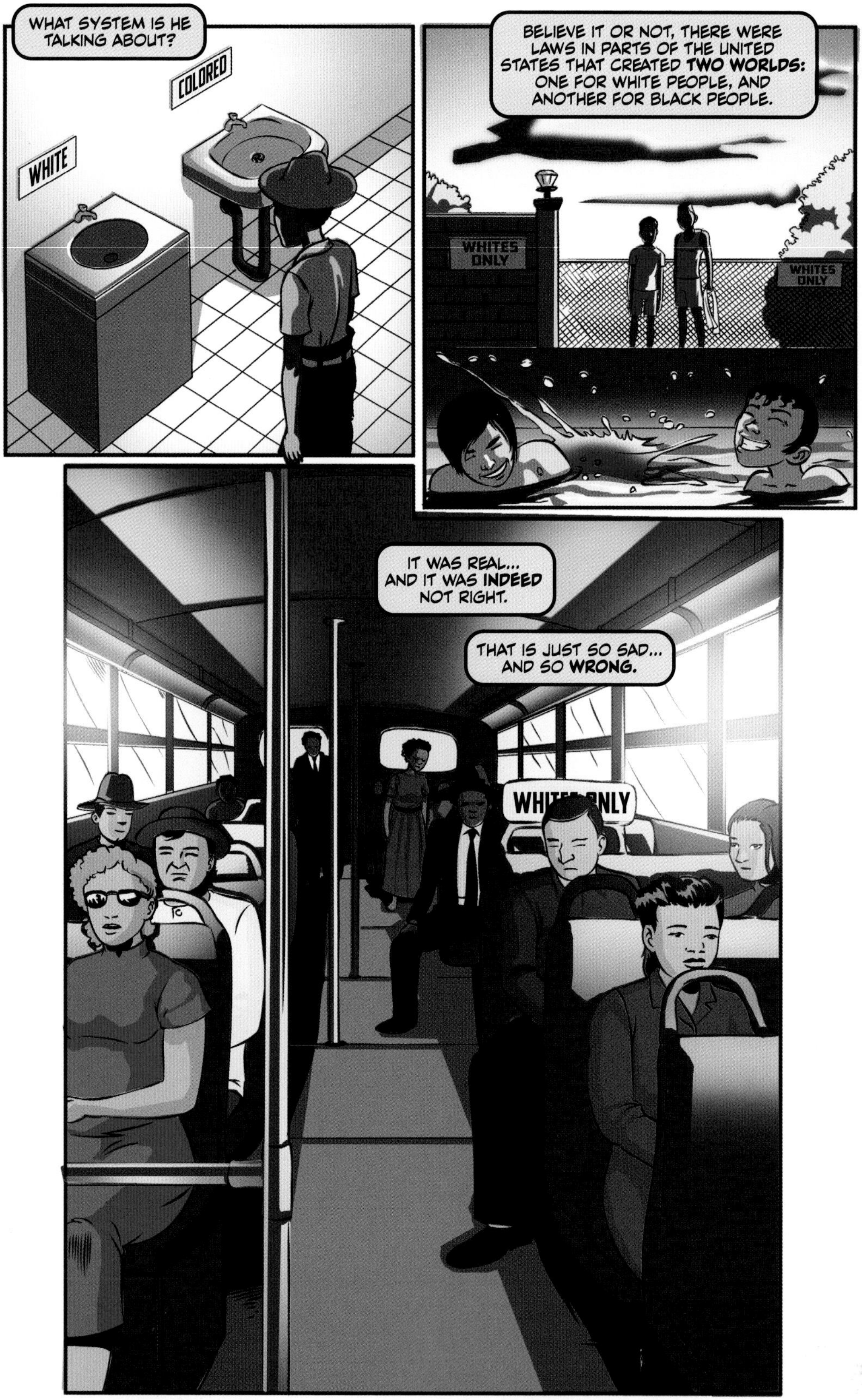
WHAT SYSTEM IS HE TALKING ABOUT?
COLORED
WHITE
BELIEVE IT OR NOT, THERE WERE LAWS IN PARTS OF THE UNITED STATES THAT CREATED **TWO WORLDS:** ONE FOR WHITE PEOPLE, AND ANOTHER FOR BLACK PEOPLE.
WHITES ONLY
WHITES ONLY
IT WAS REAL... AND IT WAS **INDEED** NOT RIGHT.
THAT IS JUST SO SAD... AND SO **WRONG.**

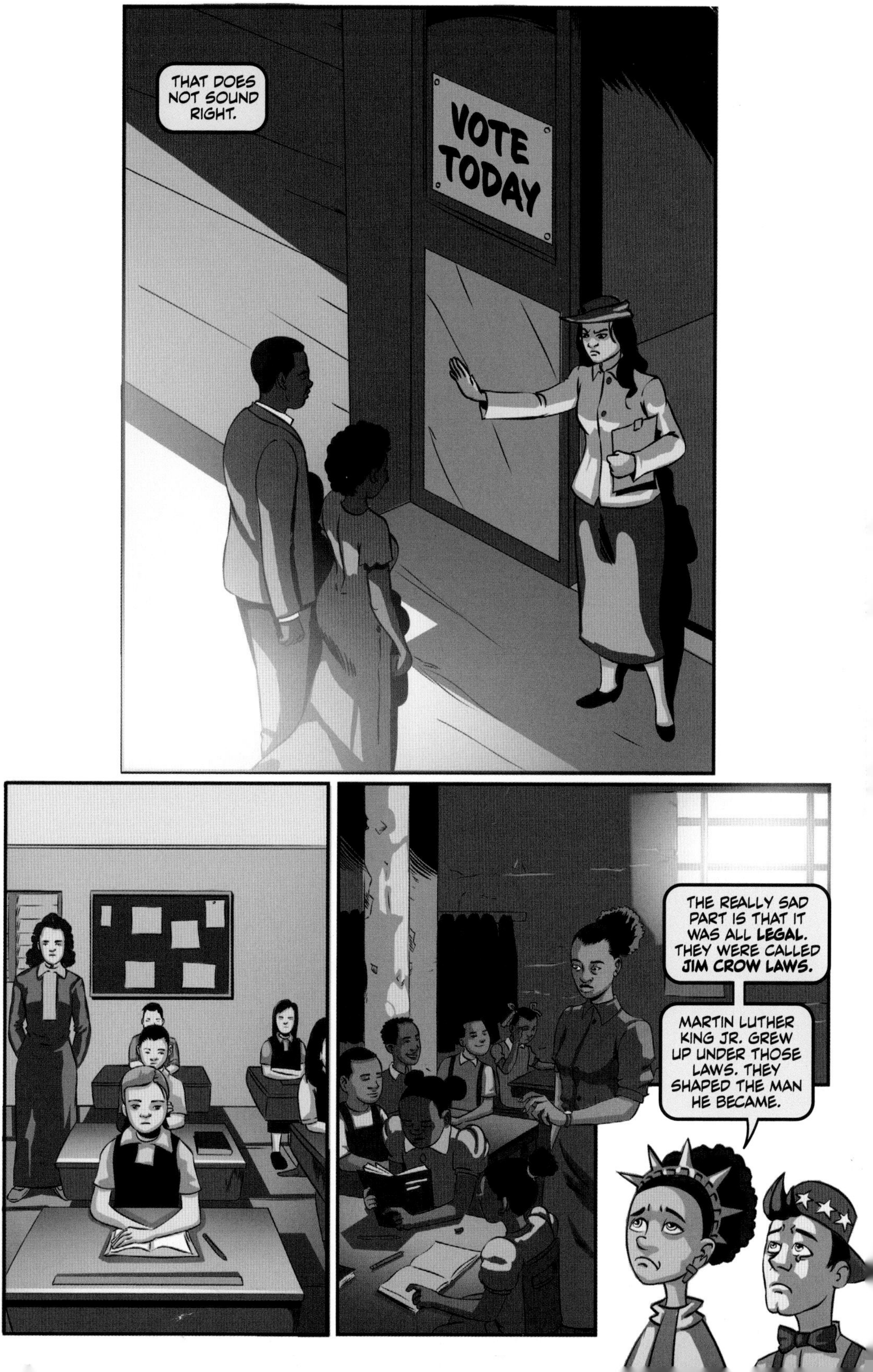
THAT DOES NOT SOUND RIGHT.
VOTE TODAY
THE REALLY SAD PART IS THAT IT WAS ALL LEGAL. THEY WERE CALLED JIM CROW LAWS.
MARTIN LUTHER KING JR. GREW UP UNDER THOSE LAWS. THEY SHAPED THE MAN HE BECAME.

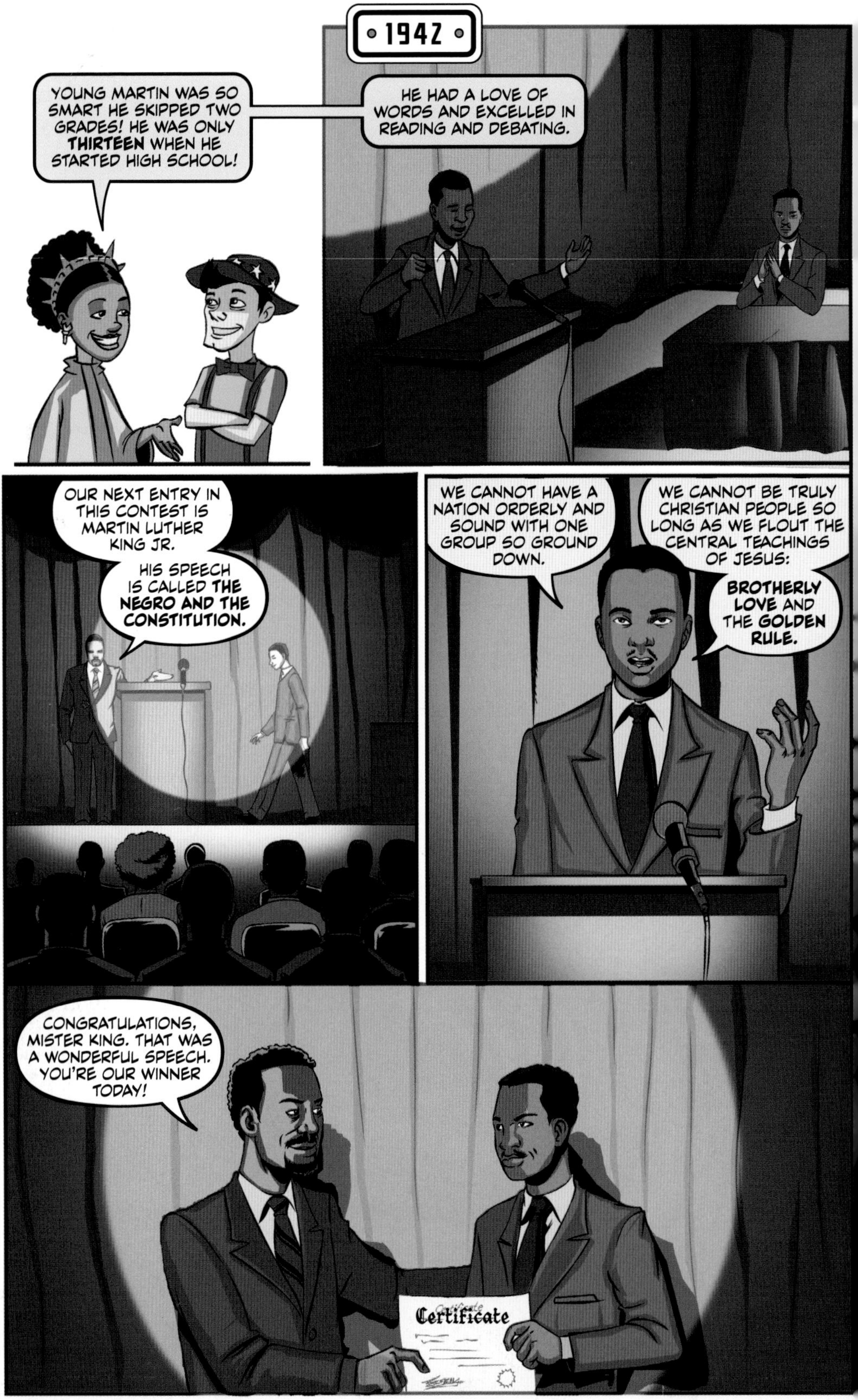
1942
YOUNG MARTIN WAS SO SMART HE SKIPPED TWO GRADES! HE WAS ONLY **THIRTEEN** WHEN HE STARTED HIGH SCHOOL!
HE HAD A LOVE OF WORDS AND EXCELLED IN READING AND DEBATING.
OUR NEXT ENTRY IN THIS CONTEST IS MARTIN LUTHER KING JR.
HIS SPEECH IS CALLED **THE NEGRO AND THE CONSTITUTION.**
WE CANNOT HAVE A NATION ORDERLY AND SOUND WITH ONE GROUP SO GROUND DOWN.
WE CANNOT BE TRULY CHRISTIAN PEOPLE SO LONG AS WE FLOUT THE CENTRAL TEACHINGS OF JESUS:
BROTHERLY LOVE AND THE **GOLDEN RULE.**
CONGRATULATIONS, MISTER KING. THAT WAS A WONDERFUL SPEECH. YOU'RE OUR WINNER TODAY!
Certificate

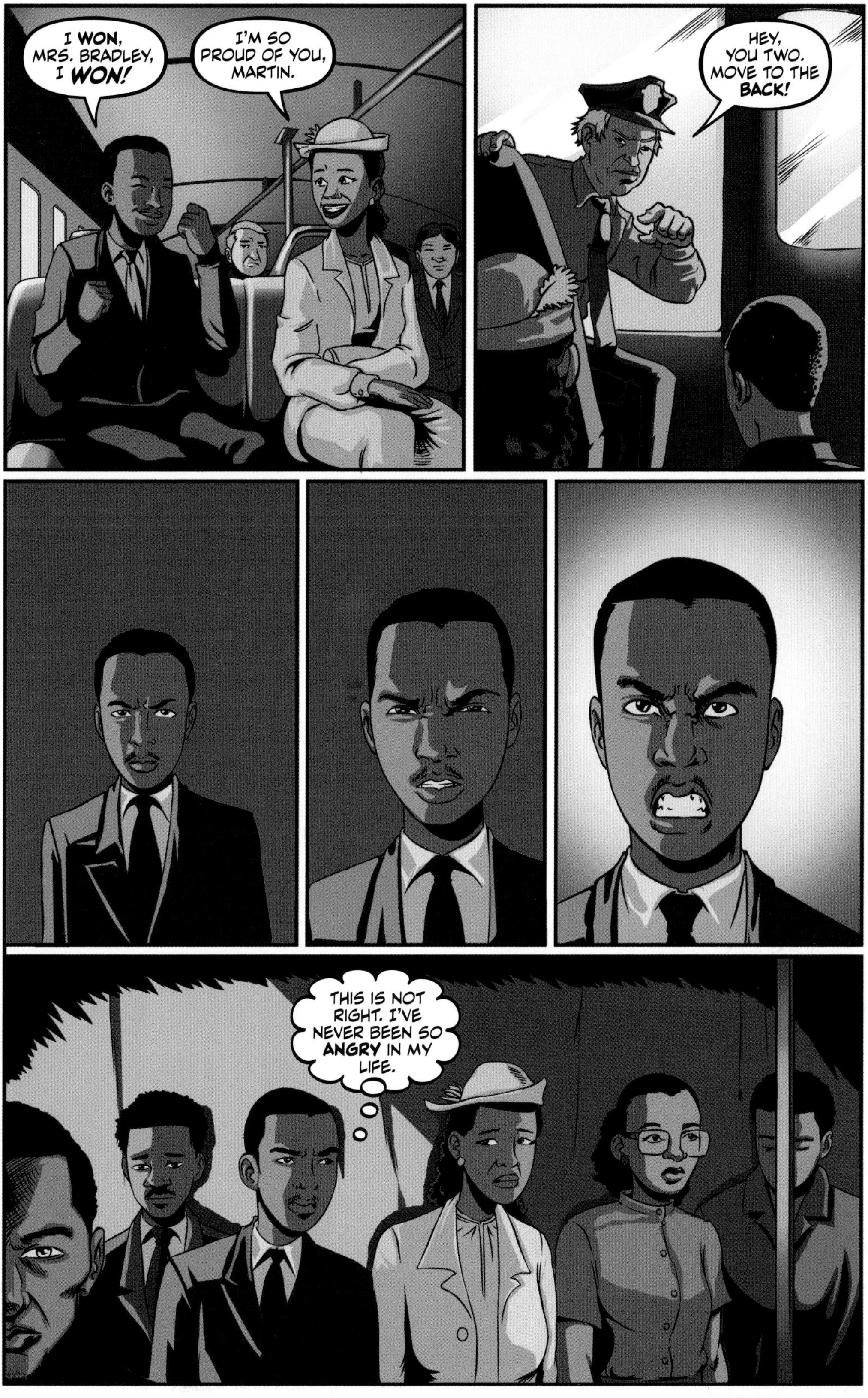
I WON, MRS. BRADLEY, I WON!
I'M SO PROUD OF YOU, MARTIN.
HEY, YOU TWO. MOVE TO THE BACK!
THIS IS NOT RIGHT. I'VE NEVER BEEN SO ANGRY IN MY LIFE.

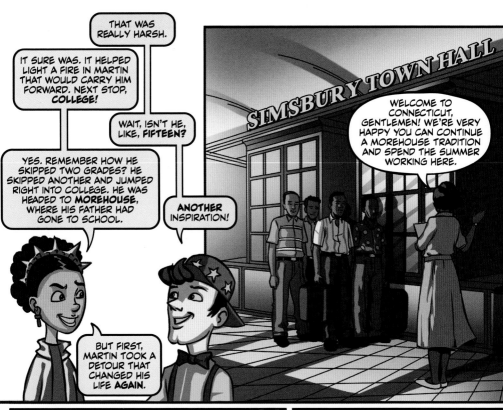

THAT WAS REALLY HARSH.

IT SURE WAS. IT HELPED LIGHT A FIRE IN MARTIN THAT WOULD CARRY HIM FORWARD. NEXT STOP, **COLLEGE!**

WAIT, ISN'T HE, LIKE, **FIFTEEN?**

YES. REMEMBER HOW HE SKIPPED TWO GRADES? HE SKIPPED ANOTHER AND JUMPED RIGHT INTO COLLEGE. HE WAS HEADED TO **MOREHOUSE,** WHERE HIS FATHER HAD GONE TO SCHOOL.

ANOTHER INSPIRATION!

BUT FIRST, MARTIN TOOK A DETOUR THAT CHANGED HIS LIFE **AGAIN.**

SIMSBURY TOWN HALL

WELCOME TO CONNECTICUT, GENTLEMEN! WE'RE VERY HAPPY YOU CAN CONTINUE A MOREHOUSE TRADITION AND SPEND THE SUMMER WORKING HERE.

THANK YOU, MA'AM. WHAT WILL WE BE DOING?

WELL, IT'S **HARD WORK,** OUT IN THE FIELDS HERE. BUT YOU'LL BE PAID, FED, AND HAVE A COMFORTABLE PLACE TO SLEEP.

WELL, SO FAR IT SOUNDS GOOD. WE'LL SEE!

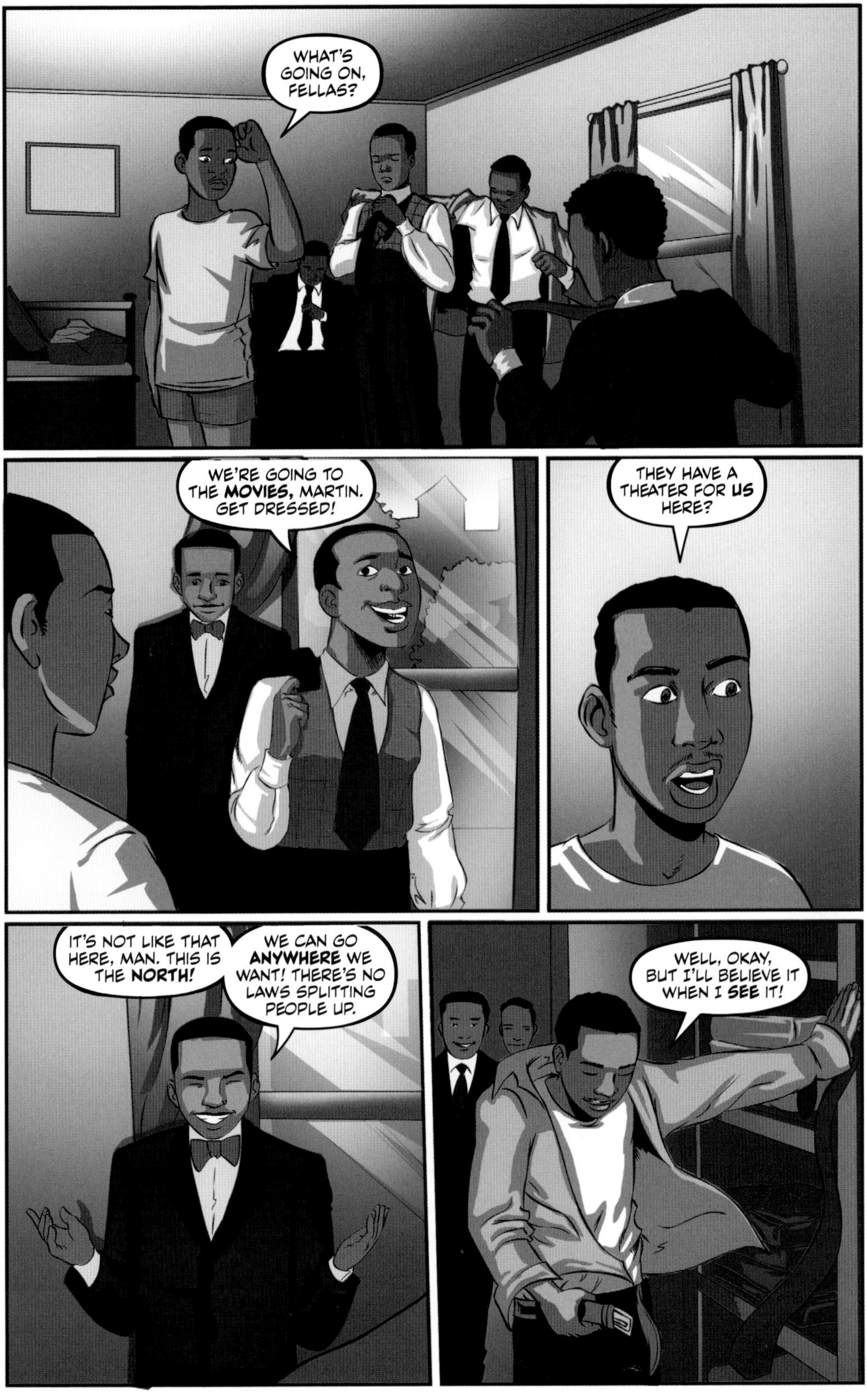
WHAT'S GOING ON, FELLAS?
WE'RE GOING TO THE **MOVIES,** MARTIN. GET DRESSED!
THEY HAVE A THEATER FOR **US** HERE?
IT'S NOT LIKE THAT HERE, MAN. THIS IS THE **NORTH!**
WE CAN GO **ANYWHERE** WE WANT! THERE'S NO LAWS SPLITTING PEOPLE UP.
WELL, OKAY, BUT I'LL BELIEVE IT WHEN I **SEE** IT!

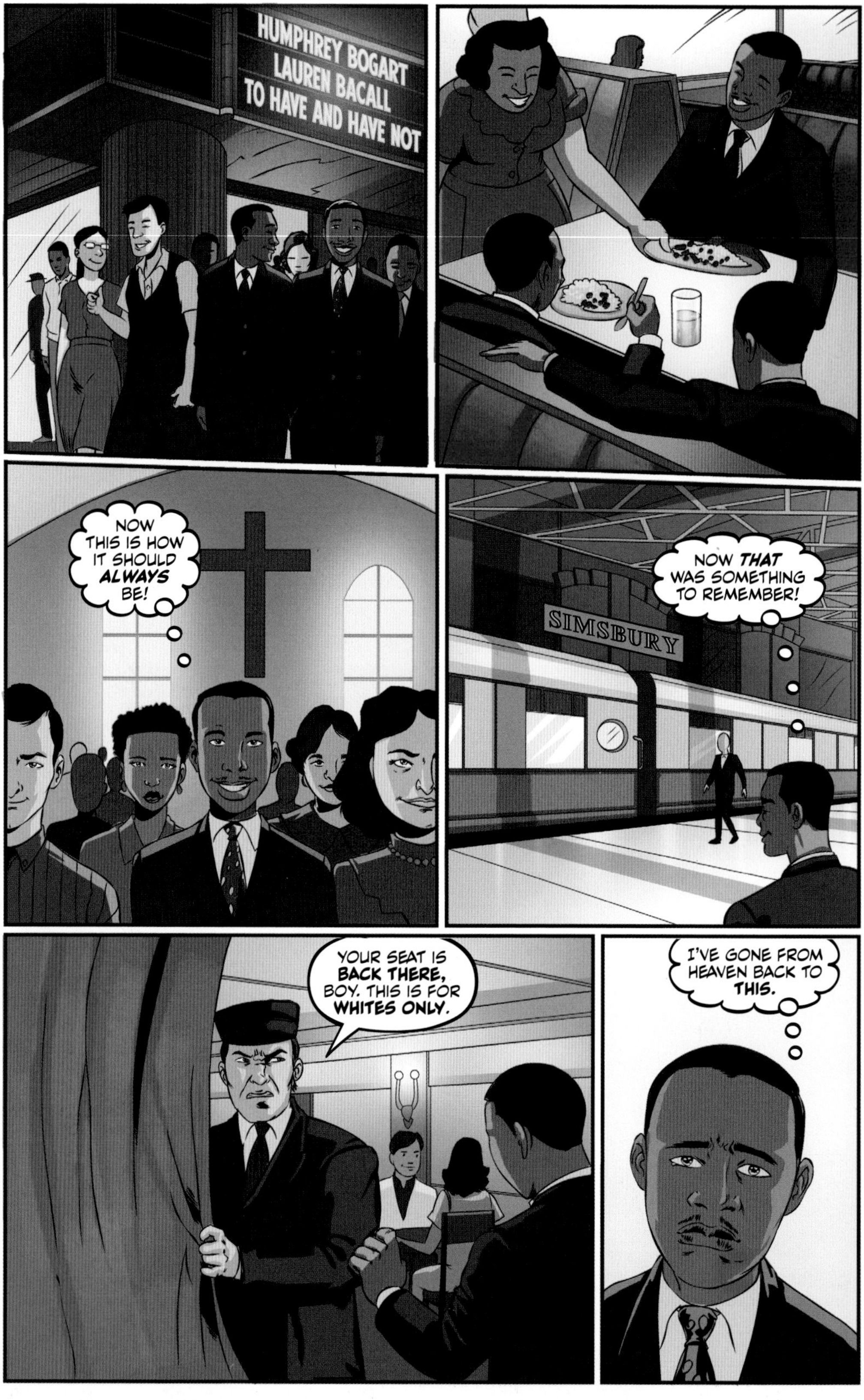
HUMPHREY BOGART
LAUREN BACALL
TO HAVE AND HAVE NOT
NOW THIS IS HOW IT SHOULD **ALWAYS** BE!
SIMSBURY
NOW ***THAT*** WAS SOMETHING TO REMEMBER!
YOUR SEAT IS **BACK THERE,** BOY. THIS IS FOR **WHITES ONLY.**
I'VE GONE FROM HEAVEN BACK TO **THIS.**

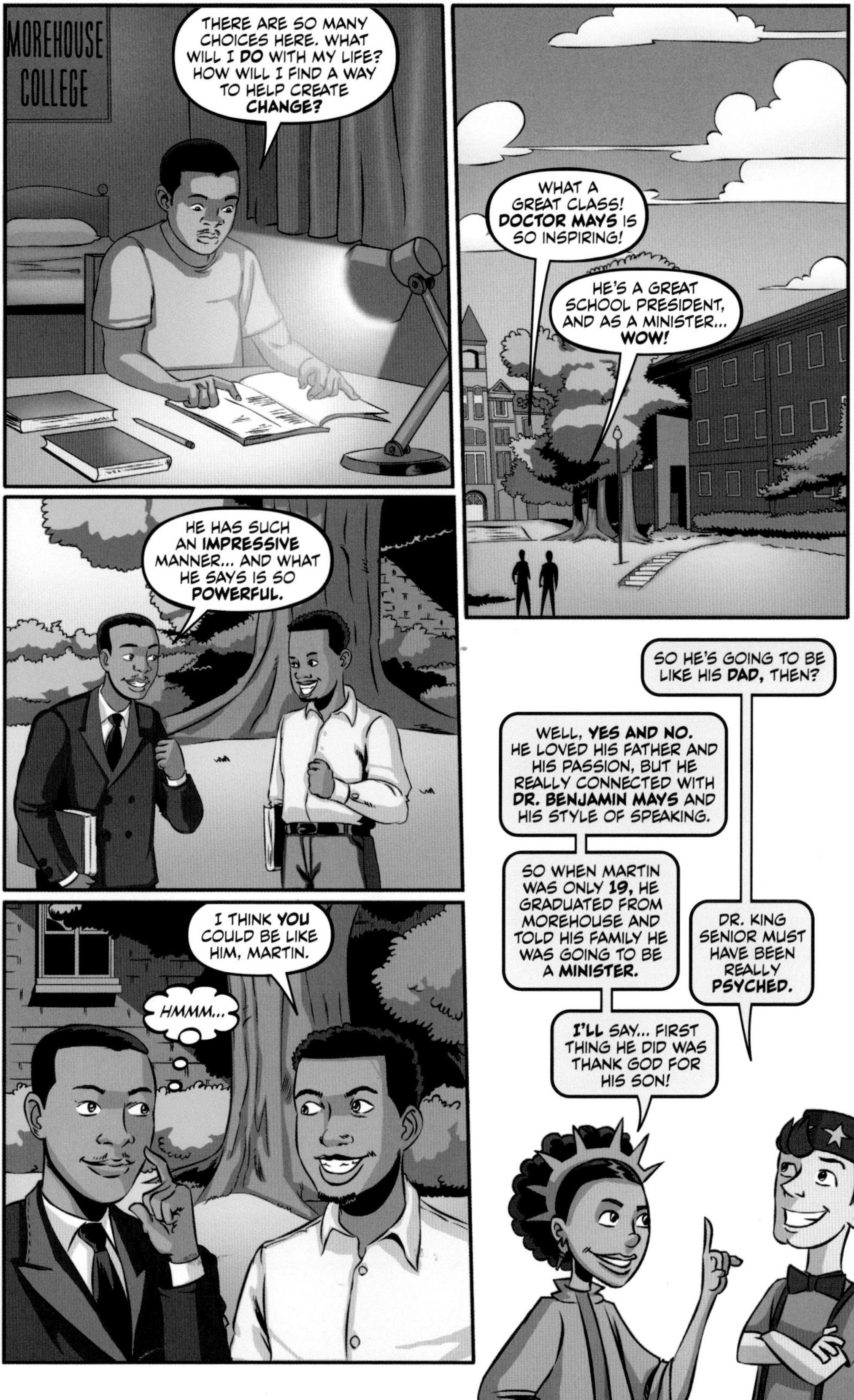
MOREHOUSE COLLEGE
THERE ARE SO MANY CHOICES HERE. WHAT WILL I DO WITH MY LIFE? HOW WILL I FIND A WAY TO HELP CREATE CHANGE?
WHAT A GREAT CLASS! DOCTOR MAYS IS SO INSPIRING!
HE'S A GREAT SCHOOL PRESIDENT, AND AS A MINISTER... WOW!
HE HAS SUCH AN IMPRESSIVE MANNER... AND WHAT HE SAYS IS SO POWERFUL.
I THINK YOU COULD BE LIKE HIM, MARTIN.
HMMM...
SO HE'S GOING TO BE LIKE HIS DAD, THEN?
WELL, YES AND NO. HE LOVED HIS FATHER AND HIS PASSION, BUT HE REALLY CONNECTED WITH DR. BENJAMIN MAYS AND HIS STYLE OF SPEAKING.
SO WHEN MARTIN WAS ONLY 19, HE GRADUATED FROM MOREHOUSE AND TOLD HIS FAMILY HE WAS GOING TO BE A MINISTER.
DR. KING SENIOR MUST HAVE BEEN REALLY PSYCHED.
I'LL SAY... FIRST THING HE DID WAS THANK GOD FOR HIS SON!

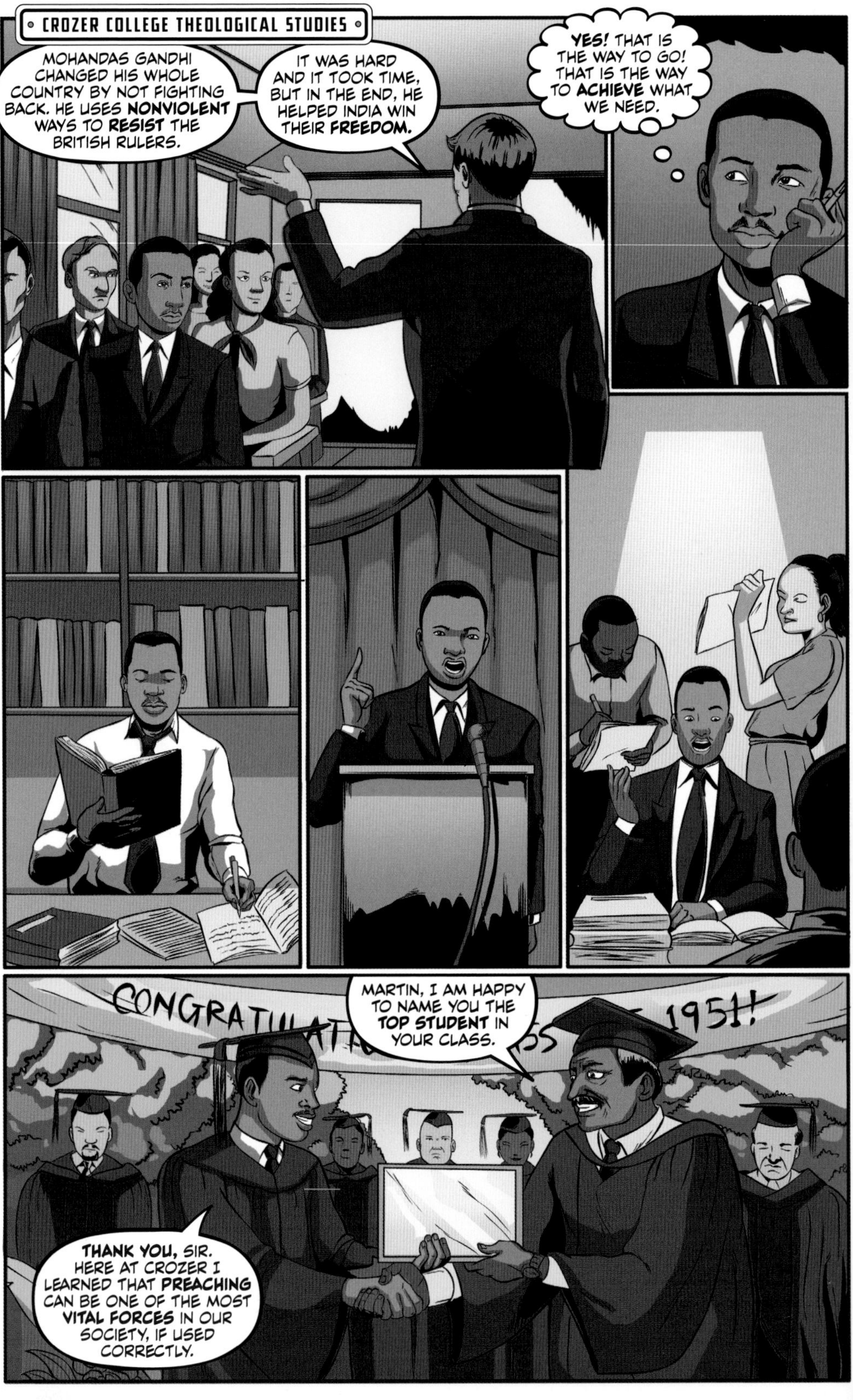
CROZER COLLEGE THEOLOGICAL STUDIES
MOHANDAS GANDHI CHANGED HIS WHOLE COUNTRY BY NOT FIGHTING BACK. HE USES **NONVIOLENT** WAYS TO **RESIST** THE BRITISH RULERS.
IT WAS HARD AND IT TOOK TIME, BUT IN THE END, HE HELPED INDIA WIN THEIR **FREEDOM.**
YES! THAT IS THE WAY TO GO! THAT IS THE WAY TO **ACHIEVE** WHAT WE NEED.
MARTIN, I AM HAPPY TO NAME YOU THE **TOP STUDENT** IN YOUR CLASS.
THANK YOU, SIR. HERE AT CROZER I LEARNED THAT **PREACHING** CAN BE ONE OF THE MOST **VITAL FORCES** IN OUR SOCIETY, IF USED CORRECTLY.

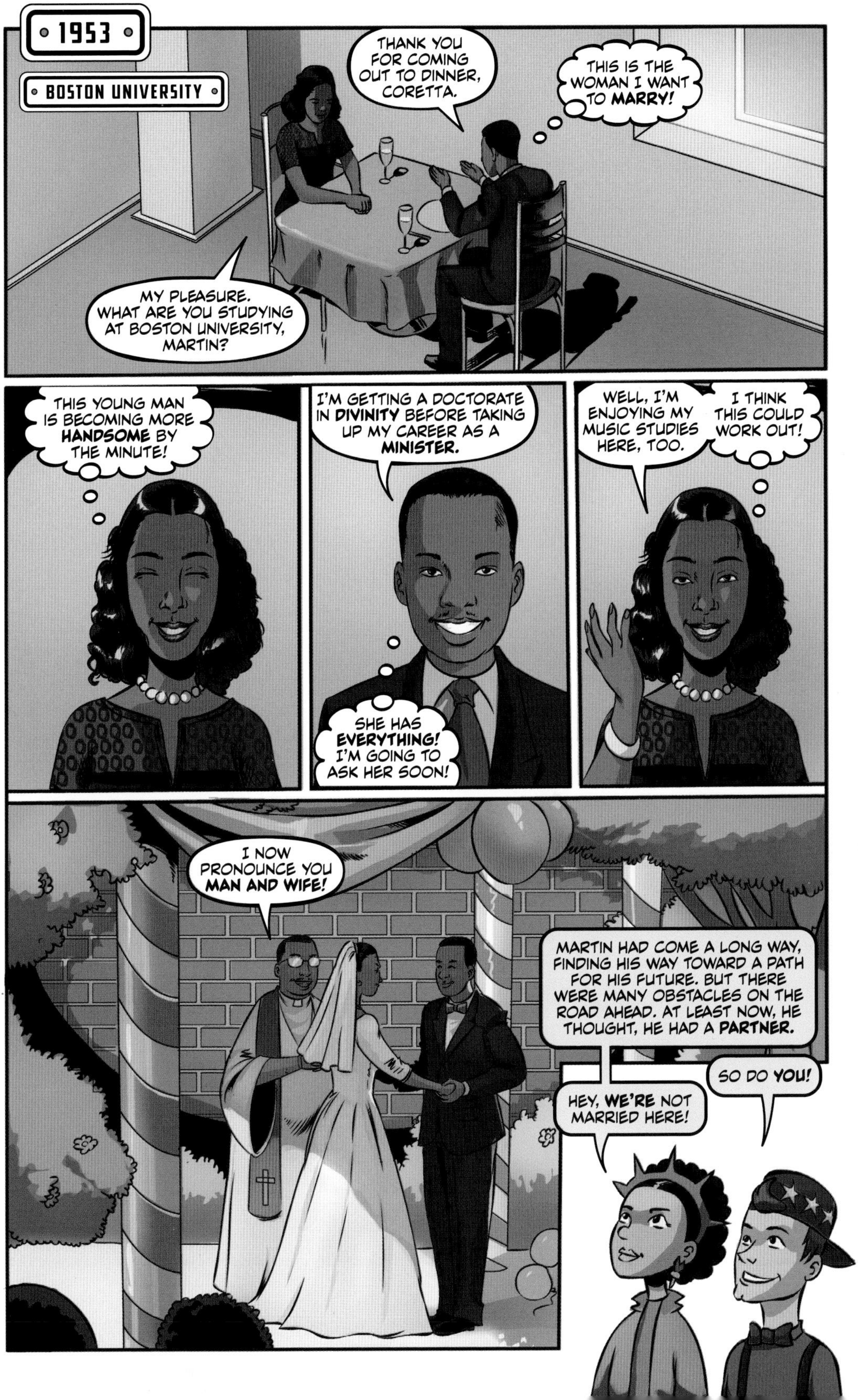
1953
BOSTON UNIVERSITY
THANK YOU FOR COMING OUT TO DINNER, CORETTA.
THIS IS THE WOMAN I WANT TO MARRY!
MY PLEASURE. WHAT ARE YOU STUDYING AT BOSTON UNIVERSITY, MARTIN?
THIS YOUNG MAN IS BECOMING MORE HANDSOME BY THE MINUTE!
I'M GETTING A DOCTORATE IN DIVINITY BEFORE TAKING UP MY CAREER AS A MINISTER.
SHE HAS EVERYTHING! I'M GOING TO ASK HER SOON!
WELL, I'M ENJOYING MY MUSIC STUDIES HERE, TOO.
I THINK THIS COULD WORK OUT!
I NOW PRONOUNCE YOU MAN AND WIFE!
MARTIN HAD COME A LONG WAY, FINDING HIS WAY TOWARD A PATH FOR HIS FUTURE. BUT THERE WERE MANY OBSTACLES ON THE ROAD AHEAD. AT LEAST NOW, HE THOUGHT, HE HAD A PARTNER.
HEY, WE'RE NOT MARRIED HERE!
SO DO YOU!

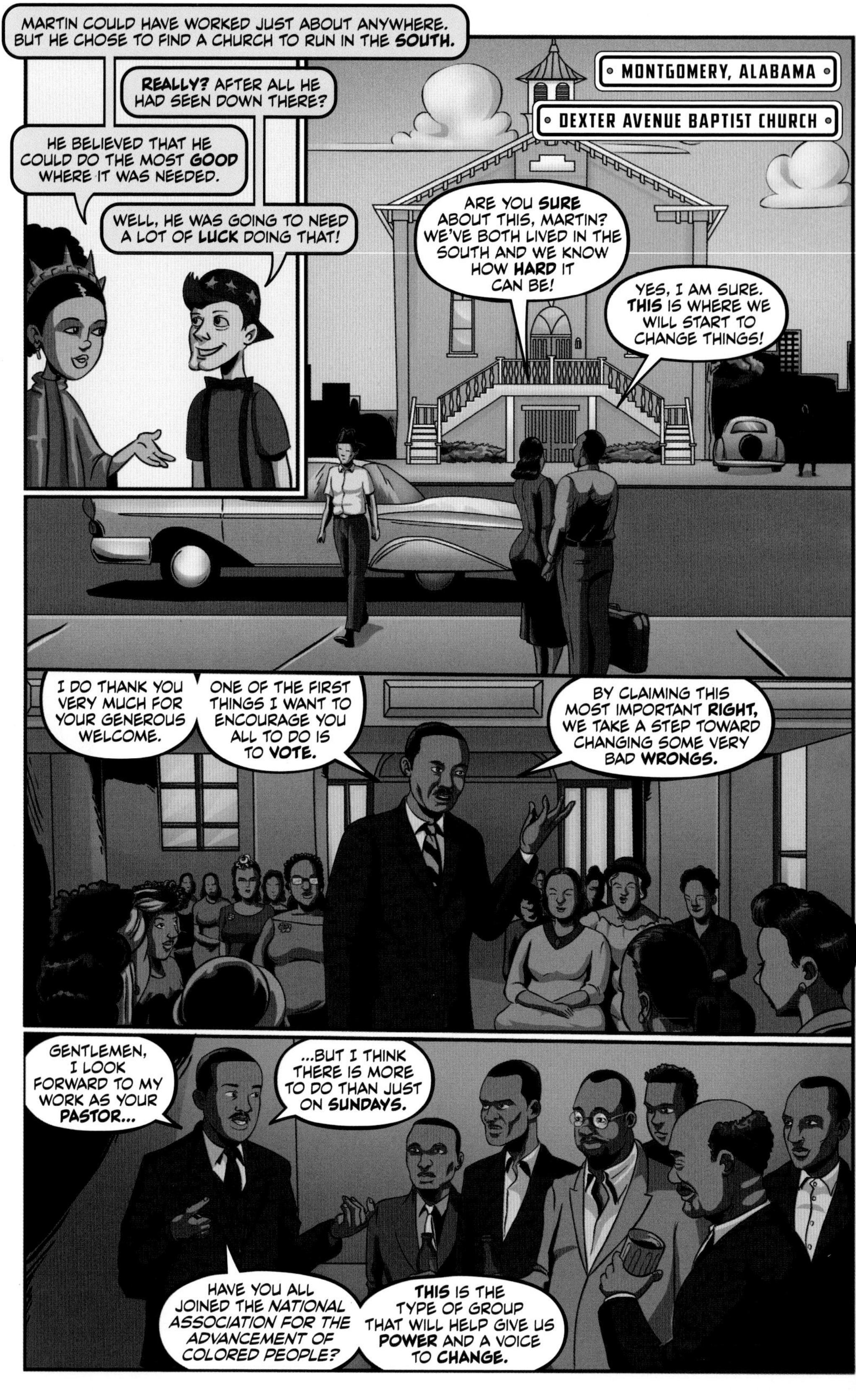
MARTIN COULD HAVE WORKED JUST ABOUT ANYWHERE. BUT HE CHOSE TO FIND A CHURCH TO RUN IN THE SOUTH.
REALLY? AFTER ALL HE HAD SEEN DOWN THERE?
HE BELIEVED THAT HE COULD DO THE MOST GOOD WHERE IT WAS NEEDED.
WELL, HE WAS GOING TO NEED A LOT OF LUCK DOING THAT!
MONTGOMERY, ALABAMA
DEXTER AVENUE BAPTIST CHURCH
ARE YOU SURE ABOUT THIS, MARTIN? WE'VE BOTH LIVED IN THE SOUTH AND WE KNOW HOW HARD IT CAN BE!
YES, I AM SURE. THIS IS WHERE WE WILL START TO CHANGE THINGS!
I DO THANK YOU VERY MUCH FOR YOUR GENEROUS WELCOME.
ONE OF THE FIRST THINGS I WANT TO ENCOURAGE YOU ALL TO DO IS TO VOTE.
BY CLAIMING THIS MOST IMPORTANT RIGHT, WE TAKE A STEP TOWARD CHANGING SOME VERY BAD WRONGS.
GENTLEMEN, I LOOK FORWARD TO MY WORK AS YOUR PASTOR...
...BUT I THINK THERE IS MORE TO DO THAN JUST ON SUNDAYS.
HAVE YOU ALL JOINED THE NATIONAL ASSOCIATION FOR THE ADVANCEMENT OF COLORED PEOPLE?
THIS IS THE TYPE OF GROUP THAT WILL HELP GIVE US POWER AND A VOICE TO CHANGE.

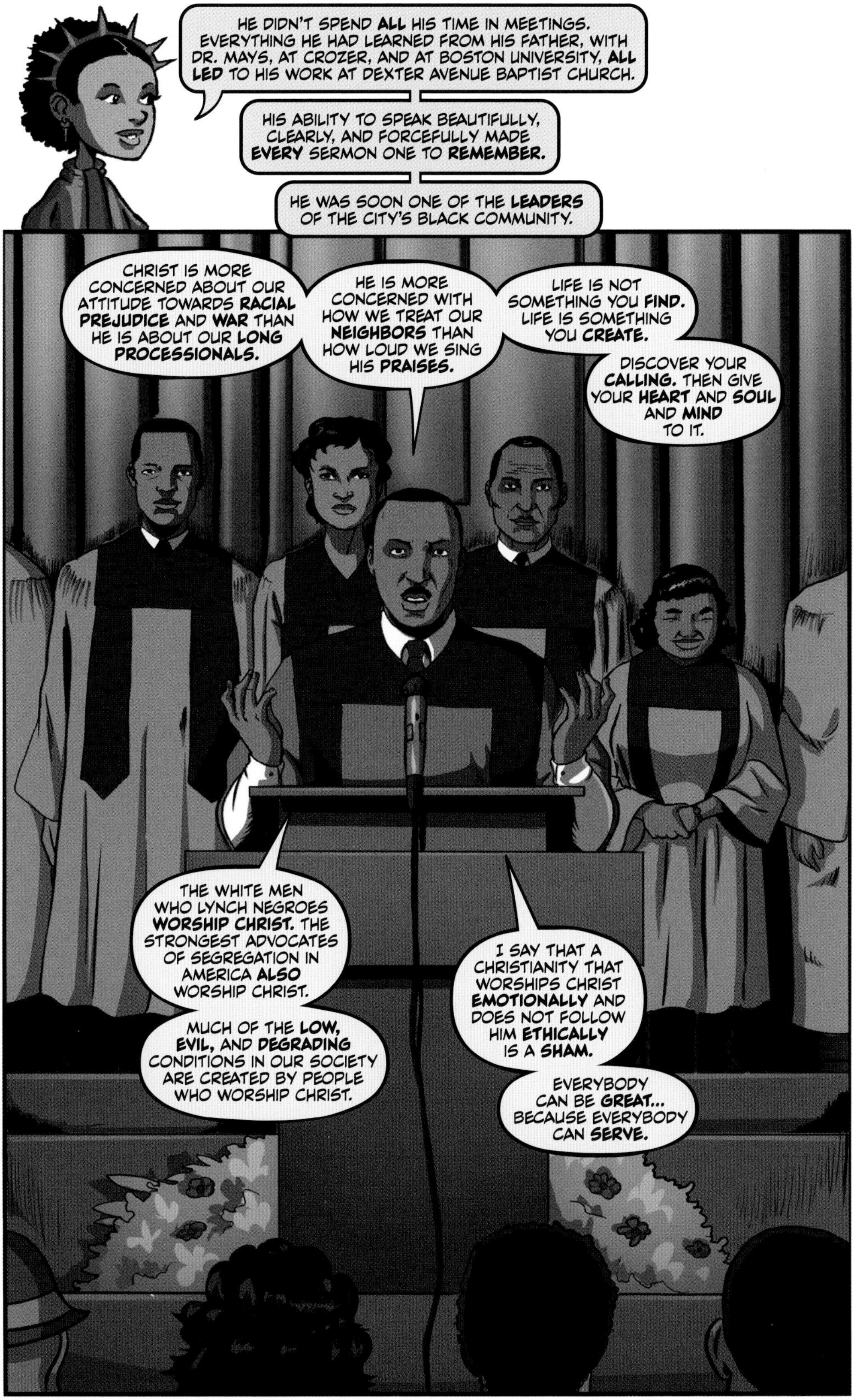
HE DIDN'T SPEND ALL HIS TIME IN MEETINGS. EVERYTHING HE HAD LEARNED FROM HIS FATHER, WITH DR. MAYS, AT CROZER, AND AT BOSTON UNIVERSITY, ALL LED TO HIS WORK AT DEXTER AVENUE BAPTIST CHURCH.
HIS ABILITY TO SPEAK BEAUTIFULLY, CLEARLY, AND FORCEFULLY MADE EVERY SERMON ONE TO REMEMBER.
HE WAS SOON ONE OF THE LEADERS OF THE CITY'S BLACK COMMUNITY.
CHRIST IS MORE CONCERNED ABOUT OUR ATTITUDE TOWARDS RACIAL PREJUDICE AND WAR THAN HE IS ABOUT OUR LONG PROCESSIONALS.
HE IS MORE CONCERNED WITH HOW WE TREAT OUR NEIGHBORS THAN HOW LOUD WE SING HIS PRAISES.
LIFE IS NOT SOMETHING YOU FIND. LIFE IS SOMETHING YOU CREATE.
DISCOVER YOUR CALLING. THEN GIVE YOUR HEART AND SOUL AND MIND TO IT.
THE WHITE MEN WHO LYNCH NEGROES WORSHIP CHRIST. THE STRONGEST ADVOCATES OF SEGREGATION IN AMERICA ALSO WORSHIP CHRIST.
MUCH OF THE LOW, EVIL, AND DEGRADING CONDITIONS IN OUR SOCIETY ARE CREATED BY PEOPLE WHO WORSHIP CHRIST.
I SAY THAT A CHRISTIANITY THAT WORSHIPS CHRIST EMOTIONALLY AND DOES NOT FOLLOW HIM ETHICALLY IS A SHAM.
EVERYBODY CAN BE GREAT... BECAUSE EVERYBODY CAN SERVE.

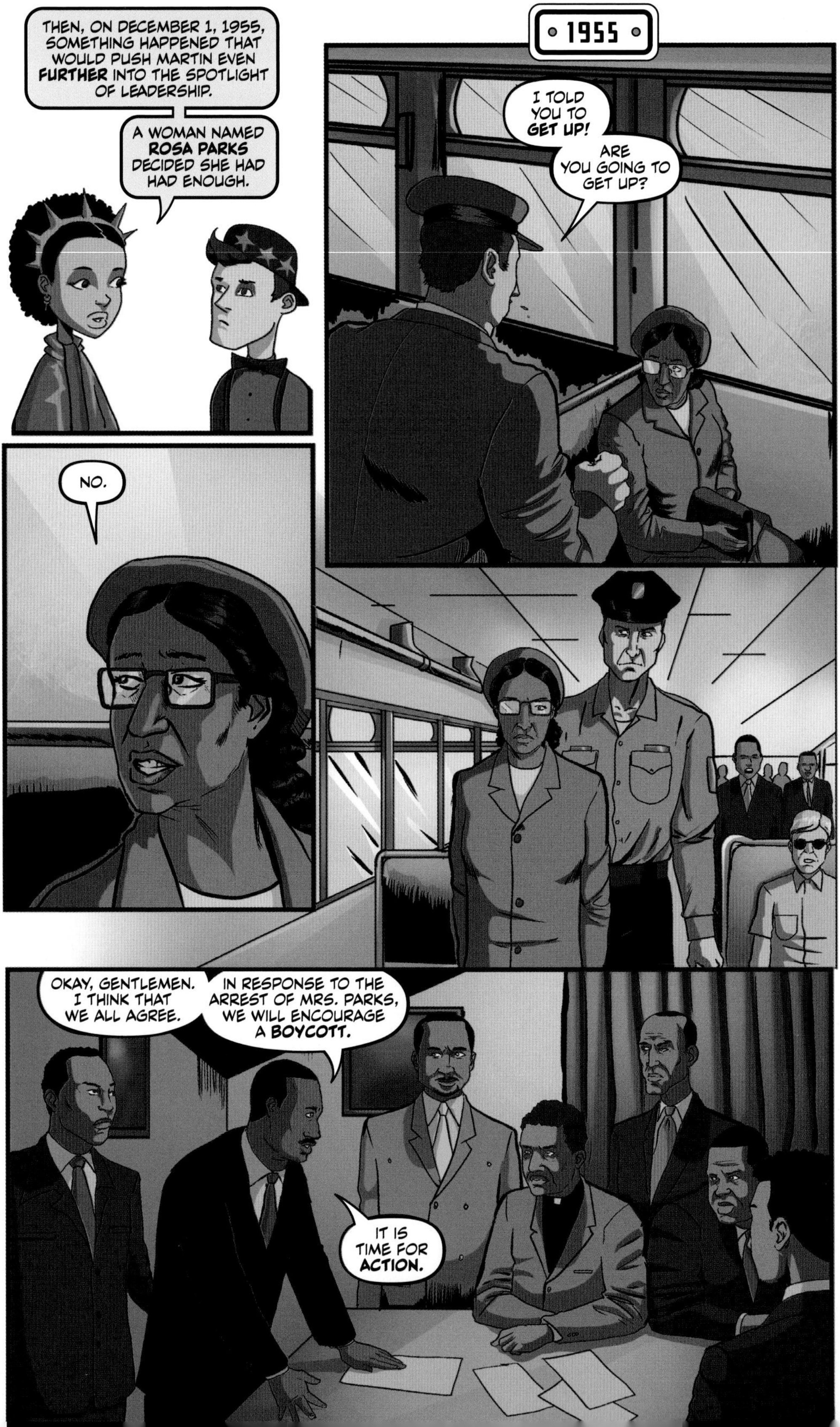
THEN, ON DECEMBER 1, 1955, SOMETHING HAPPENED THAT WOULD PUSH MARTIN EVEN FURTHER INTO THE SPOTLIGHT OF LEADERSHIP.
A WOMAN NAMED ROSA PARKS DECIDED SHE HAD HAD ENOUGH.
1955
I TOLD YOU TO GET UP!
ARE YOU GOING TO GET UP?
NO.
OKAY, GENTLEMEN. I THINK THAT WE ALL AGREE.
IN RESPONSE TO THE ARREST OF MRS. PARKS, WE WILL ENCOURAGE A BOYCOTT.
IT IS TIME FOR ACTION.

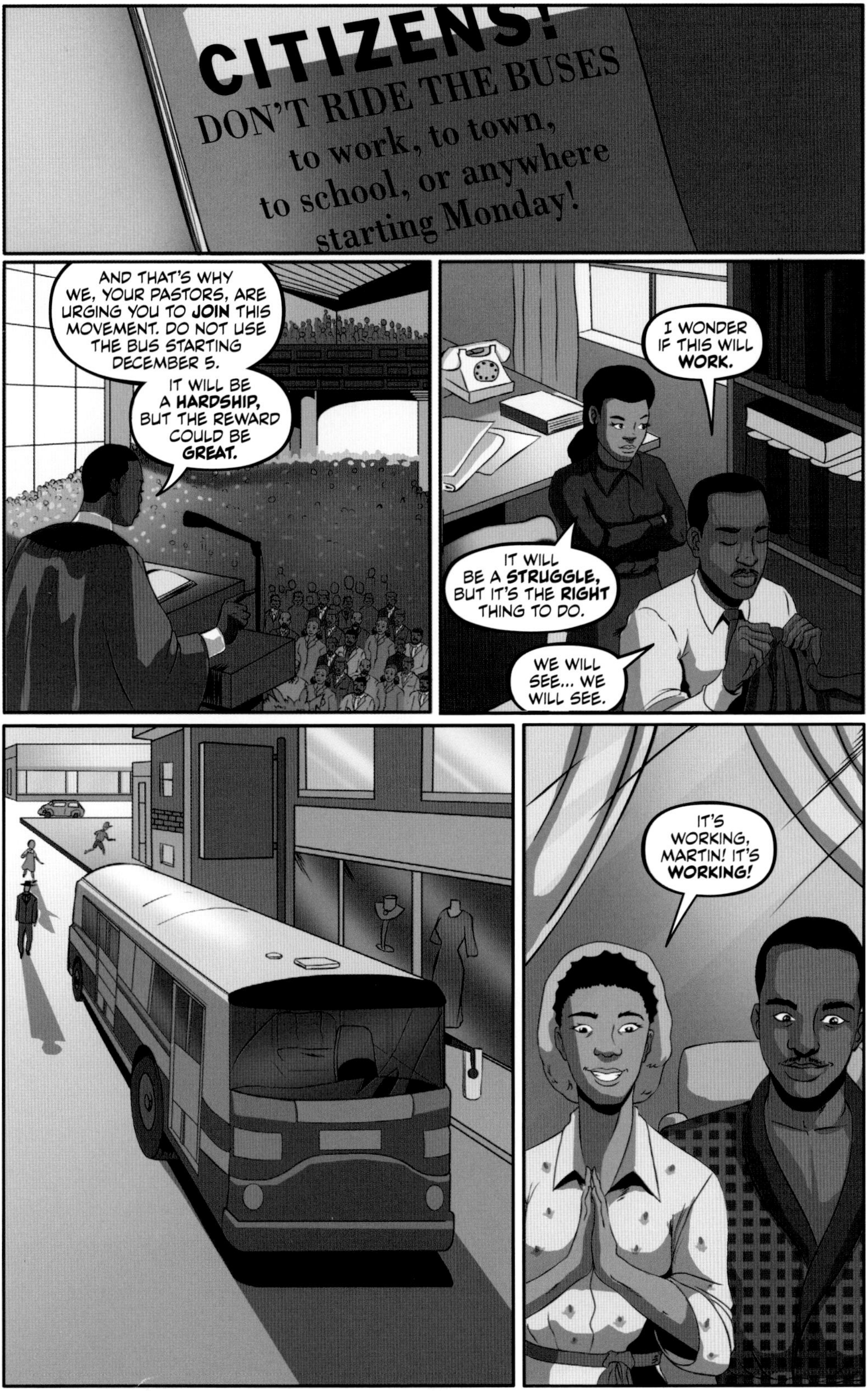
CITIZENS!
DON'T RIDE THE BUSES
to work, to town,
to school, or anywhere
starting Monday!
AND THAT'S WHY WE, YOUR PASTORS, ARE URGING YOU TO **JOIN** THIS MOVEMENT. DO NOT USE THE BUS STARTING DECEMBER 5.
IT WILL BE A **HARDSHIP,** BUT THE REWARD COULD BE **GREAT.**
I WONDER IF THIS WILL **WORK.**
IT WILL BE A **STRUGGLE,** BUT IT'S THE **RIGHT** THING TO DO.
WE WILL SEE... WE WILL SEE.
IT'S WORKING, MARTIN! IT'S **WORKING!**

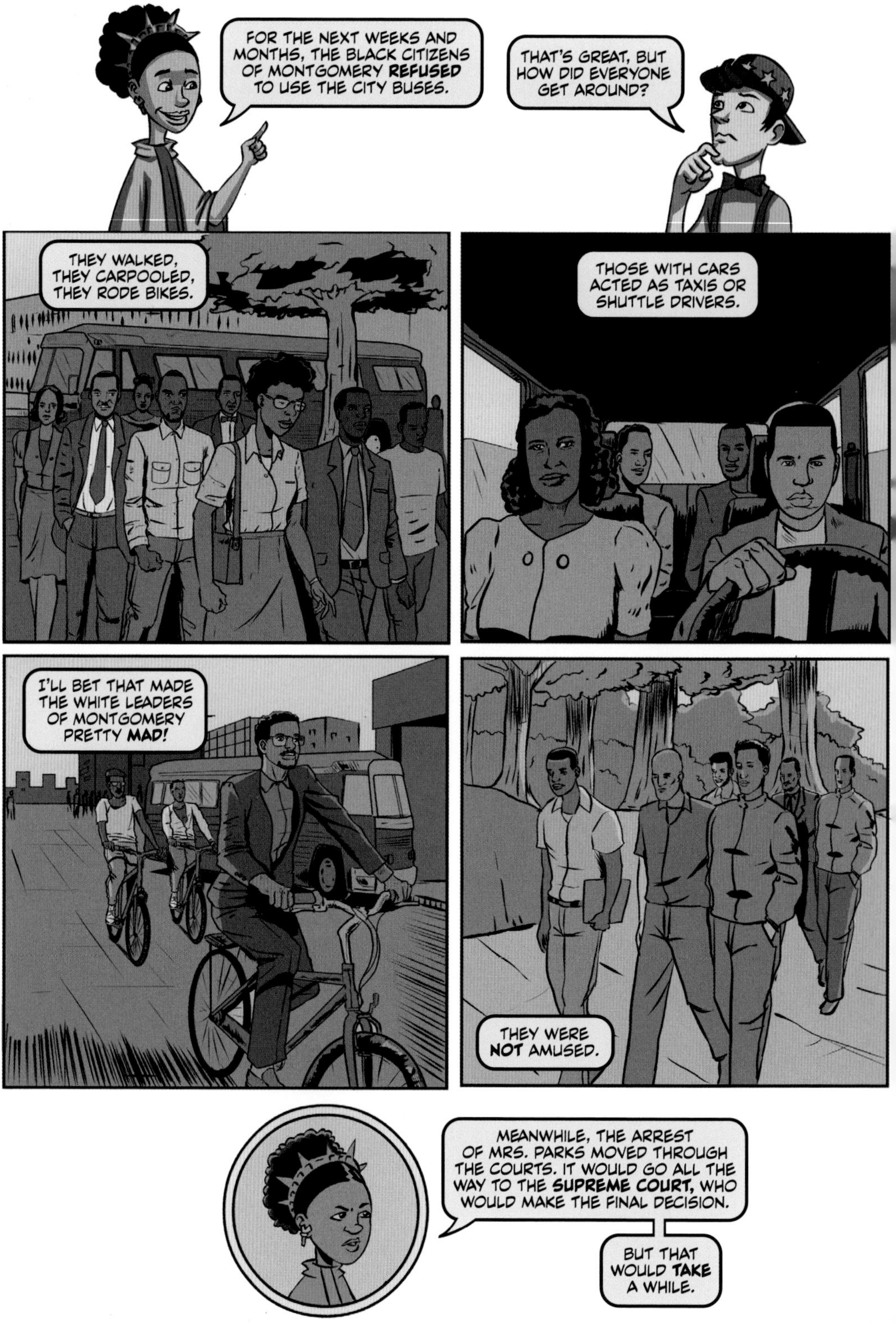
FOR THE NEXT WEEKS AND MONTHS, THE BLACK CITIZENS OF MONTGOMERY **REFUSED** TO USE THE CITY BUSES.
THAT'S GREAT, BUT HOW DID EVERYONE GET AROUND?
THEY WALKED, THEY CARPOOLED, THEY RODE BIKES.
THOSE WITH CARS ACTED AS TAXIS OR SHUTTLE DRIVERS.
I'LL BET THAT MADE THE WHITE LEADERS OF MONTGOMERY PRETTY **MAD!**
THEY WERE **NOT** AMUSED.
MEANWHILE, THE ARREST OF MRS. PARKS MOVED THROUGH THE COURTS. IT WOULD GO ALL THE WAY TO THE **SUPREME COURT,** WHO WOULD MAKE THE FINAL DECISION.
BUT THAT WOULD **TAKE** A WHILE.

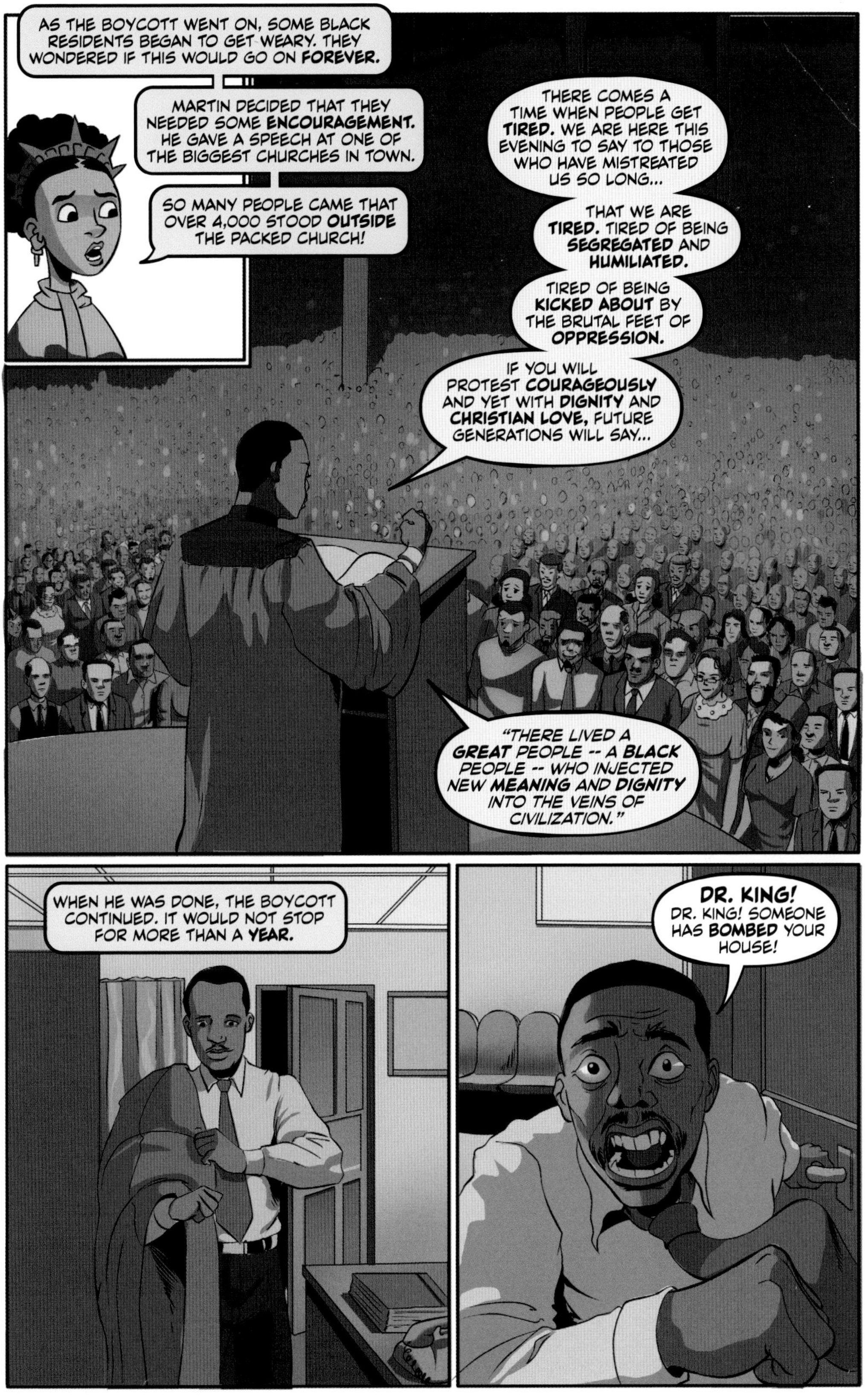
AS THE BOYCOTT WENT ON, SOME BLACK RESIDENTS BEGAN TO GET WEARY. THEY WONDERED IF THIS WOULD GO ON **FOREVER.**
MARTIN DECIDED THAT THEY NEEDED SOME **ENCOURAGEMENT.** HE GAVE A SPEECH AT ONE OF THE BIGGEST CHURCHES IN TOWN.
SO MANY PEOPLE CAME THAT OVER 4,000 STOOD **OUTSIDE** THE PACKED CHURCH!
THERE COMES A TIME WHEN PEOPLE GET **TIRED.** WE ARE HERE THIS EVENING TO SAY TO THOSE WHO HAVE MISTREATED US SO LONG...
THAT WE ARE **TIRED.** TIRED OF BEING **SEGREGATED** AND **HUMILIATED.**
TIRED OF BEING **KICKED ABOUT** BY THE BRUTAL FEET OF **OPPRESSION.**
IF YOU WILL PROTEST **COURAGEOUSLY** AND YET WITH **DIGNITY** AND **CHRISTIAN LOVE,** FUTURE GENERATIONS WILL SAY...
*"THERE LIVED A **GREAT** PEOPLE -- A **BLACK** PEOPLE -- WHO INJECTED NEW **MEANING** AND **DIGNITY** INTO THE VEINS OF CIVILIZATION."*
WHEN HE WAS DONE, THE BOYCOTT CONTINUED. IT WOULD NOT STOP FOR MORE THAN A **YEAR.**
DR. KING! DR. KING! SOMEONE HAS **BOMBED** YOUR HOUSE!

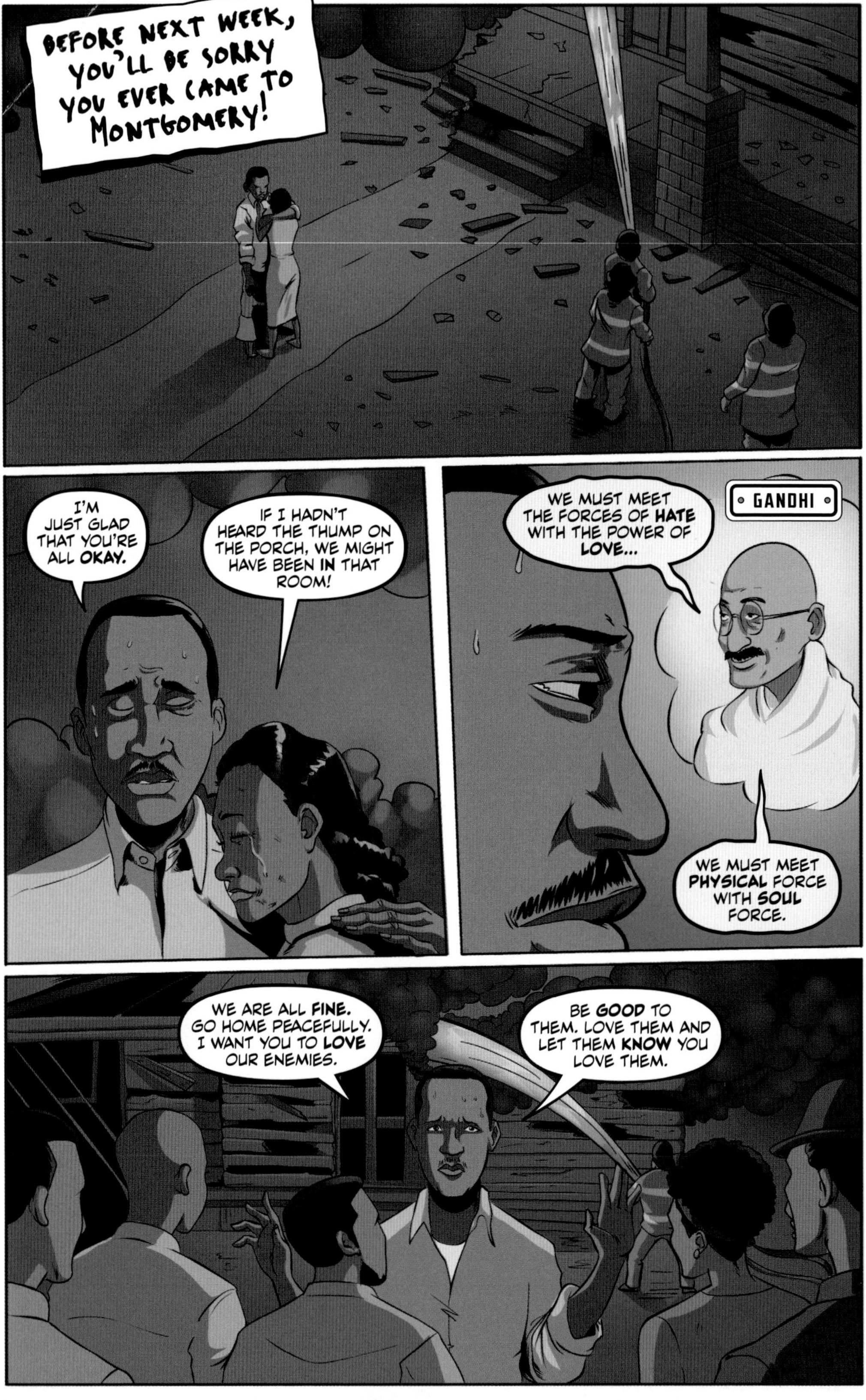

BEFORE NEXT WEEK, YOU'LL BE SORRY YOU EVER CAME TO MONTGOMERY!
I'M JUST GLAD THAT YOU'RE ALL **OKAY.**
IF I HADN'T HEARD THE THUMP ON THE PORCH, WE MIGHT HAVE BEEN **IN** THAT ROOM!
WE MUST MEET THE FORCES OF **HATE** WITH THE POWER OF **LOVE...**
GANDHI
WE MUST MEET **PHYSICAL** FORCE WITH **SOUL** FORCE.
WE ARE ALL **FINE.** GO HOME PEACEFULLY. I WANT YOU TO **LOVE** OUR ENEMIES.
BE **GOOD** TO THEM. LOVE THEM AND LET THEM **KNOW** YOU LOVE THEM.

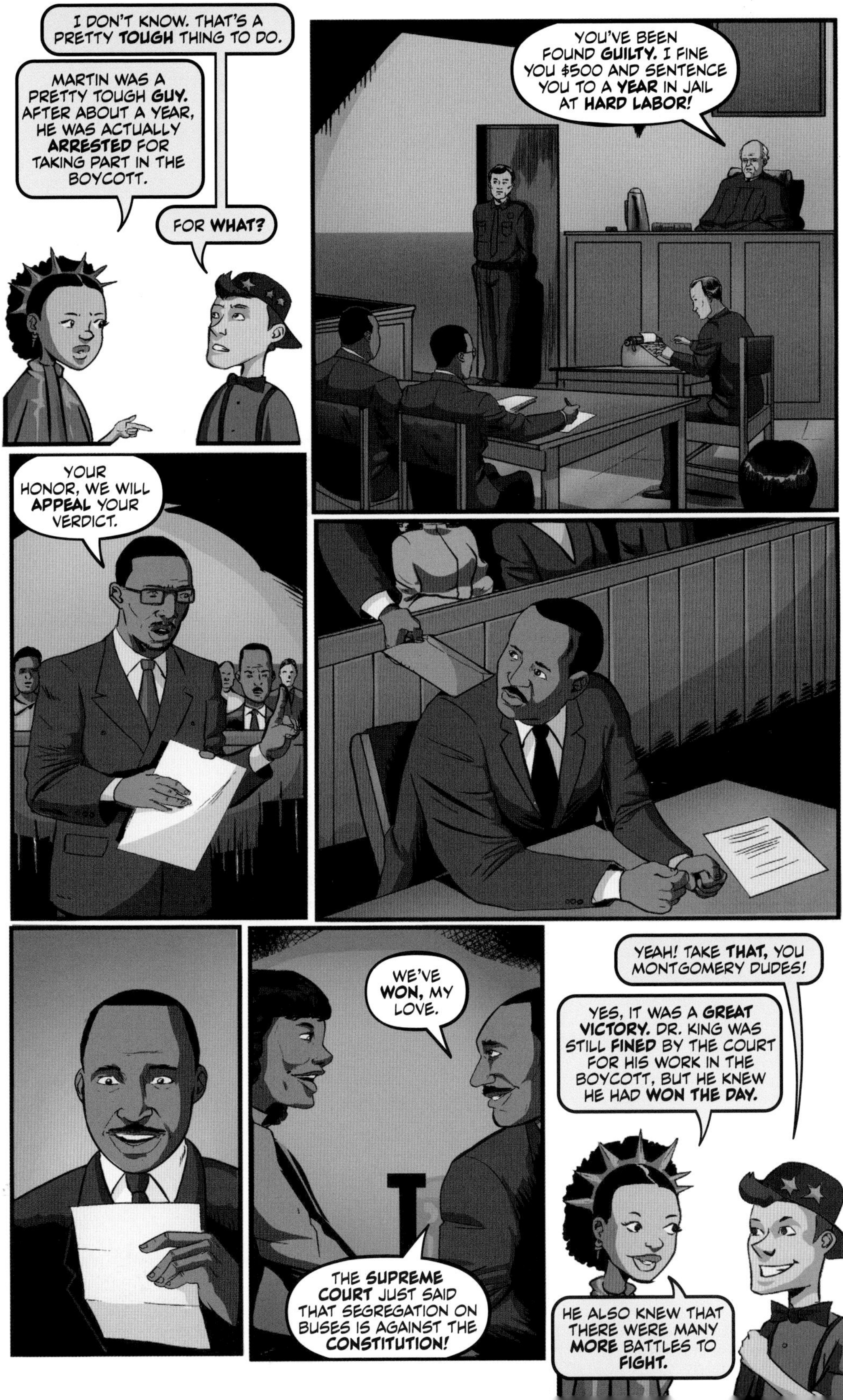
I DON'T KNOW. THAT'S A PRETTY TOUGH THING TO DO.
MARTIN WAS A PRETTY TOUGH GUY. AFTER ABOUT A YEAR, HE WAS ACTUALLY ARRESTED FOR TAKING PART IN THE BOYCOTT.
FOR WHAT?
YOU'VE BEEN FOUND GUILTY. I FINE YOU $500 AND SENTENCE YOU TO A YEAR IN JAIL AT HARD LABOR!
YOUR HONOR, WE WILL APPEAL YOUR VERDICT.
WE'VE WON, MY LOVE.
THE SUPREME COURT JUST SAID THAT SEGREGATION ON BUSES IS AGAINST THE CONSTITUTION!
YEAH! TAKE THAT, YOU MONTGOMERY DUDES!
YES, IT WAS A GREAT VICTORY. DR. KING WAS STILL FINED BY THE COURT FOR HIS WORK IN THE BOYCOTT, BUT HE KNEW HE HAD WON THE DAY.
HE ALSO KNEW THAT THERE WERE MANY MORE BATTLES TO FIGHT.

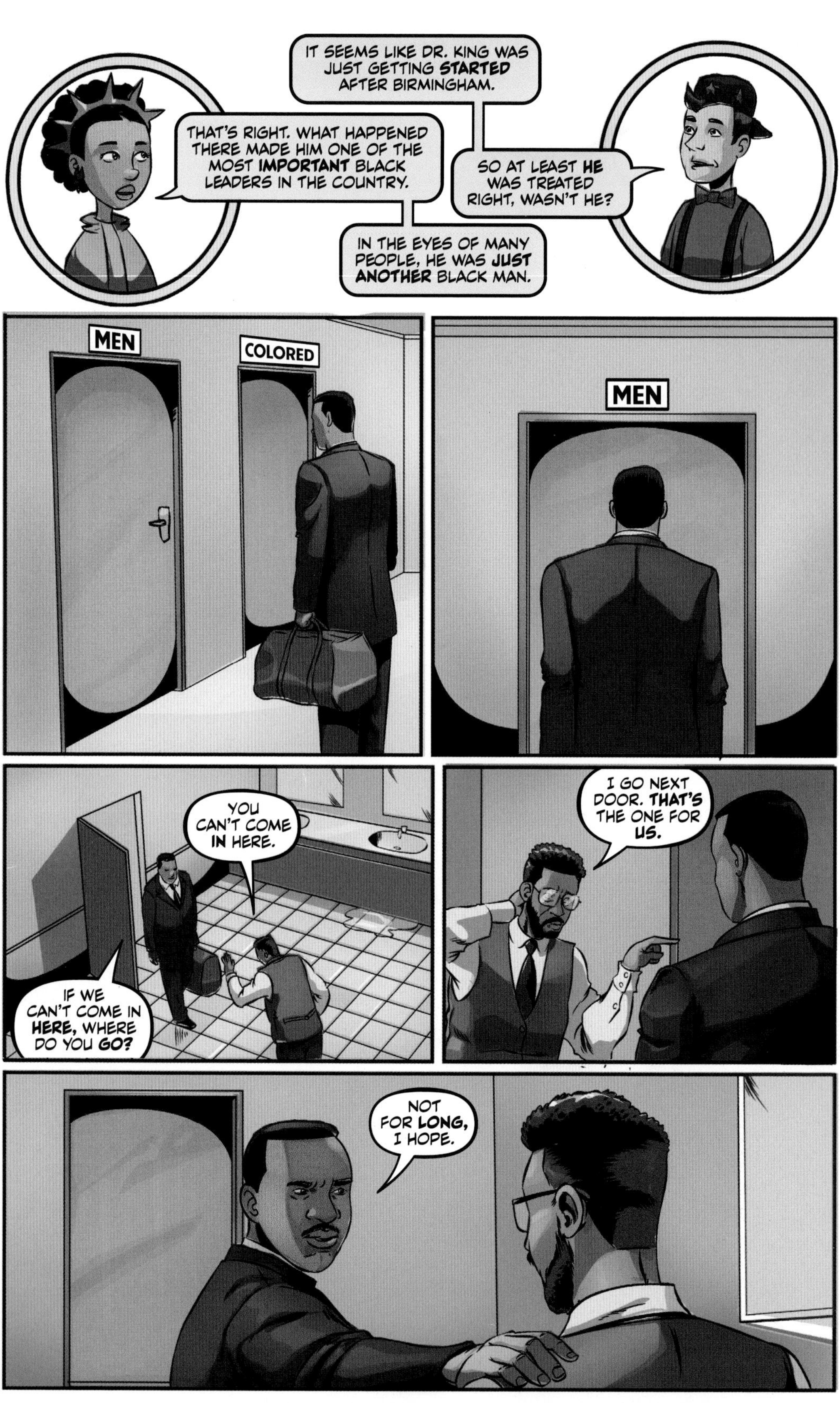
IT SEEMS LIKE DR. KING WAS JUST GETTING STARTED AFTER BIRMINGHAM.
THAT'S RIGHT. WHAT HAPPENED THERE MADE HIM ONE OF THE MOST IMPORTANT BLACK LEADERS IN THE COUNTRY.
SO AT LEAST HE WAS TREATED RIGHT, WASN'T HE?
IN THE EYES OF MANY PEOPLE, HE WAS JUST ANOTHER BLACK MAN.
MEN
COLORED
MEN
YOU CAN'T COME IN HERE.
IF WE CAN'T COME IN HERE, WHERE DO YOU GO?
I GO NEXT DOOR. THAT'S THE ONE FOR US.
NOT FOR LONG, I HOPE.

DIDN'T HE ACTUALLY TRAVEL TO **AFRICA** AROUND THEN?

YOU'VE DONE YOUR **HOMEWORK**, SAM! YES, DR. KING WAS INVITED TO VISIT **GHANA**, A NEW NATION IN AFRICA. THE PRIME MINISTER WANTED THIS IMPORTANT AMERICAN LEADER TO SEE **HISTORY** HAPPENING.

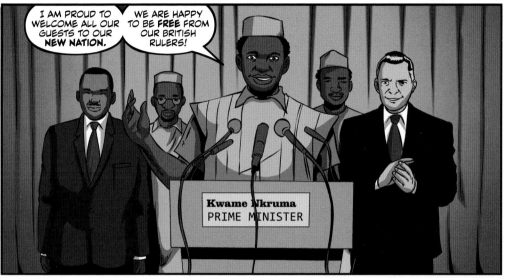

I AM PROUD TO WELCOME ALL OUR GUESTS TO OUR **NEW NATION.**

WE ARE HAPPY TO BE **FREE** FROM OUR BRITISH RULERS!

Kwame Nkruma
PRIME MINISTER

BUT HE WASN'T THE **ONLY** AMERICAN THERE, RIGHT?

DR. KING, HAPPY TO MEET YOU.

VICE PRESIDENT RICHARD NIXON

I'M GLAD YOU'RE HERE, TOO, MR. VICE PRESIDENT. BUT I WANT YOU TO COME DOWN TO **ALABAMA.**

PEOPLE THERE ARE **STILL WAITING** FOR THE FREEDOM GHANA IS CELEBRATING **TODAY.**

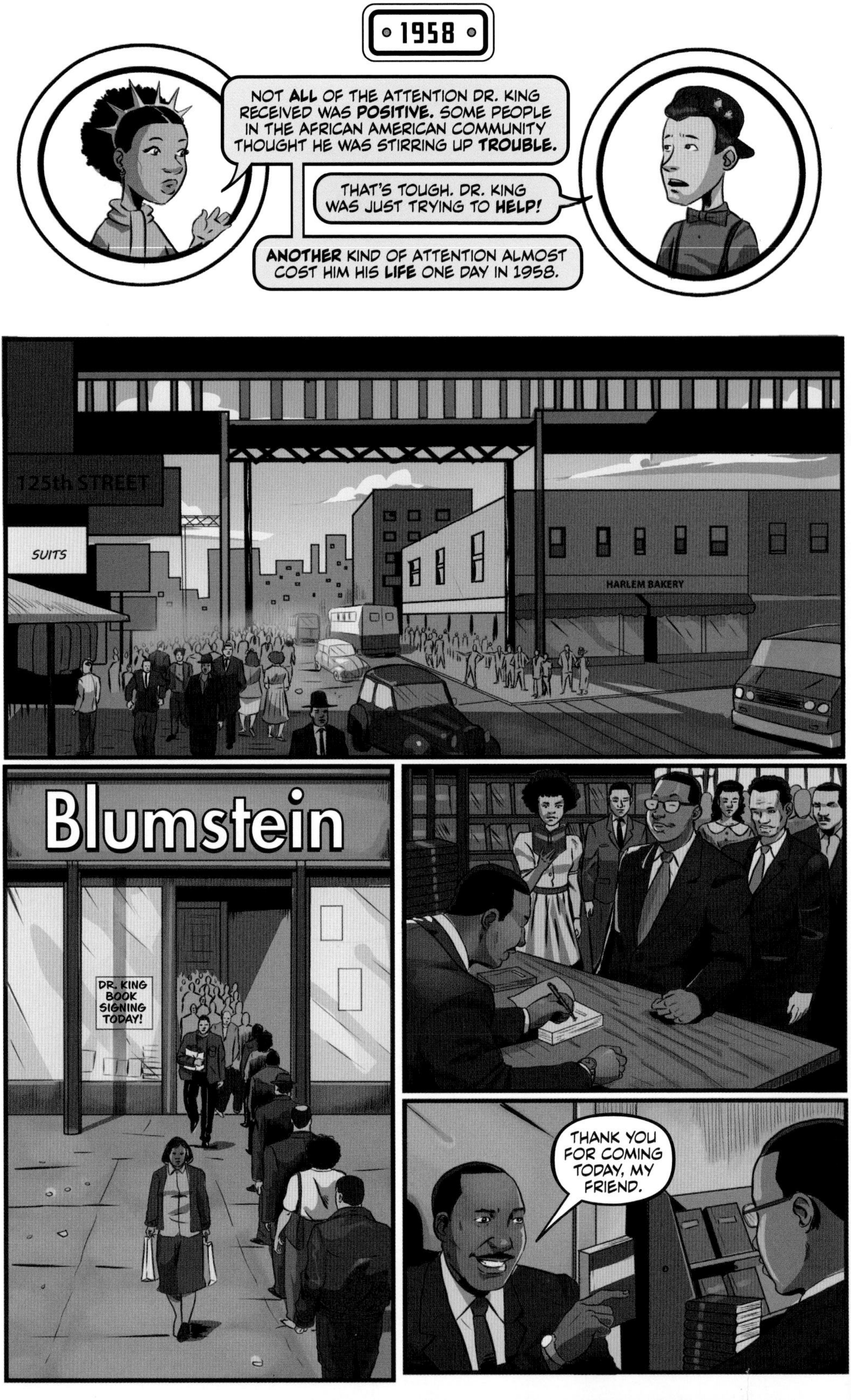
1958
NOT ALL OF THE ATTENTION DR. KING RECEIVED WAS POSITIVE. SOME PEOPLE IN THE AFRICAN AMERICAN COMMUNITY THOUGHT HE WAS STIRRING UP TROUBLE.
THAT'S TOUGH. DR. KING WAS JUST TRYING TO HELP!
ANOTHER KIND OF ATTENTION ALMOST COST HIM HIS LIFE ONE DAY IN 1958.
125th STREET
SUITS
HARLEM BAKERY
Blumstein
DR. KING BOOK SIGNING TODAY!
THANK YOU FOR COMING TODAY, MY FRIEND.

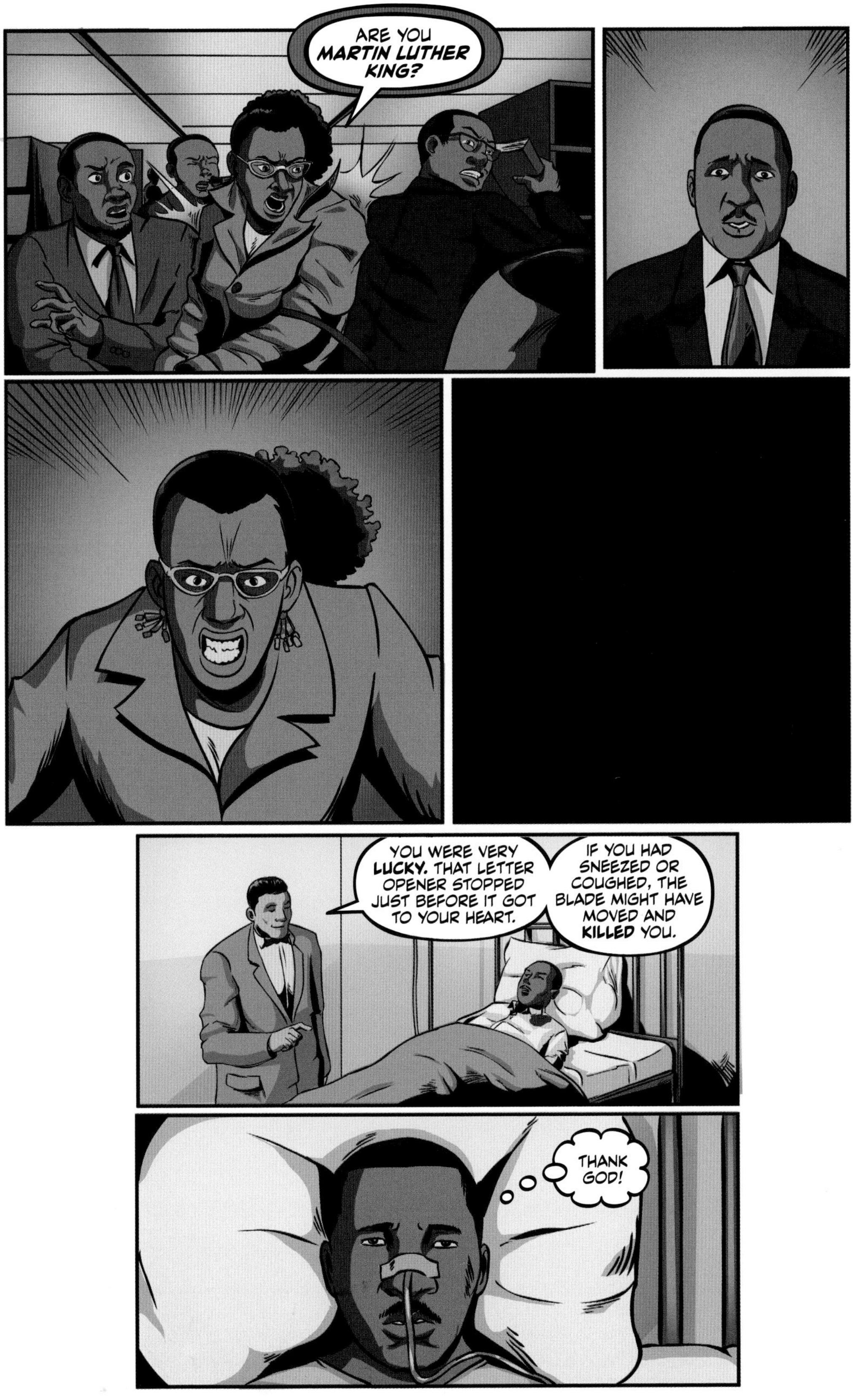
ARE YOU MARTIN LUTHER KING?
YOU WERE VERY LUCKY. THAT LETTER OPENER STOPPED JUST BEFORE IT GOT TO YOUR HEART.
IF YOU HAD SNEEZED OR COUGHED, THE BLADE MIGHT HAVE MOVED AND KILLED YOU.
THANK GOD!

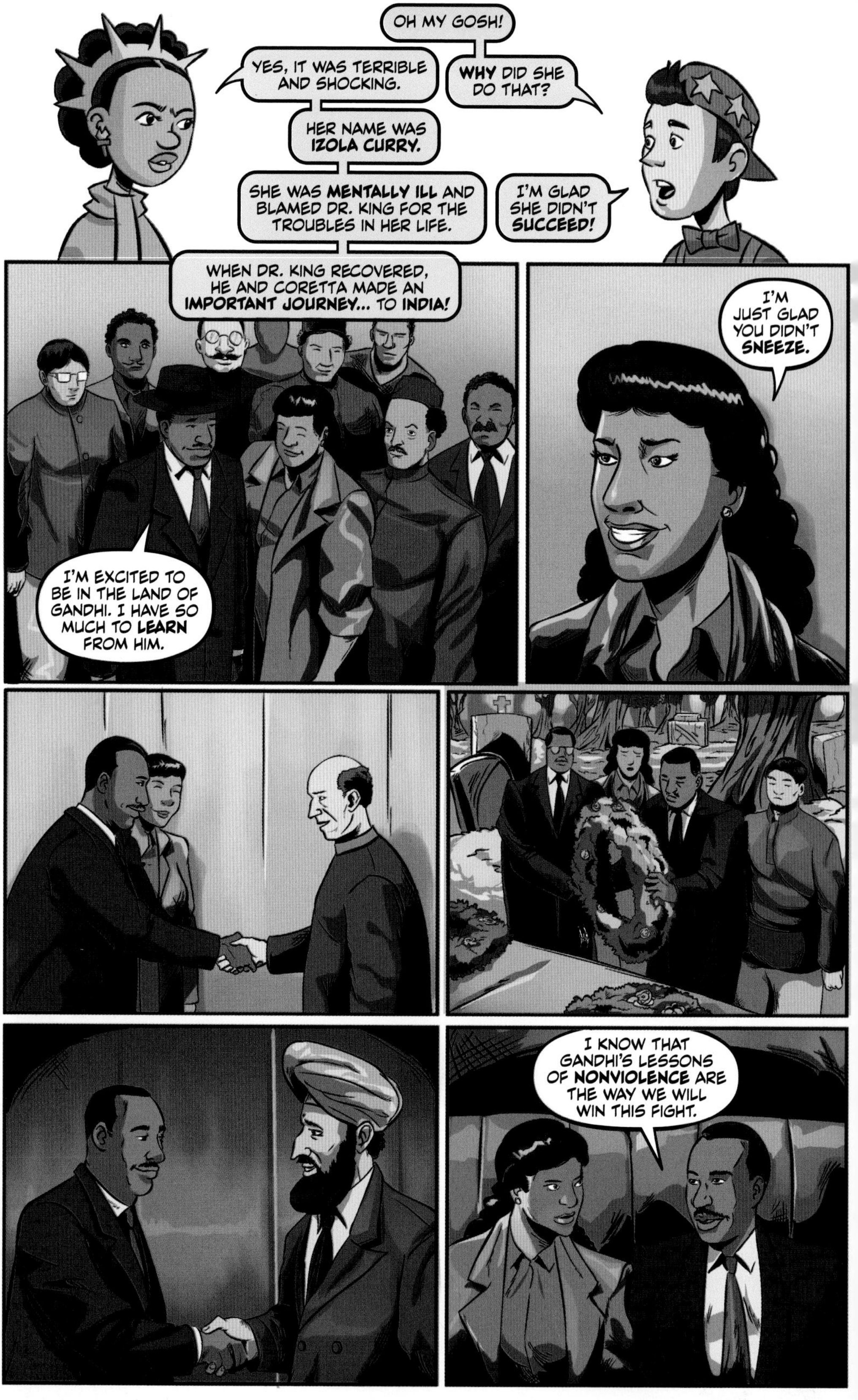
OH MY GOSH!
YES, IT WAS TERRIBLE AND SHOCKING.
WHY DID SHE DO THAT?
HER NAME WAS IZOLA CURRY.
SHE WAS MENTALLY ILL AND BLAMED DR. KING FOR THE TROUBLES IN HER LIFE.
I'M GLAD SHE DIDN'T SUCCEED!
WHEN DR. KING RECOVERED, HE AND CORETTA MADE AN IMPORTANT JOURNEY... TO INDIA!
I'M EXCITED TO BE IN THE LAND OF GANDHI. I HAVE SO MUCH TO LEARN FROM HIM.
I'M JUST GLAD YOU DIDN'T SNEEZE.
I KNOW THAT GANDHI'S LESSONS OF NONVIOLENCE ARE THE WAY WE WILL WIN THIS FIGHT.

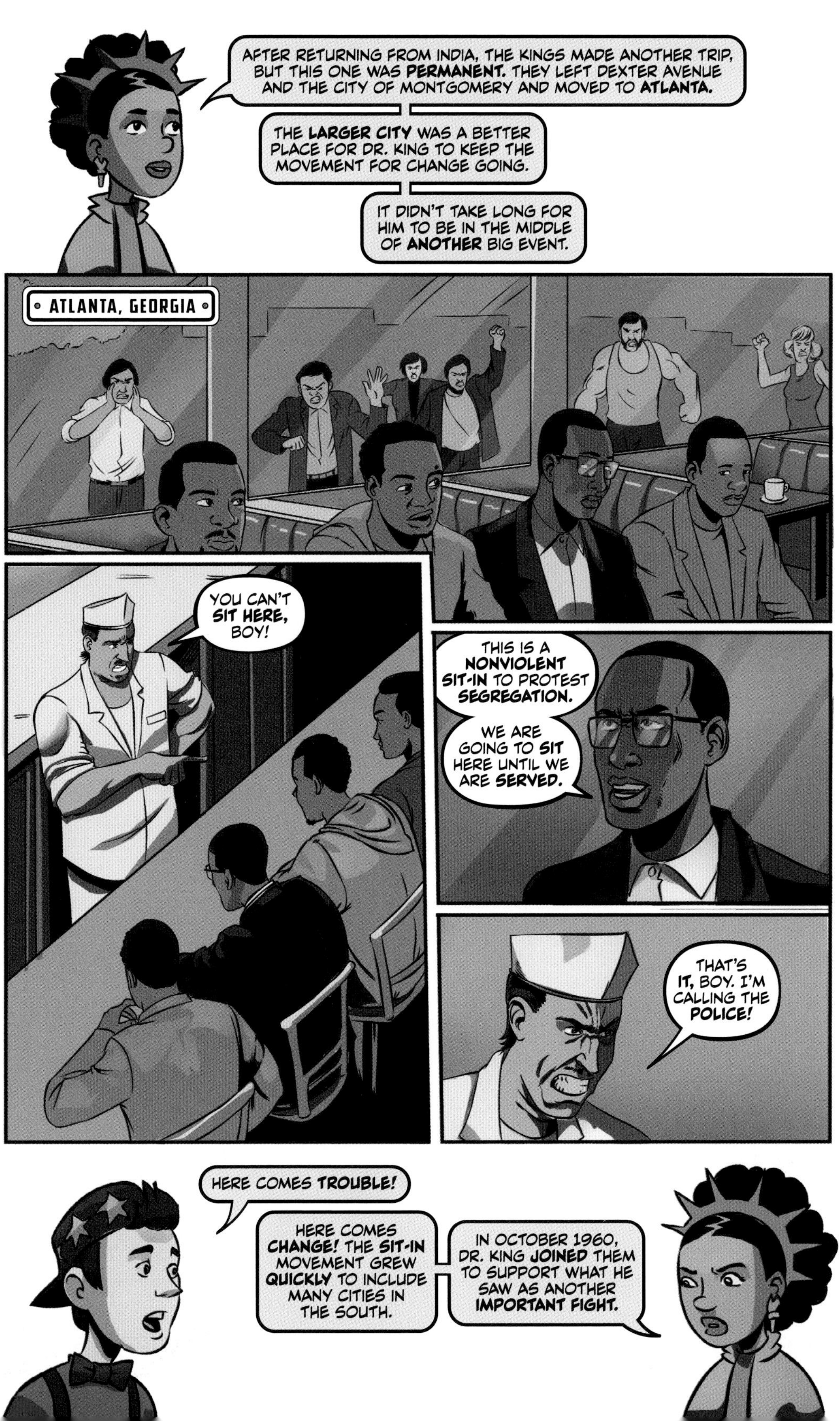
AFTER RETURNING FROM INDIA, THE KINGS MADE ANOTHER TRIP, BUT THIS ONE WAS PERMANENT. THEY LEFT DEXTER AVENUE AND THE CITY OF MONTGOMERY AND MOVED TO ATLANTA.
THE LARGER CITY WAS A BETTER PLACE FOR DR. KING TO KEEP THE MOVEMENT FOR CHANGE GOING.
IT DIDN'T TAKE LONG FOR HIM TO BE IN THE MIDDLE OF ANOTHER BIG EVENT.
ATLANTA, GEORGIA
YOU CAN'T SIT HERE, BOY!
THIS IS A NONVIOLENT SIT-IN TO PROTEST SEGREGATION.
WE ARE GOING TO SIT HERE UNTIL WE ARE SERVED.
THAT'S IT, BOY. I'M CALLING THE POLICE!
HERE COMES TROUBLE!
HERE COMES CHANGE! THE SIT-IN MOVEMENT GREW QUICKLY TO INCLUDE MANY CITIES IN THE SOUTH.
IN OCTOBER 1960, DR. KING JOINED THEM TO SUPPORT WHAT HE SAW AS ANOTHER IMPORTANT FIGHT.

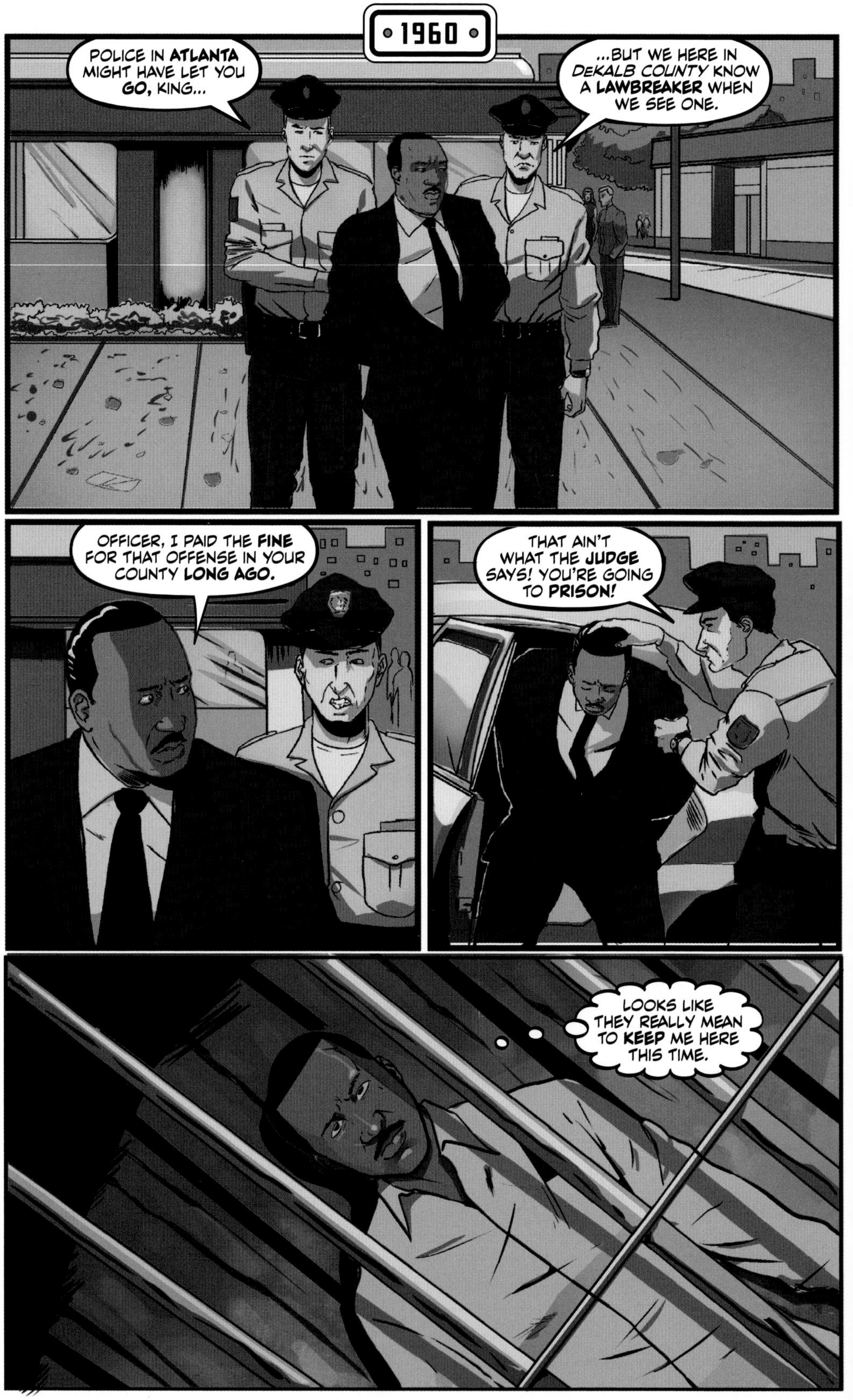
1960
POLICE IN ATLANTA MIGHT HAVE LET YOU GO, KING...
...BUT WE HERE IN DEKALB COUNTY KNOW A LAWBREAKER WHEN WE SEE ONE.
OFFICER, I PAID THE FINE FOR THAT OFFENSE IN YOUR COUNTY LONG AGO.
THAT AIN'T WHAT THE JUDGE SAYS! YOU'RE GOING TO PRISON!
LOOKS LIKE THEY REALLY MEAN TO KEEP ME HERE THIS TIME.

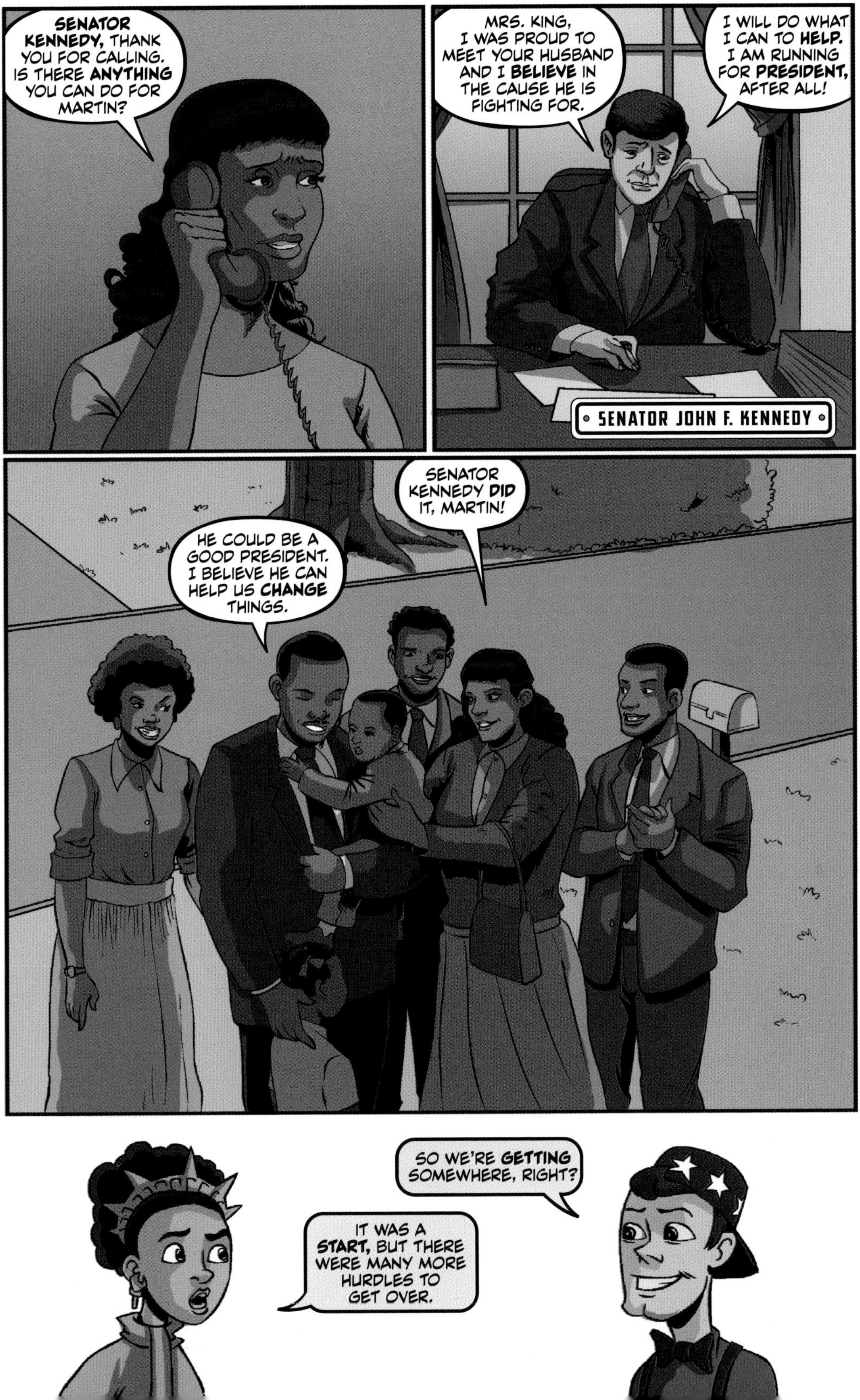
SENATOR KENNEDY, THANK YOU FOR CALLING. IS THERE ANYTHING YOU CAN DO FOR MARTIN?
MRS. KING, I WAS PROUD TO MEET YOUR HUSBAND AND I BELIEVE IN THE CAUSE HE IS FIGHTING FOR.
I WILL DO WHAT I CAN TO HELP. I AM RUNNING FOR PRESIDENT, AFTER ALL!
SENATOR JOHN F. KENNEDY
SENATOR KENNEDY DID IT, MARTIN!
HE COULD BE A GOOD PRESIDENT. I BELIEVE HE CAN HELP US CHANGE THINGS.
SO WE'RE GETTING SOMEWHERE, RIGHT?
IT WAS A START, BUT THERE WERE MANY MORE HURDLES TO GET OVER.

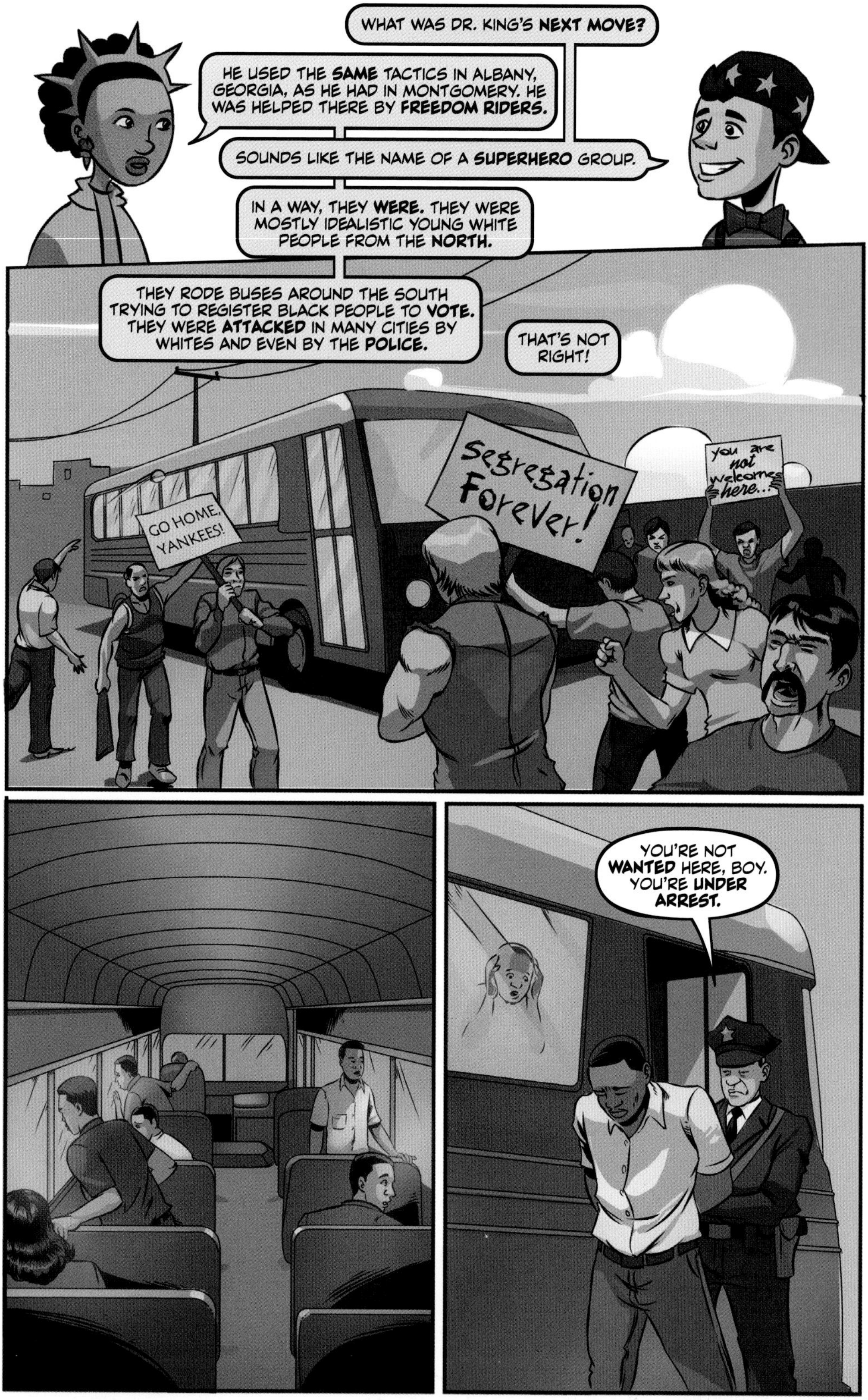
WHAT WAS DR. KING'S NEXT MOVE?
HE USED THE SAME TACTICS IN ALBANY, GEORGIA, AS HE HAD IN MONTGOMERY. HE WAS HELPED THERE BY FREEDOM RIDERS.
SOUNDS LIKE THE NAME OF A SUPERHERO GROUP.
IN A WAY, THEY WERE. THEY WERE MOSTLY IDEALISTIC YOUNG WHITE PEOPLE FROM THE NORTH.
THEY RODE BUSES AROUND THE SOUTH TRYING TO REGISTER BLACK PEOPLE TO VOTE. THEY WERE ATTACKED IN MANY CITIES BY WHITES AND EVEN BY THE POLICE.
THAT'S NOT RIGHT!
Segregation Forever!
you are not welcome here...
GO HOME, YANKEES!
YOU'RE NOT WANTED HERE, BOY. YOU'RE UNDER ARREST.

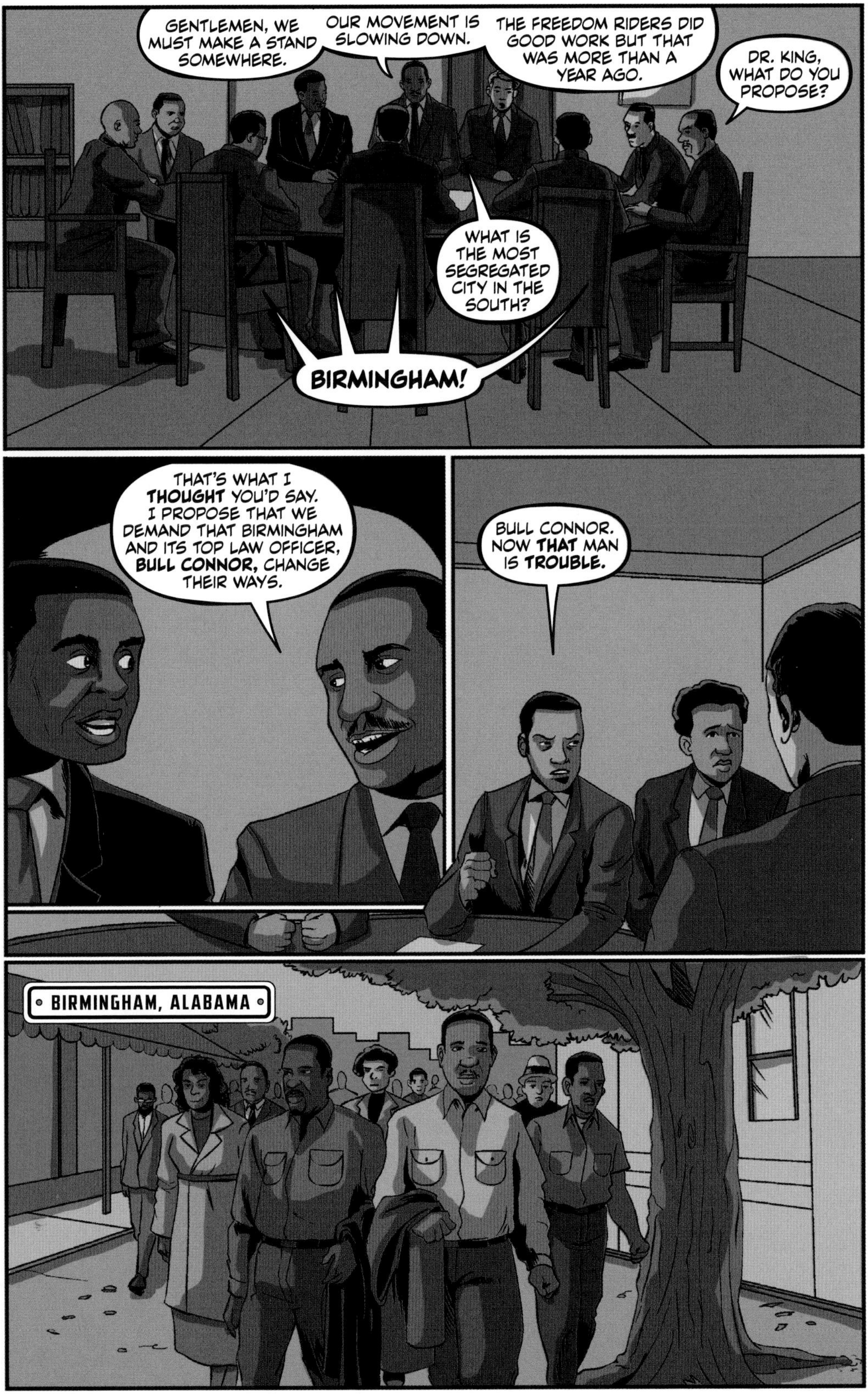
GENTLEMEN, WE MUST MAKE A STAND SOMEWHERE.
OUR MOVEMENT IS SLOWING DOWN.
THE FREEDOM RIDERS DID GOOD WORK BUT THAT WAS MORE THAN A YEAR AGO.
DR. KING, WHAT DO YOU PROPOSE?
WHAT IS THE MOST SEGREGATED CITY IN THE SOUTH?
BIRMINGHAM!
THAT'S WHAT I THOUGHT YOU'D SAY. I PROPOSE THAT WE DEMAND THAT BIRMINGHAM AND ITS TOP LAW OFFICER, BULL CONNOR, CHANGE THEIR WAYS.
BULL CONNOR. NOW THAT MAN IS TROUBLE.
BIRMINGHAM, ALABAMA

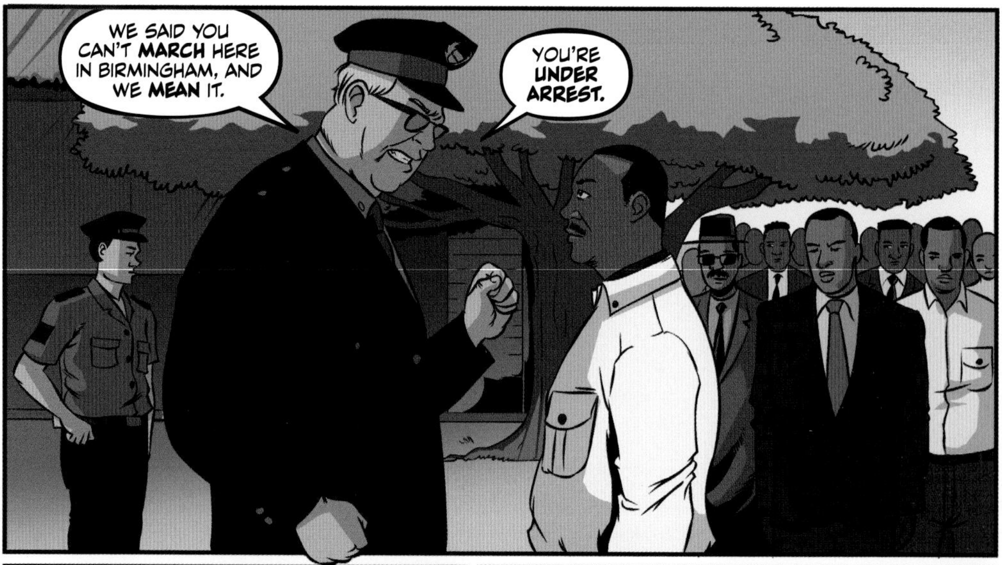
WE SAID YOU CAN'T MARCH HERE IN BIRMINGHAM, AND WE MEAN IT.
YOU'RE UNDER ARREST.

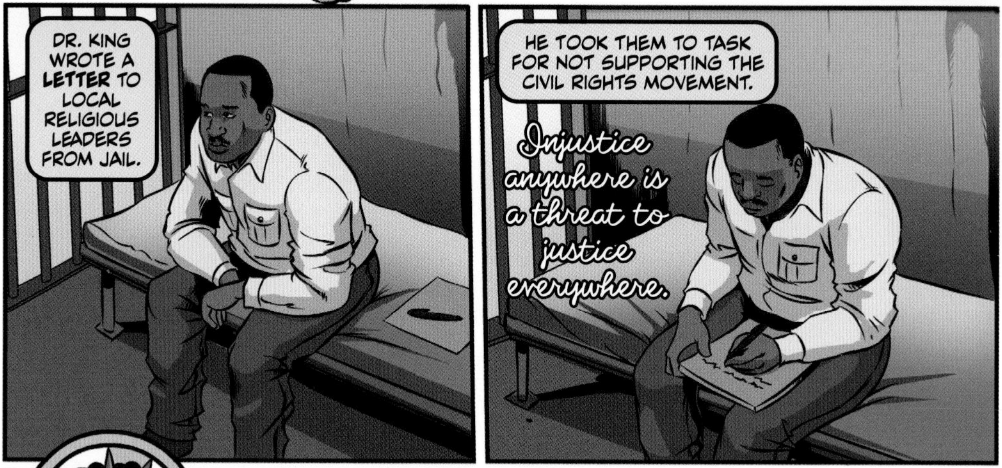
DR. KING WROTE A LETTER TO LOCAL RELIGIOUS LEADERS FROM JAIL.
HE TOOK THEM TO TASK FOR NOT SUPPORTING THE CIVIL RIGHTS MOVEMENT.
Injustice anywhere is a threat to justice everywhere.

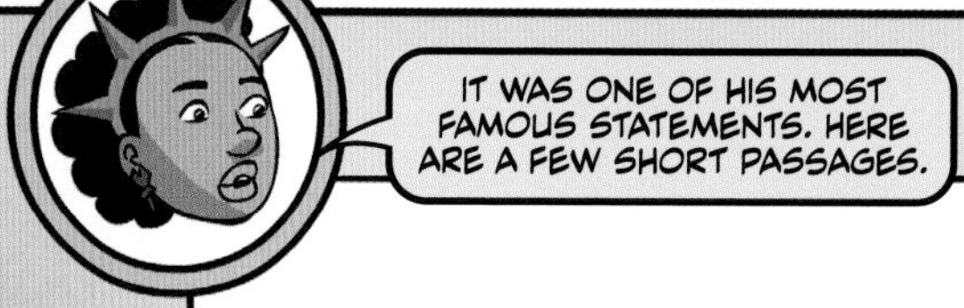
IT WAS ONE OF HIS MOST FAMOUS STATEMENTS. HERE ARE A FEW SHORT PASSAGES.

Martin Luther King, Jr.
Birmingham City Jail
April 16, 1963

One has not only a legal but a moral responsibility to obey just laws. Conversely, one has a moral responsibility to disobey unjust laws.

I doubt that you would have so warmly commended the police force if you had seen its dogs sinking their teeth into unarmed, nonviolent Negroes.

Let us all hope that the dark clouds of racial prejudice will soon pass away and the deep fog of misunderstanding will be lifted from our fear-drenched communities, and in some not too distant tomorrow the radiant stars of love and brotherhood will shine over our great nation with all their scintillating beauty.

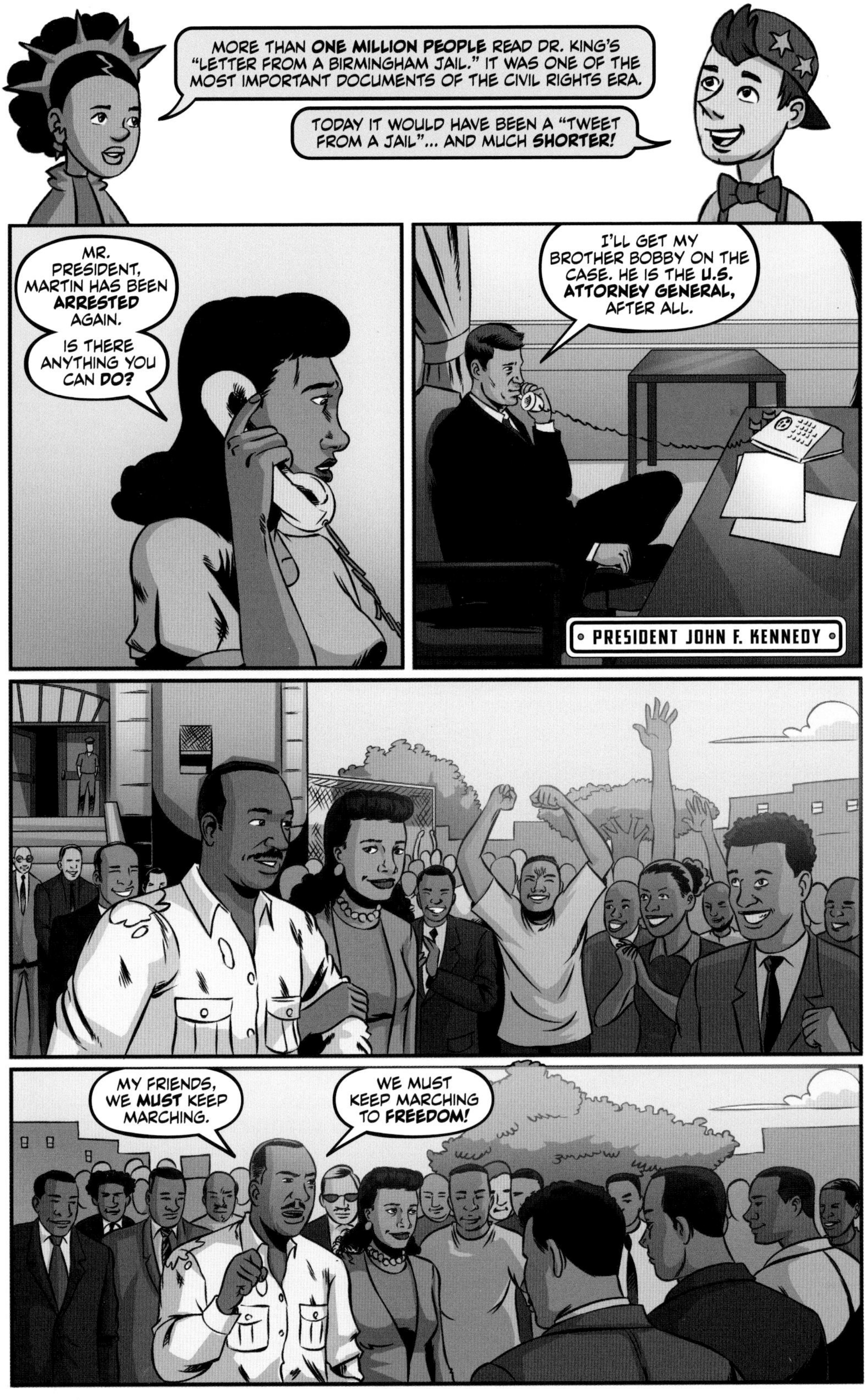
MORE THAN ONE MILLION PEOPLE READ DR. KING'S "LETTER FROM A BIRMINGHAM JAIL." IT WAS ONE OF THE MOST IMPORTANT DOCUMENTS OF THE CIVIL RIGHTS ERA.
TODAY IT WOULD HAVE BEEN A "TWEET FROM A JAIL"... AND MUCH SHORTER!
MR. PRESIDENT, MARTIN HAS BEEN ARRESTED AGAIN.
IS THERE ANYTHING YOU CAN DO?
I'LL GET MY BROTHER BOBBY ON THE CASE. HE IS THE U.S. ATTORNEY GENERAL, AFTER ALL.
PRESIDENT JOHN F. KENNEDY
MY FRIENDS, WE MUST KEEP MARCHING.
WE MUST KEEP MARCHING TO FREEDOM!

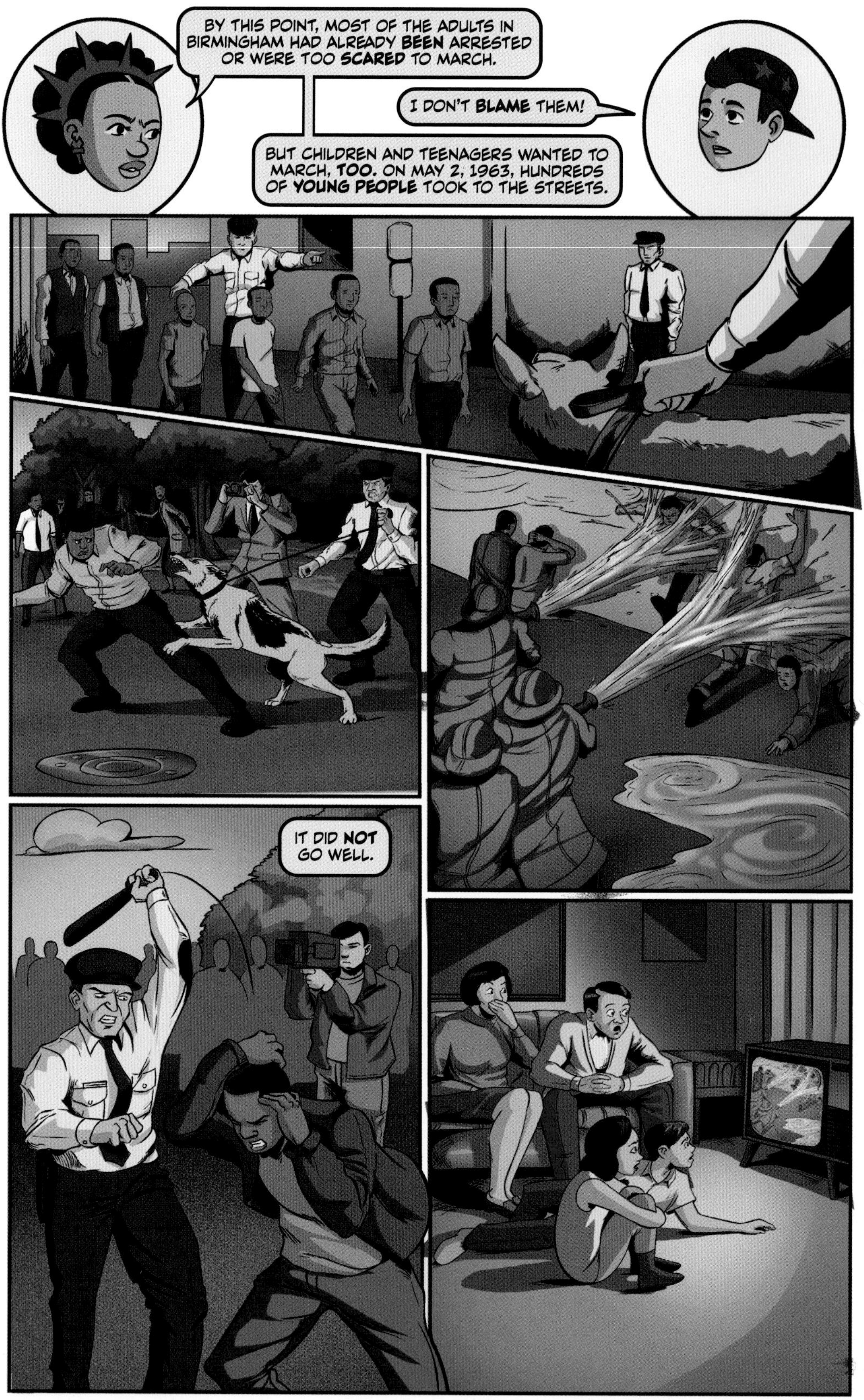

BY THIS POINT, MOST OF THE ADULTS IN BIRMINGHAM HAD ALREADY BEEN ARRESTED OR WERE TOO SCARED TO MARCH.
I DON'T BLAME THEM!
BUT CHILDREN AND TEENAGERS WANTED TO MARCH, TOO. ON MAY 2, 1963, HUNDREDS OF YOUNG PEOPLE TOOK TO THE STREETS.
IT DID NOT GO WELL.

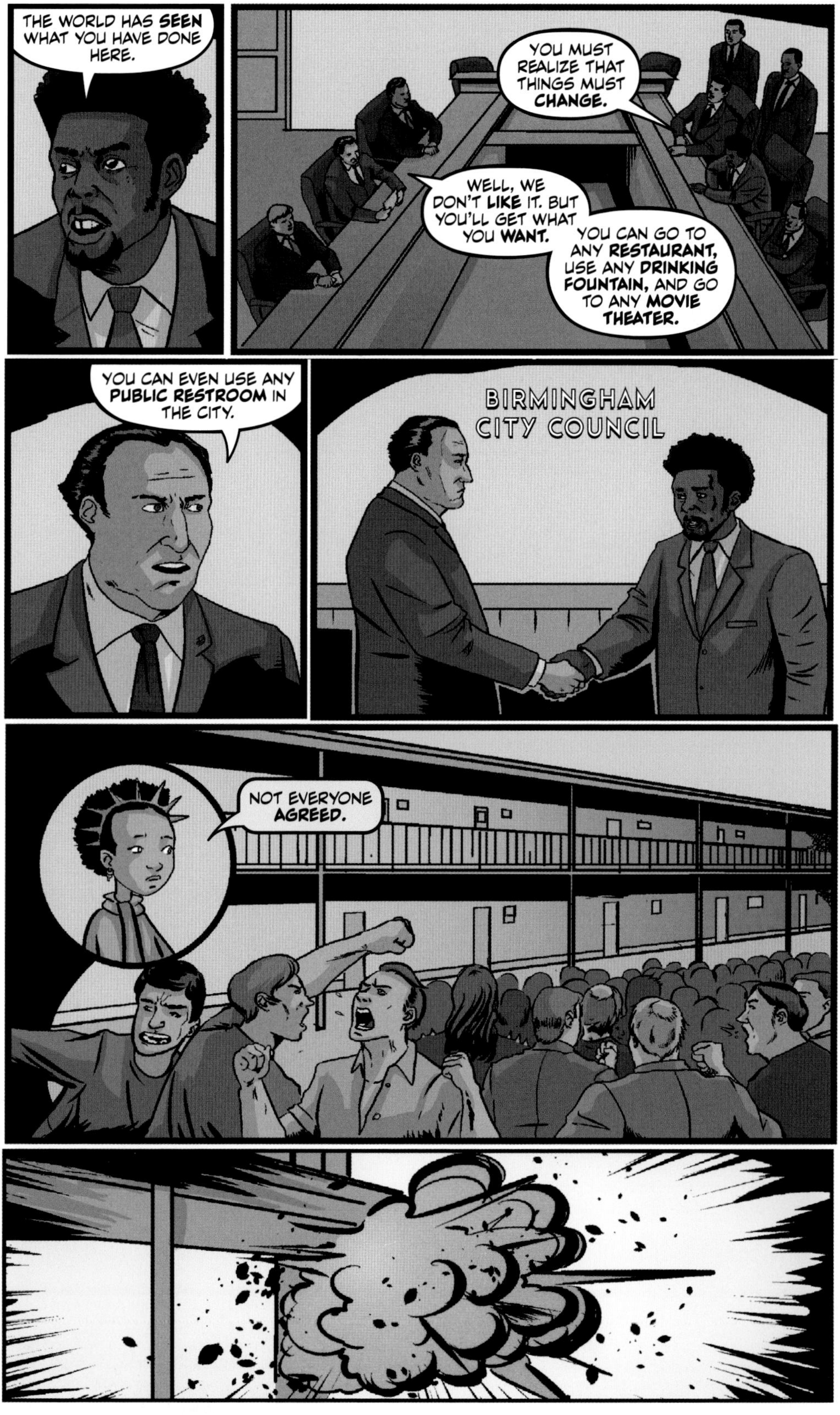
THE WORLD HAS SEEN WHAT YOU HAVE DONE HERE.
YOU MUST REALIZE THAT THINGS MUST CHANGE.
WELL, WE DON'T LIKE IT. BUT YOU'LL GET WHAT YOU WANT.
YOU CAN GO TO ANY RESTAURANT, USE ANY DRINKING FOUNTAIN, AND GO TO ANY MOVIE THEATER.
YOU CAN EVEN USE ANY PUBLIC RESTROOM IN THE CITY.
BIRMINGHAM CITY COUNCIL
NOT EVERYONE AGREED.

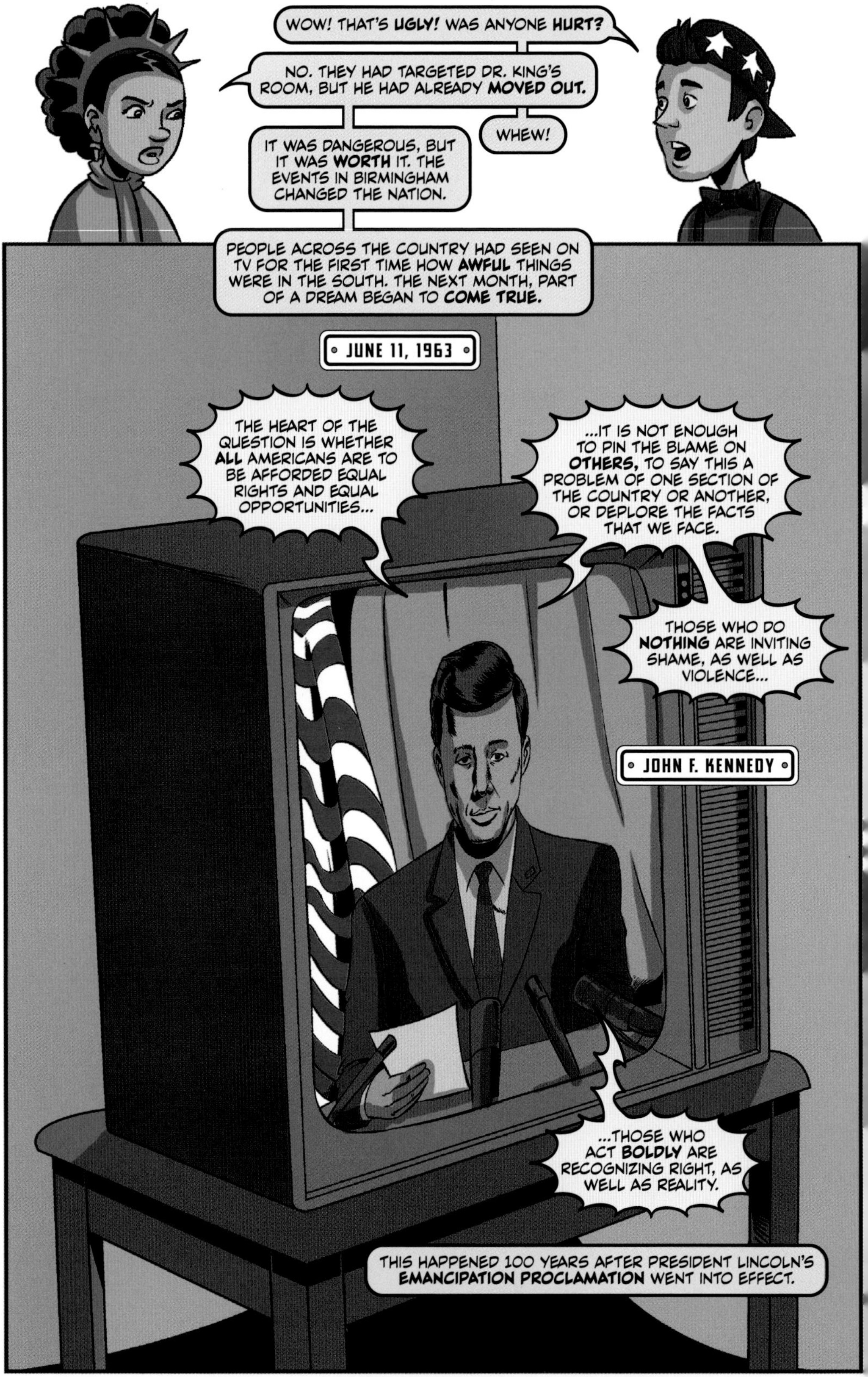
WOW! THAT'S UGLY! WAS ANYONE HURT?
NO. THEY HAD TARGETED DR. KING'S ROOM, BUT HE HAD ALREADY MOVED OUT.
WHEW!
IT WAS DANGEROUS, BUT IT WAS WORTH IT. THE EVENTS IN BIRMINGHAM CHANGED THE NATION.
PEOPLE ACROSS THE COUNTRY HAD SEEN ON TV FOR THE FIRST TIME HOW AWFUL THINGS WERE IN THE SOUTH. THE NEXT MONTH, PART OF A DREAM BEGAN TO COME TRUE.
JUNE 11, 1963
THE HEART OF THE QUESTION IS WHETHER ALL AMERICANS ARE TO BE AFFORDED EQUAL RIGHTS AND EQUAL OPPORTUNITIES...
...IT IS NOT ENOUGH TO PIN THE BLAME ON OTHERS, TO SAY THIS A PROBLEM OF ONE SECTION OF THE COUNTRY OR ANOTHER, OR DEPLORE THE FACTS THAT WE FACE.
THOSE WHO DO NOTHING ARE INVITING SHAME, AS WELL AS VIOLENCE...
JOHN F. KENNEDY
...THOSE WHO ACT BOLDLY ARE RECOGNIZING RIGHT, AS WELL AS REALITY.
THIS HAPPENED 100 YEARS AFTER PRESIDENT LINCOLN'S EMANCIPATION PROCLAMATION WENT INTO EFFECT.

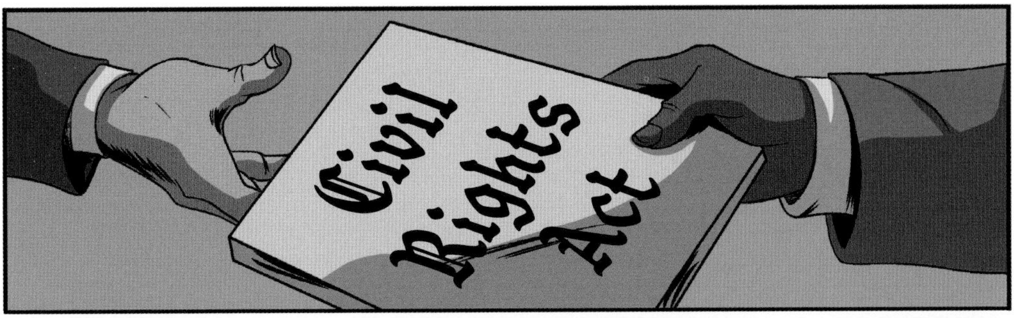
Civil Rights Act

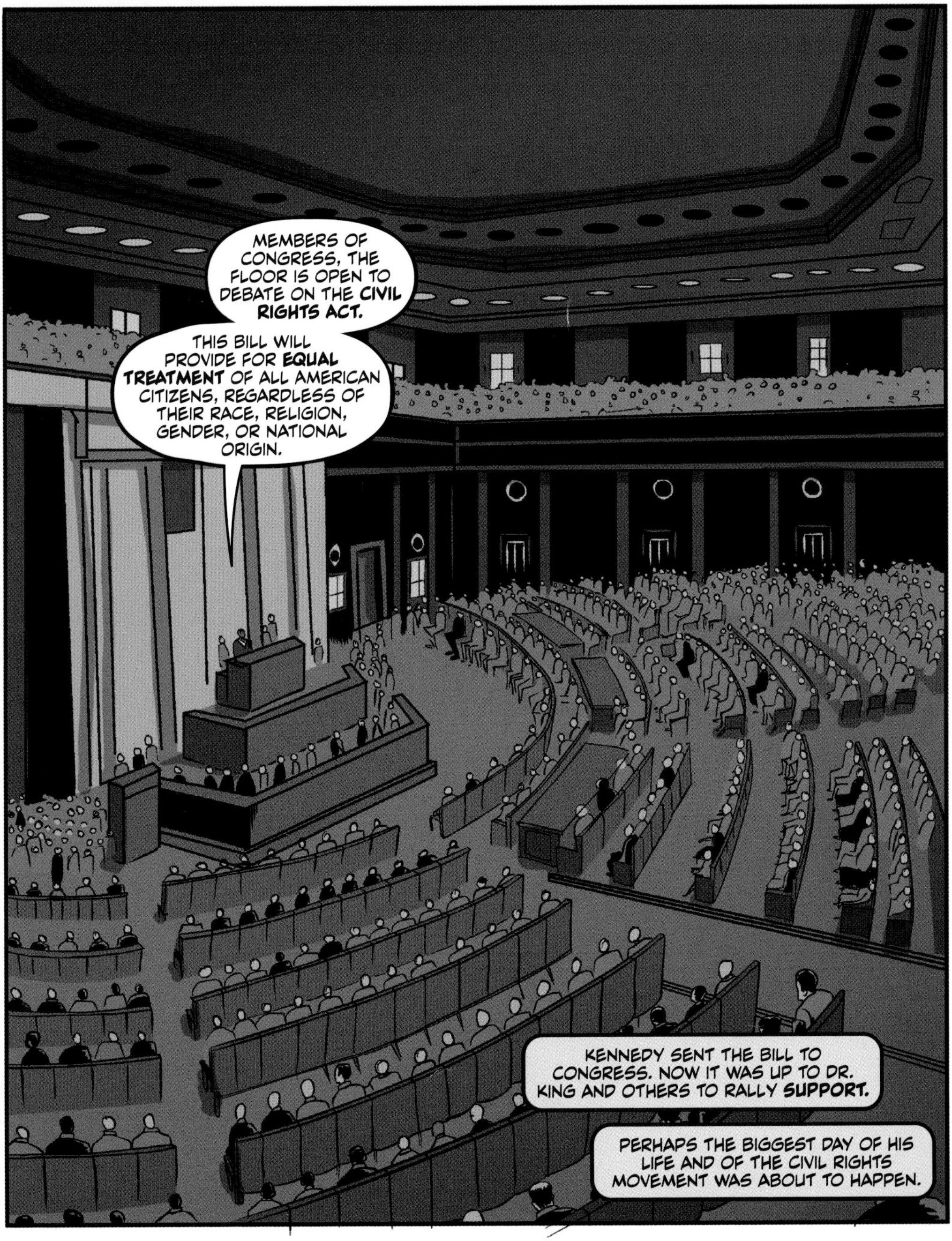
MEMBERS OF CONGRESS, THE FLOOR IS OPEN TO DEBATE ON THE **CIVIL RIGHTS ACT.**
THIS BILL WILL PROVIDE FOR **EQUAL TREATMENT** OF ALL AMERICAN CITIZENS, REGARDLESS OF THEIR RACE, RELIGION, GENDER, OR NATIONAL ORIGIN.
KENNEDY SENT THE BILL TO CONGRESS. NOW IT WAS UP TO DR. KING AND OTHERS TO RALLY **SUPPORT.**
PERHAPS THE BIGGEST DAY OF HIS LIFE AND OF THE CIVIL RIGHTS MOVEMENT WAS ABOUT TO HAPPEN.

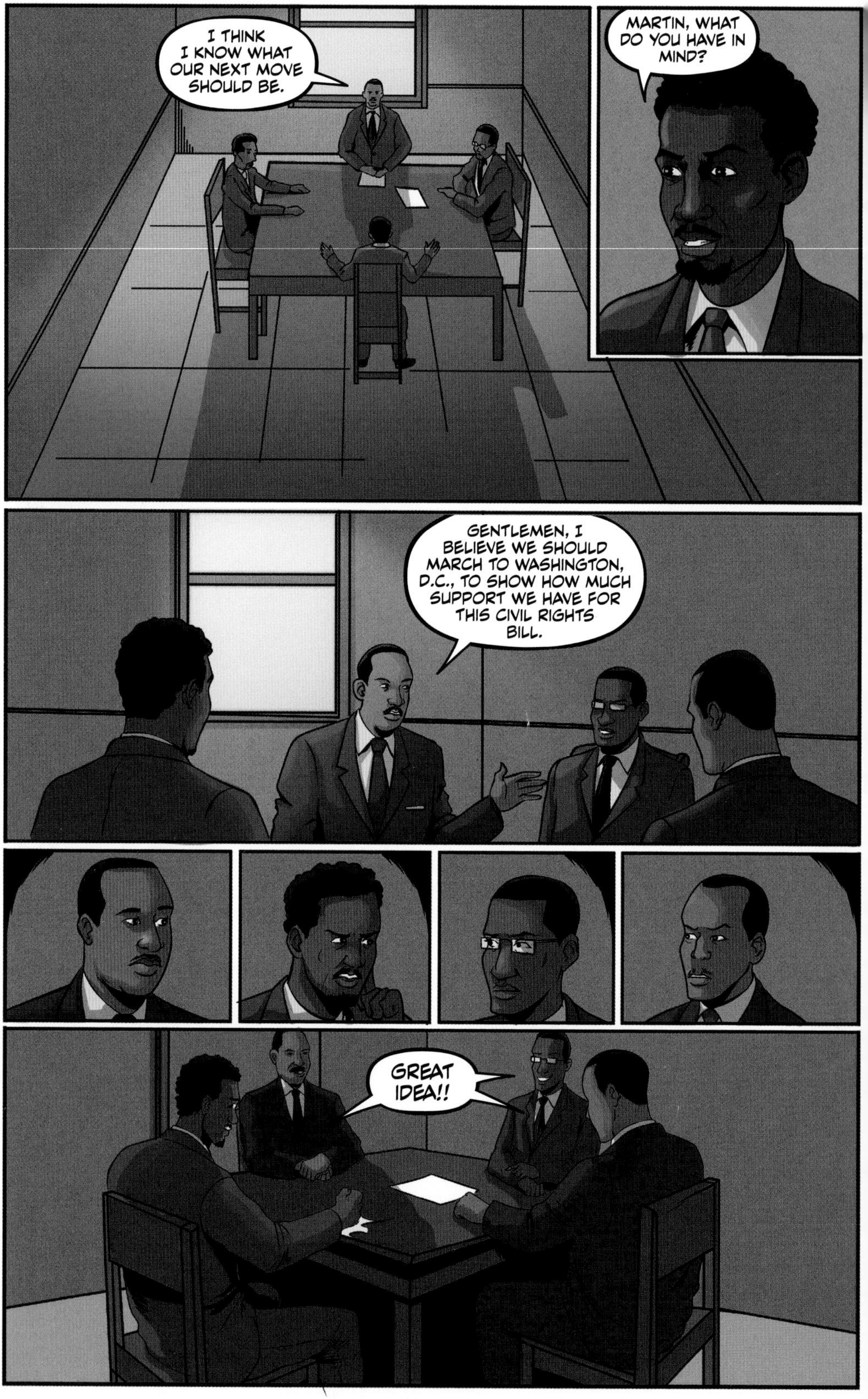

I THINK I KNOW WHAT OUR NEXT MOVE SHOULD BE.
MARTIN, WHAT DO YOU HAVE IN MIND?
GENTLEMEN, I BELIEVE WE SHOULD MARCH TO WASHINGTON, D.C., TO SHOW HOW MUCH SUPPORT WE HAVE FOR THIS CIVIL RIGHTS BILL.
GREAT IDEA!!

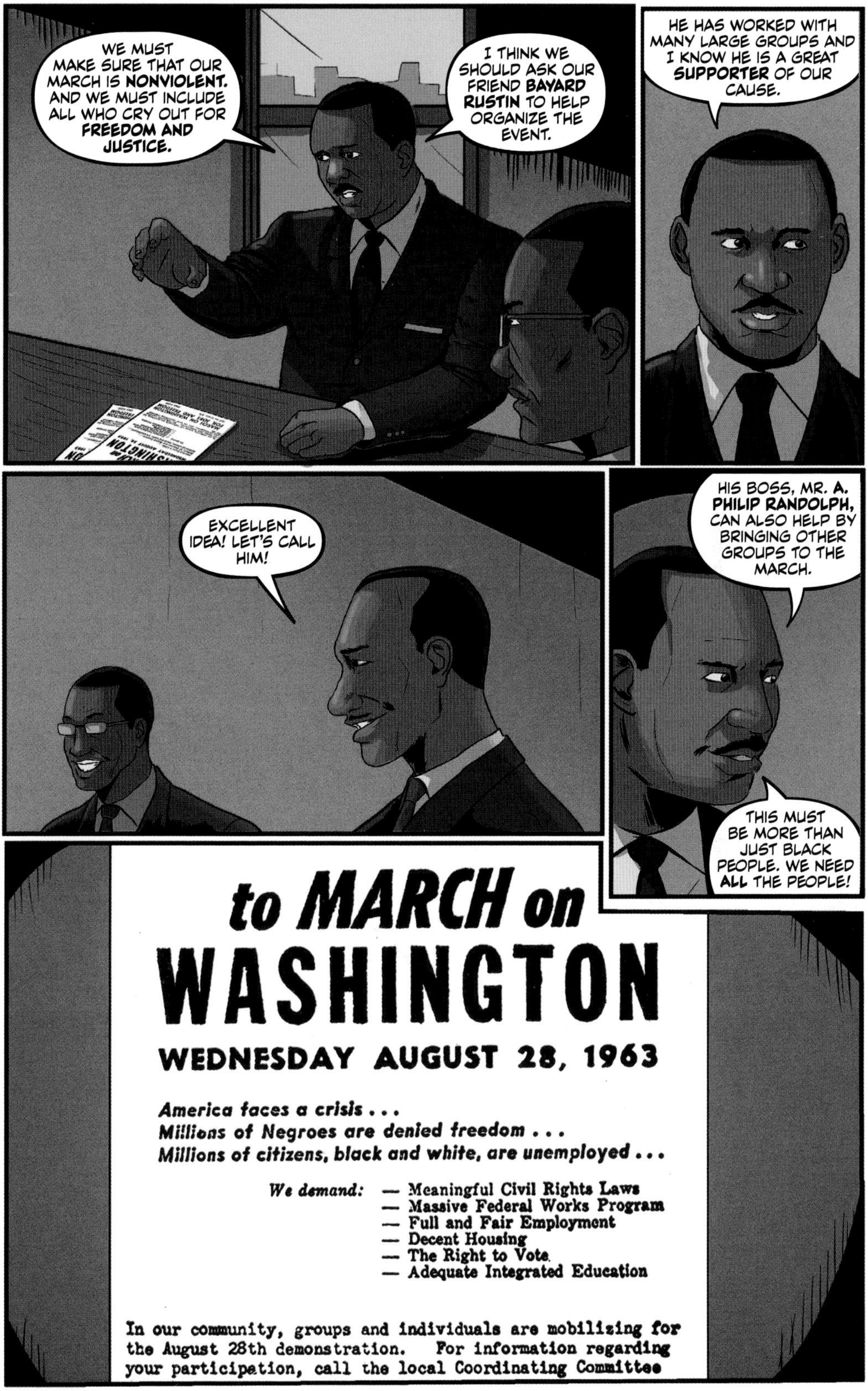
WE MUST MAKE SURE THAT OUR MARCH IS NONVIOLENT. AND WE MUST INCLUDE ALL WHO CRY OUT FOR FREEDOM AND JUSTICE.
I THINK WE SHOULD ASK OUR FRIEND BAYARD RUSTIN TO HELP ORGANIZE THE EVENT.
HE HAS WORKED WITH MANY LARGE GROUPS AND I KNOW HE IS A GREAT SUPPORTER OF OUR CAUSE.
EXCELLENT IDEA! LET'S CALL HIM!
HIS BOSS, MR. A. PHILIP RANDOLPH, CAN ALSO HELP BY BRINGING OTHER GROUPS TO THE MARCH.
THIS MUST BE MORE THAN JUST BLACK PEOPLE. WE NEED ALL THE PEOPLE!
to MARCH on
WASHINGTON
WEDNESDAY AUGUST 28, 1963
America faces a crisis . . .
Millions of Negroes are denied freedom . . .
Millions of citizens, black and white, are unemployed . . .
We demand: — Meaningful Civil Rights Laws
— Massive Federal Works Program
— Full and Fair Employment
— Decent Housing
— The Right to Vote
— Adequate Integrated Education
In our community, groups and individuals are mobilizing for the August 28th demonstration. For information regarding your participation, call the local Coordinating Committee

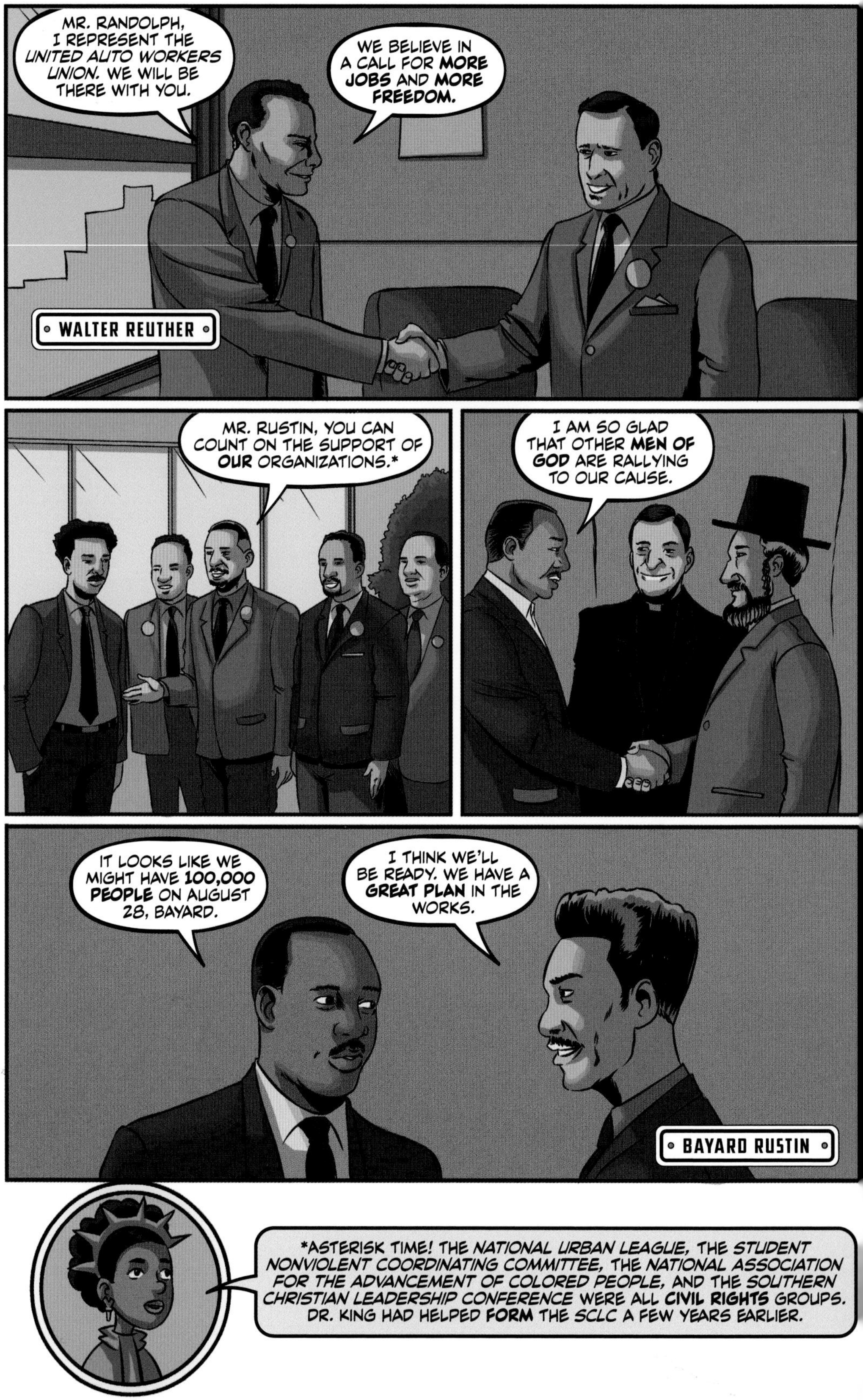
MR. RANDOLPH, I REPRESENT THE *UNITED AUTO WORKERS UNION*. WE WILL BE THERE WITH YOU.
WE BELIEVE IN A CALL FOR **MORE JOBS** AND **MORE FREEDOM.**
WALTER REUTHER
MR. RUSTIN, YOU CAN COUNT ON THE SUPPORT OF **OUR** ORGANIZATIONS.*
I AM SO GLAD THAT OTHER **MEN OF GOD** ARE RALLYING TO OUR CAUSE.
IT LOOKS LIKE WE MIGHT HAVE **100,000 PEOPLE** ON AUGUST 28, BAYARD.
I THINK WE'LL BE READY. WE HAVE A **GREAT PLAN** IN THE WORKS.
BAYARD RUSTIN
*ASTERISK TIME! THE *NATIONAL URBAN LEAGUE*, THE *STUDENT NONVIOLENT COORDINATING COMMITTEE*, THE *NATIONAL ASSOCIATION FOR THE ADVANCEMENT OF COLORED PEOPLE*, AND THE *SOUTHERN CHRISTIAN LEADERSHIP CONFERENCE* WERE ALL **CIVIL RIGHTS** GROUPS. DR. KING HAD HELPED **FORM** THE SCLC A FEW YEARS EARLIER.

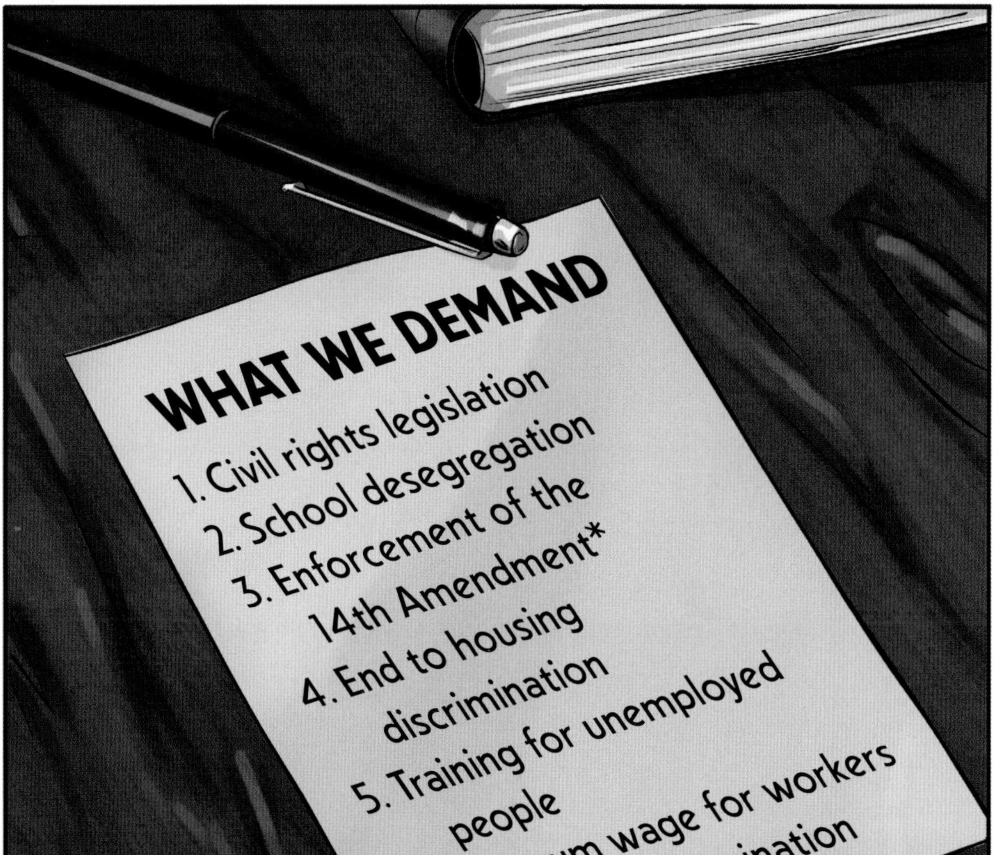
WHAT WE DEMAND
1. Civil rights legislation
2. School desegregation
3. Enforcement of the 14th Amendment*
4. End to housing discrimination
5. Training for unemployed people
6. Minimum wage for workers
7. No labor discrimination
BE PART OF THE MARCH!
AUGUST 28
WASHINGTON, D.C.

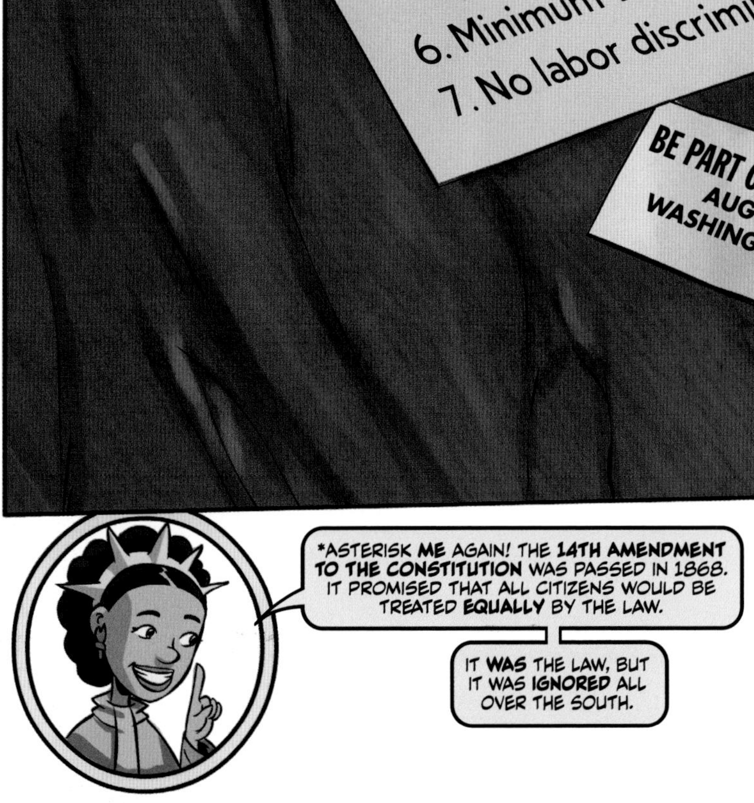
*ASTERISK ME AGAIN! THE 14TH AMENDMENT TO THE CONSTITUTION WAS PASSED IN 1868. IT PROMISED THAT ALL CITIZENS WOULD BE TREATED EQUALLY BY THE LAW.
IT WAS THE LAW, BUT IT WAS IGNORED ALL OVER THE SOUTH.

• AUGUST 28, 1963 •

RUSTIN AND HIS MANY "BUS CAPTAINS" WERE READY FOR A **BIG CROWD**. EACH BUS HAD A PERSON TO LEAD THE RIDERS TO THE MARCH. BUT THE ORGANIZERS GOT MUCH **MORE** THAN THEY EXPECTED.

I KNOW! I SAW THE PICTURE BACK ON PAGE FIVE... THAT'S A **LOT** OF PEOPLE!

MORE THAN **250,000 PEOPLE** PACKED THE NATIONAL MALL IN FRONT OF THE LINCOLN MEMORIAL. THEY WERE WITNESSES TO HISTORY. THE FIRST PEOPLE THEY HEARD WERE FAMOUS SINGERS, THERE TO SUPPORT THE MARCH.

• CAMILLA WILLIAMS •

O SAY CAN YOU SEE...

• JOAN BAEZ •

WE SHALL OVERCOME, WE SHALL OVERCOME...

• ODETTA •

OH FREEDOM, OH FREEDOM, OH FREEDOM OVER ME! AND BEFORE I'D BE A SLAVE I'LL BE BURIED IN MY GRAVE!

WHEN THE SHIP COMES IN...

• BOB DYLAN •

• PETER, PAUL AND MARY •

IF I HAD A HAMMER...

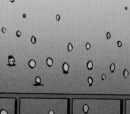

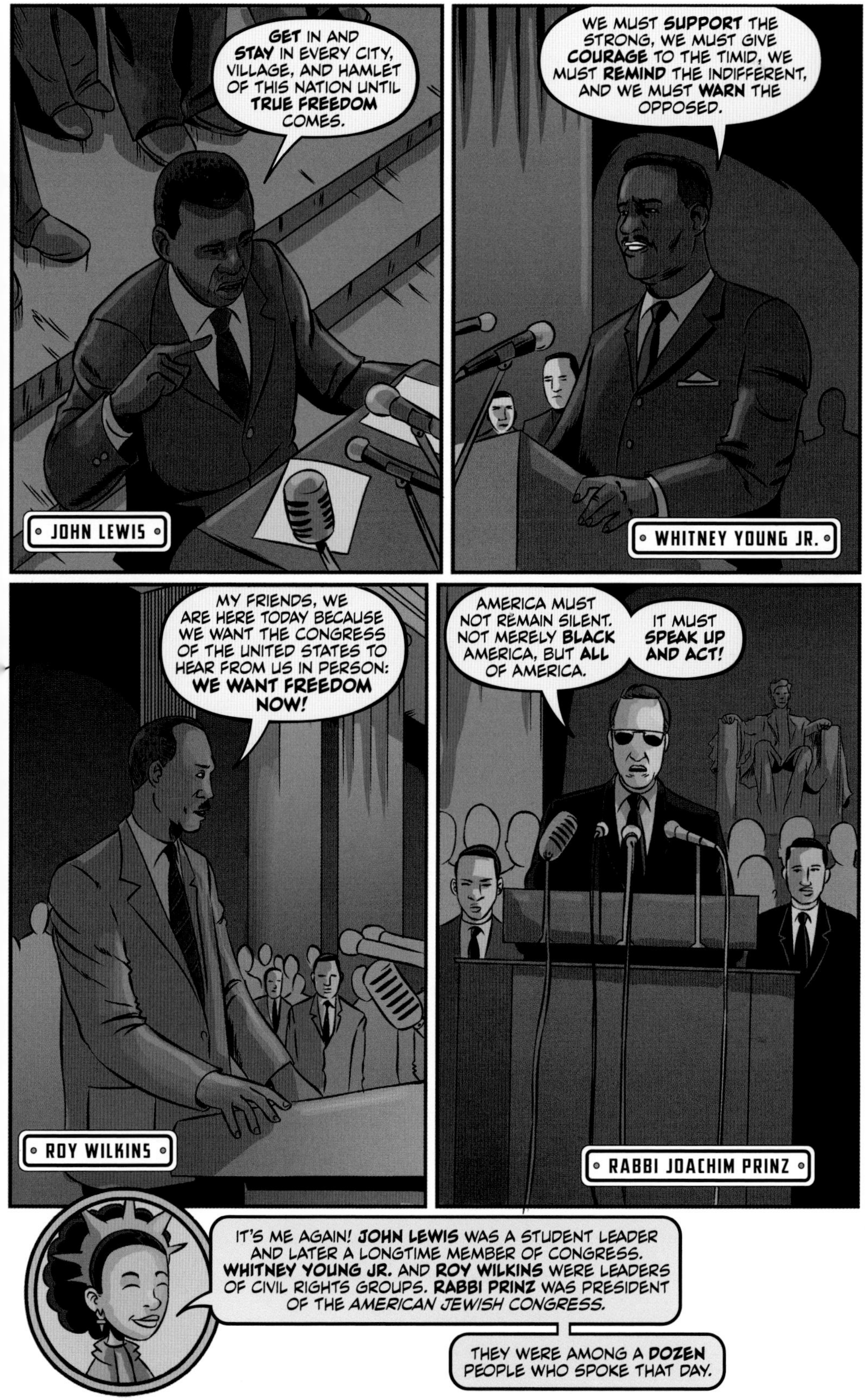
GET IN AND STAY IN EVERY CITY, VILLAGE, AND HAMLET OF THIS NATION UNTIL TRUE FREEDOM COMES.
JOHN LEWIS
WE MUST SUPPORT THE STRONG, WE MUST GIVE COURAGE TO THE TIMID, WE MUST REMIND THE INDIFFERENT, AND WE MUST WARN THE OPPOSED.
WHITNEY YOUNG JR.
MY FRIENDS, WE ARE HERE TODAY BECAUSE WE WANT THE CONGRESS OF THE UNITED STATES TO HEAR FROM US IN PERSON: WE WANT FREEDOM NOW!
ROY WILKINS
AMERICA MUST NOT REMAIN SILENT. NOT MERELY BLACK AMERICA, BUT ALL OF AMERICA.
IT MUST SPEAK UP AND ACT!
RABBI JOACHIM PRINZ
IT'S ME AGAIN! JOHN LEWIS WAS A STUDENT LEADER AND LATER A LONGTIME MEMBER OF CONGRESS. WHITNEY YOUNG JR. AND ROY WILKINS WERE LEADERS OF CIVIL RIGHTS GROUPS. RABBI PRINZ WAS PRESIDENT OF THE AMERICAN JEWISH CONGRESS.
THEY WERE AMONG A DOZEN PEOPLE WHO SPOKE THAT DAY.

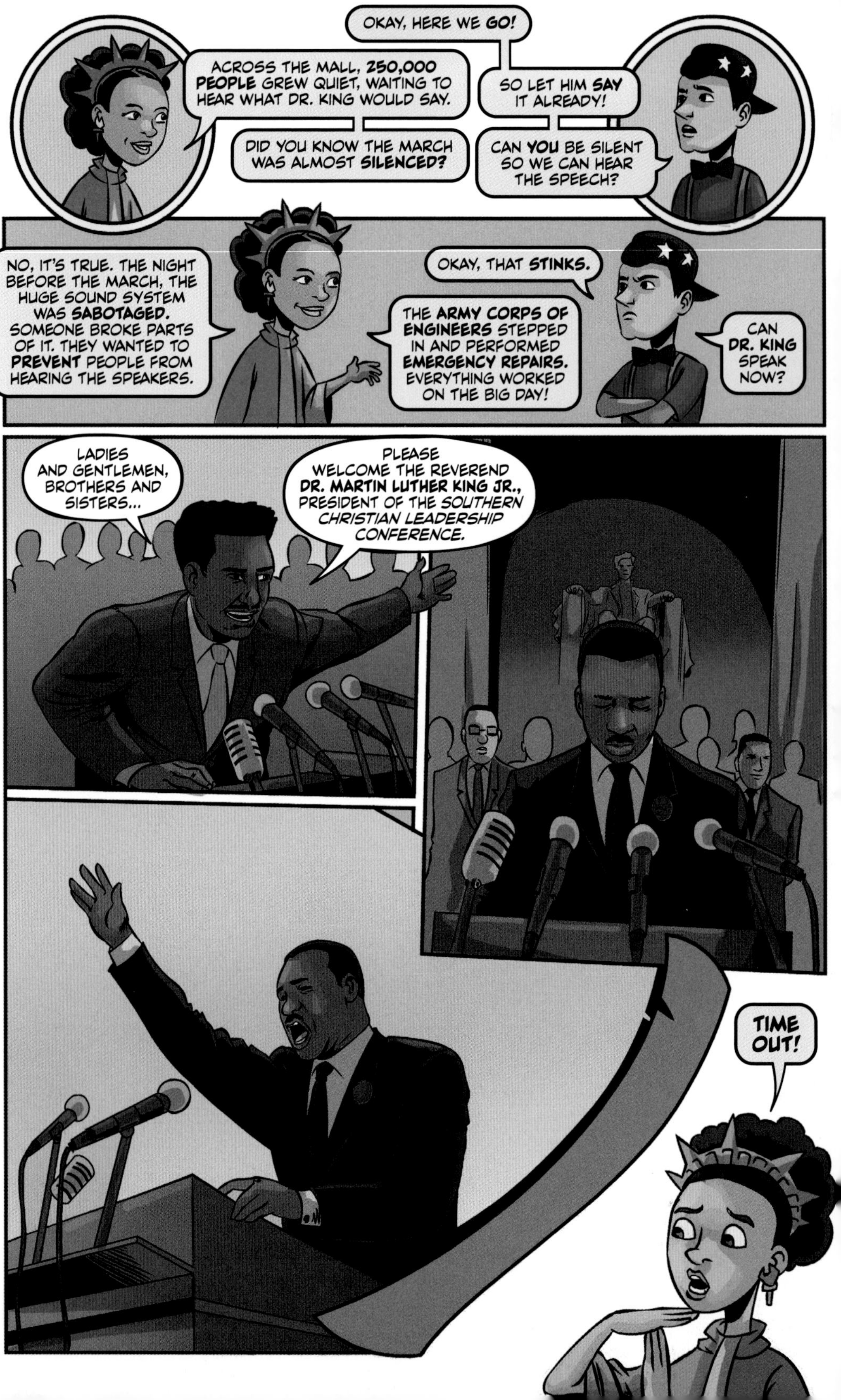
ACROSS THE MALL, 250,000 PEOPLE GREW QUIET, WAITING TO HEAR WHAT DR. KING WOULD SAY.
OKAY, HERE WE GO!
SO LET HIM SAY IT ALREADY!
DID YOU KNOW THE MARCH WAS ALMOST SILENCED?
CAN YOU BE SILENT SO WE CAN HEAR THE SPEECH?
NO, IT'S TRUE. THE NIGHT BEFORE THE MARCH, THE HUGE SOUND SYSTEM WAS SABOTAGED. SOMEONE BROKE PARTS OF IT. THEY WANTED TO PREVENT PEOPLE FROM HEARING THE SPEAKERS.
OKAY, THAT STINKS.
THE ARMY CORPS OF ENGINEERS STEPPED IN AND PERFORMED EMERGENCY REPAIRS. EVERYTHING WORKED ON THE BIG DAY!
CAN DR. KING SPEAK NOW?
LADIES AND GENTLEMEN, BROTHERS AND SISTERS...
PLEASE WELCOME THE REVEREND DR. MARTIN LUTHER KING JR., PRESIDENT OF THE SOUTHERN CHRISTIAN LEADERSHIP CONFERENCE.
TIME OUT!

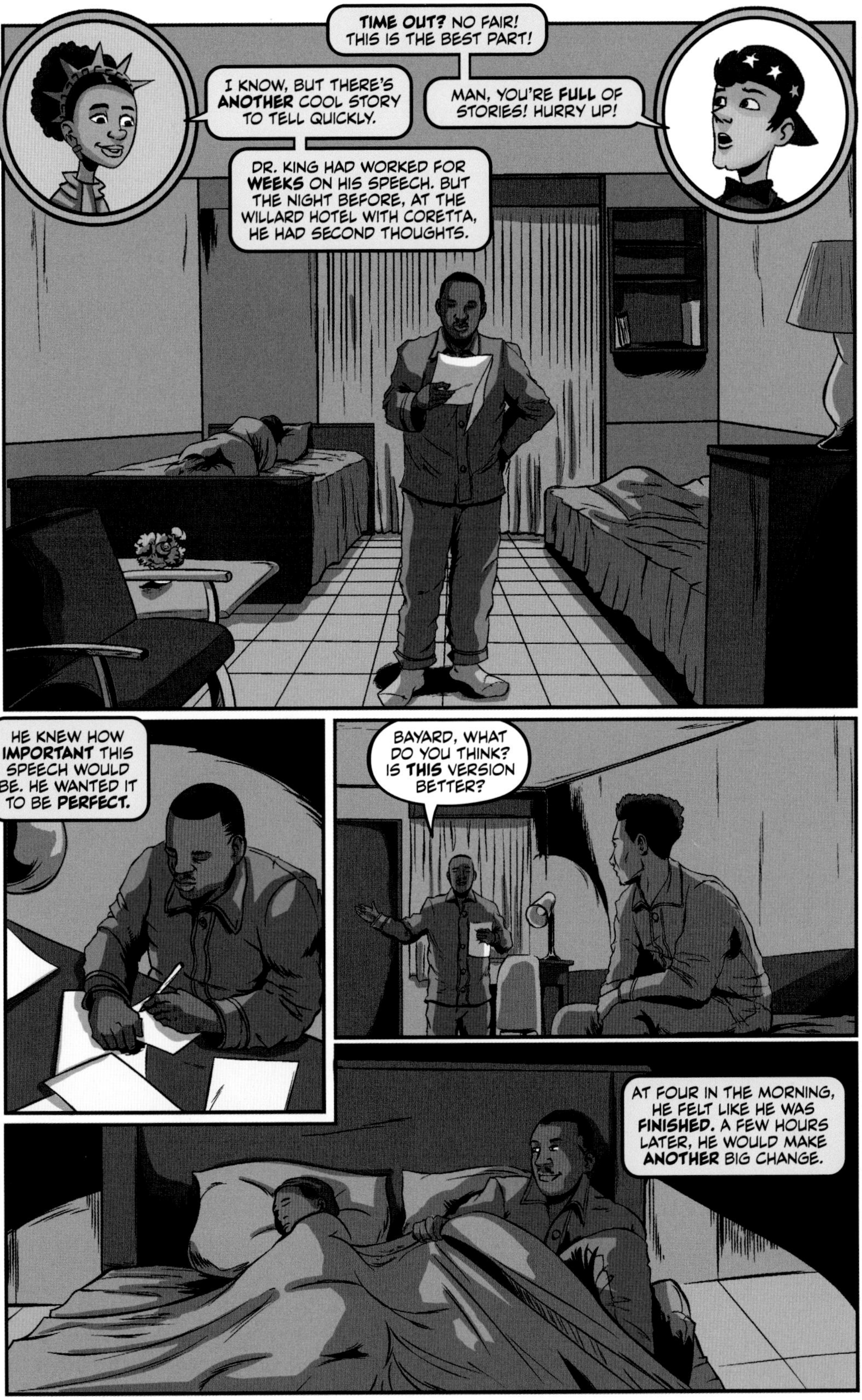
TIME OUT? NO FAIR! THIS IS THE BEST PART!
I KNOW, BUT THERE'S ANOTHER COOL STORY TO TELL QUICKLY.
MAN, YOU'RE FULL OF STORIES! HURRY UP!
DR. KING HAD WORKED FOR WEEKS ON HIS SPEECH. BUT THE NIGHT BEFORE, AT THE WILLARD HOTEL WITH CORETTA, HE HAD SECOND THOUGHTS.
HE KNEW HOW IMPORTANT THIS SPEECH WOULD BE. HE WANTED IT TO BE PERFECT.
BAYARD, WHAT DO YOU THINK? IS THIS VERSION BETTER?
AT FOUR IN THE MORNING, HE FELT LIKE HE WAS FINISHED. A FEW HOURS LATER, HE WOULD MAKE ANOTHER BIG CHANGE.

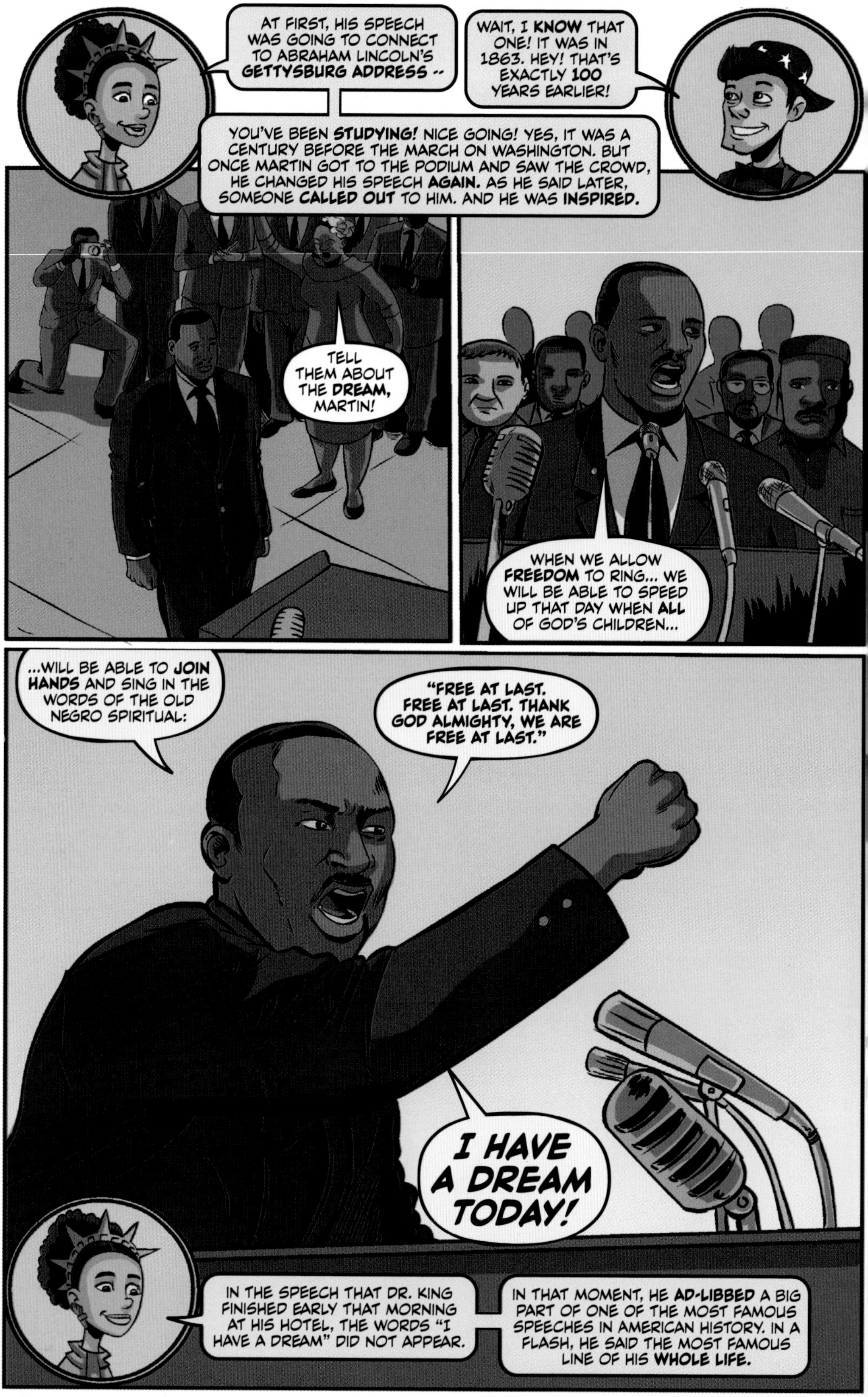

AT FIRST, HIS SPEECH WAS GOING TO CONNECT TO ABRAHAM LINCOLN'S GETTYSBURG ADDRESS --
WAIT, I KNOW THAT ONE! IT WAS IN 1863. HEY! THAT'S EXACTLY 100 YEARS EARLIER!
YOU'VE BEEN STUDYING! NICE GOING! YES, IT WAS A CENTURY BEFORE THE MARCH ON WASHINGTON. BUT ONCE MARTIN GOT TO THE PODIUM AND SAW THE CROWD, HE CHANGED HIS SPEECH AGAIN. AS HE SAID LATER, SOMEONE CALLED OUT TO HIM. AND HE WAS INSPIRED.
TELL THEM ABOUT THE DREAM, MARTIN!
WHEN WE ALLOW FREEDOM TO RING... WE WILL BE ABLE TO SPEED UP THAT DAY WHEN ALL OF GOD'S CHILDREN...
...WILL BE ABLE TO JOIN HANDS AND SING IN THE WORDS OF THE OLD NEGRO SPIRITUAL:
"FREE AT LAST. FREE AT LAST. THANK GOD ALMIGHTY, WE ARE FREE AT LAST."
I HAVE A DREAM TODAY!
IN THE SPEECH THAT DR. KING FINISHED EARLY THAT MORNING AT HIS HOTEL, THE WORDS "I HAVE A DREAM" DID NOT APPEAR.
IN THAT MOMENT, HE AD-LIBBED A BIG PART OF ONE OF THE MOST FAMOUS SPEECHES IN AMERICAN HISTORY. IN A FLASH, HE SAID THE MOST FAMOUS LINE OF HIS WHOLE LIFE.

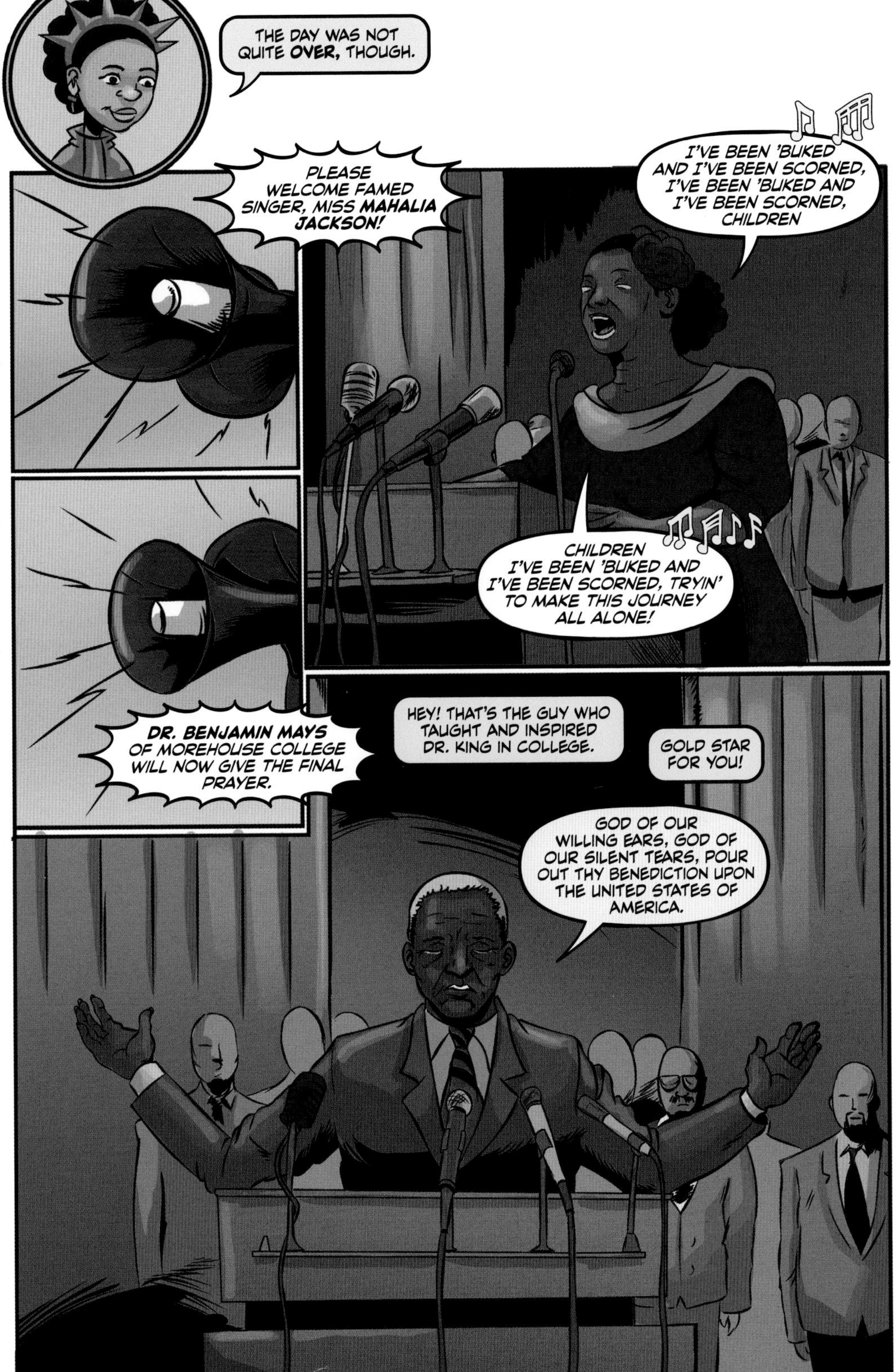
THE DAY WAS NOT QUITE OVER, THOUGH.
PLEASE WELCOME FAMED SINGER, MISS MAHALIA JACKSON!
I'VE BEEN 'BUKED AND I'VE BEEN SCORNED, I'VE BEEN 'BUKED AND I'VE BEEN SCORNED, CHILDREN
CHILDREN I'VE BEEN 'BUKED AND I'VE BEEN SCORNED, TRYIN' TO MAKE THIS JOURNEY ALL ALONE!
DR. BENJAMIN MAYS OF MOREHOUSE COLLEGE WILL NOW GIVE THE FINAL PRAYER.
HEY! THAT'S THE GUY WHO TAUGHT AND INSPIRED DR. KING IN COLLEGE.
GOLD STAR FOR YOU!
GOD OF OUR WILLING EARS, GOD OF OUR SILENT TEARS, POUR OUT THY BENEDICTION UPON THE UNITED STATES OF AMERICA.

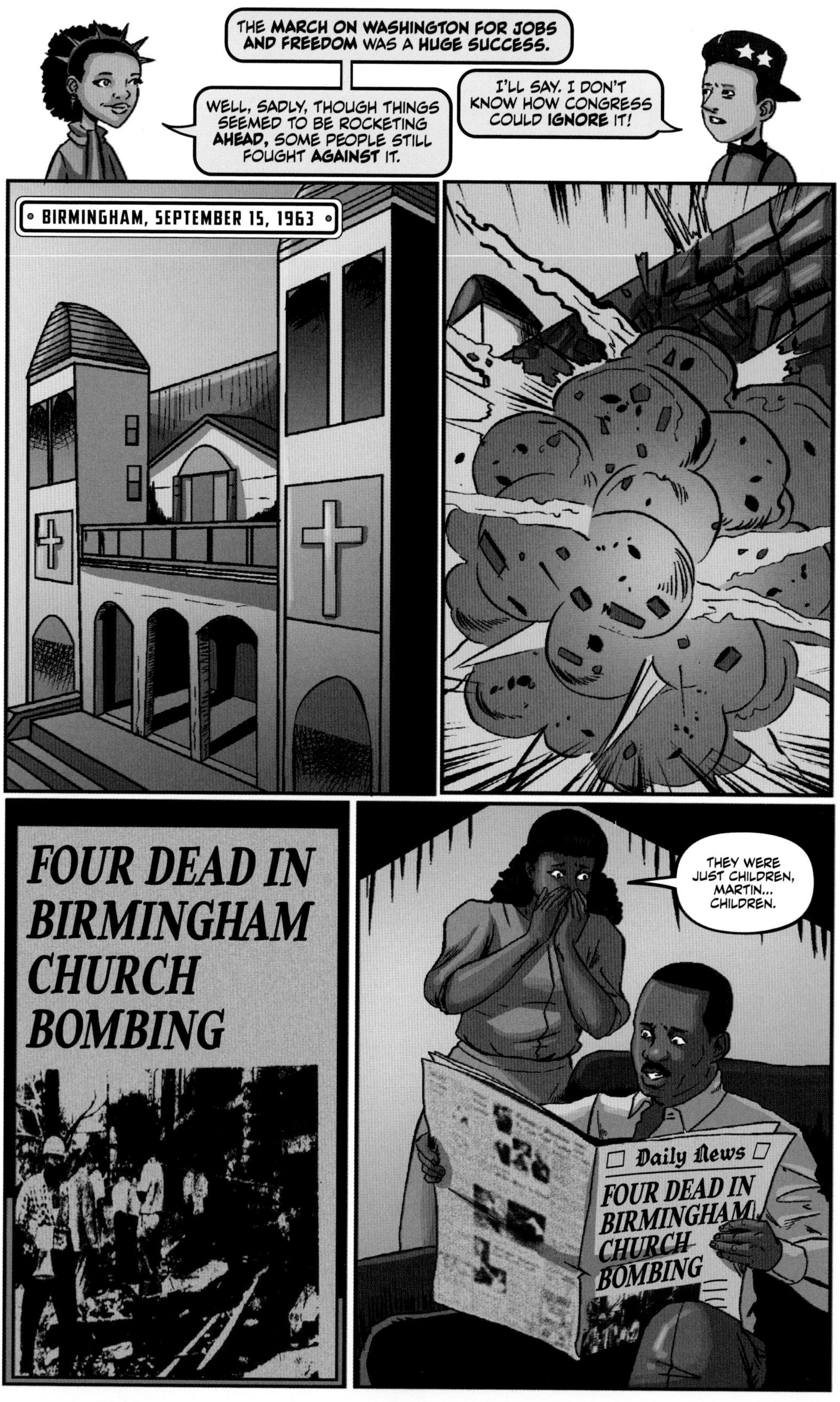
THE MARCH ON WASHINGTON FOR JOBS AND FREEDOM WAS A HUGE SUCCESS.
I'LL SAY. I DON'T KNOW HOW CONGRESS COULD IGNORE IT!
WELL, SADLY, THOUGH THINGS SEEMED TO BE ROCKETING AHEAD, SOME PEOPLE STILL FOUGHT AGAINST IT.
BIRMINGHAM, SEPTEMBER 15, 1963
FOUR DEAD IN BIRMINGHAM CHURCH BOMBING
THEY WERE JUST CHILDREN, MARTIN... CHILDREN.
Daily News
FOUR DEAD IN BIRMINGHAM CHURCH BOMBING

DALLAS, NOVEMBER 22, 1963

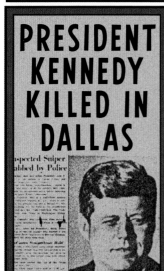

PRESIDENT KENNEDY KILLED IN DALLAS

I DON'T THINK I'LL LIVE TO BE FORTY.

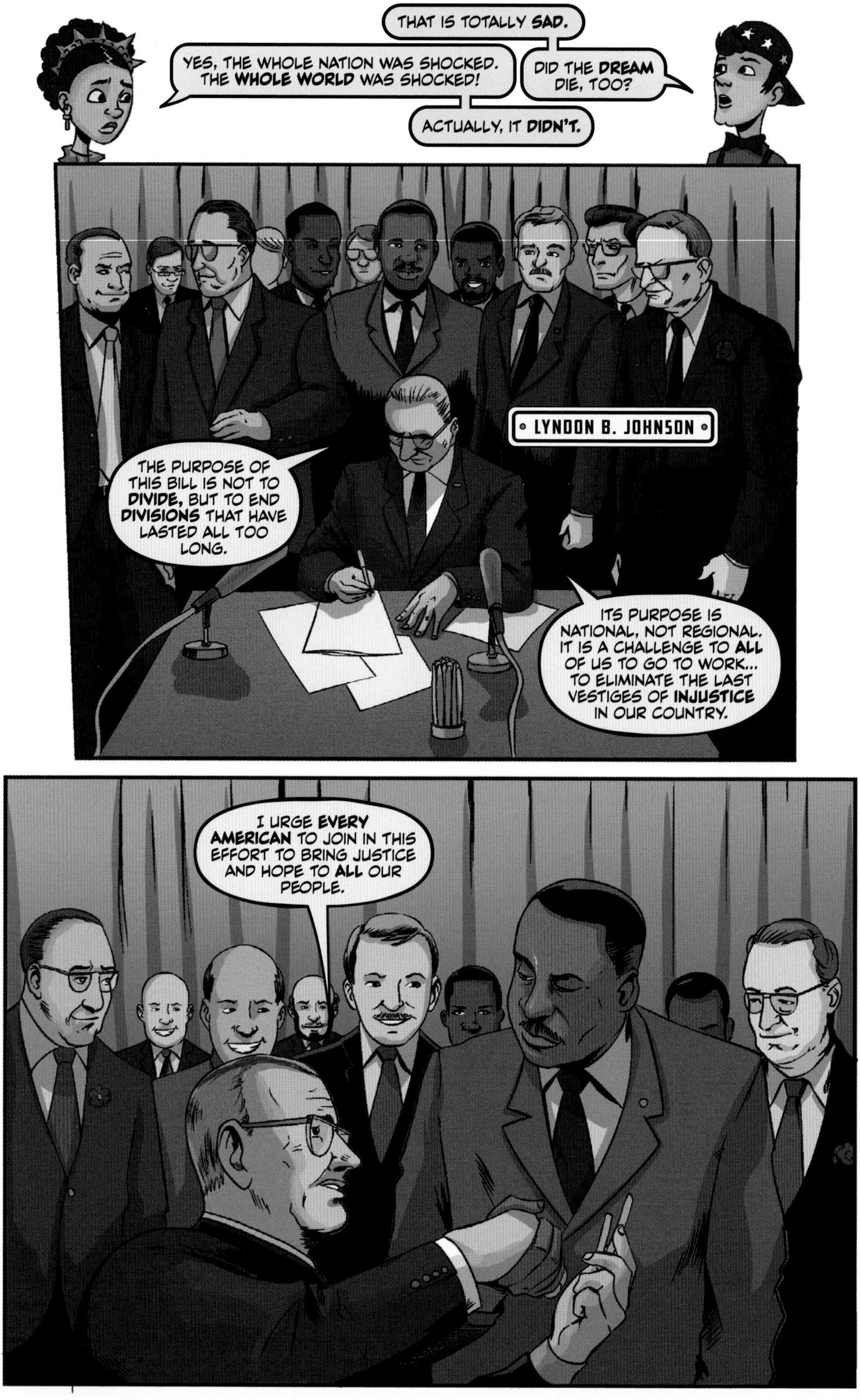

THAT IS TOTALLY SAD.
YES, THE WHOLE NATION WAS SHOCKED. THE WHOLE WORLD WAS SHOCKED!
DID THE DREAM DIE, TOO?
ACTUALLY, IT DIDN'T.
LYNDON B. JOHNSON
THE PURPOSE OF THIS BILL IS NOT TO DIVIDE, BUT TO END DIVISIONS THAT HAVE LASTED ALL TOO LONG.
ITS PURPOSE IS NATIONAL, NOT REGIONAL. IT IS A CHALLENGE TO ALL OF US TO GO TO WORK... TO ELIMINATE THE LAST VESTIGES OF INJUSTICE IN OUR COUNTRY.
I URGE EVERY AMERICAN TO JOIN IN THIS EFFORT TO BRING JUSTICE AND HOPE TO ALL OUR PEOPLE.

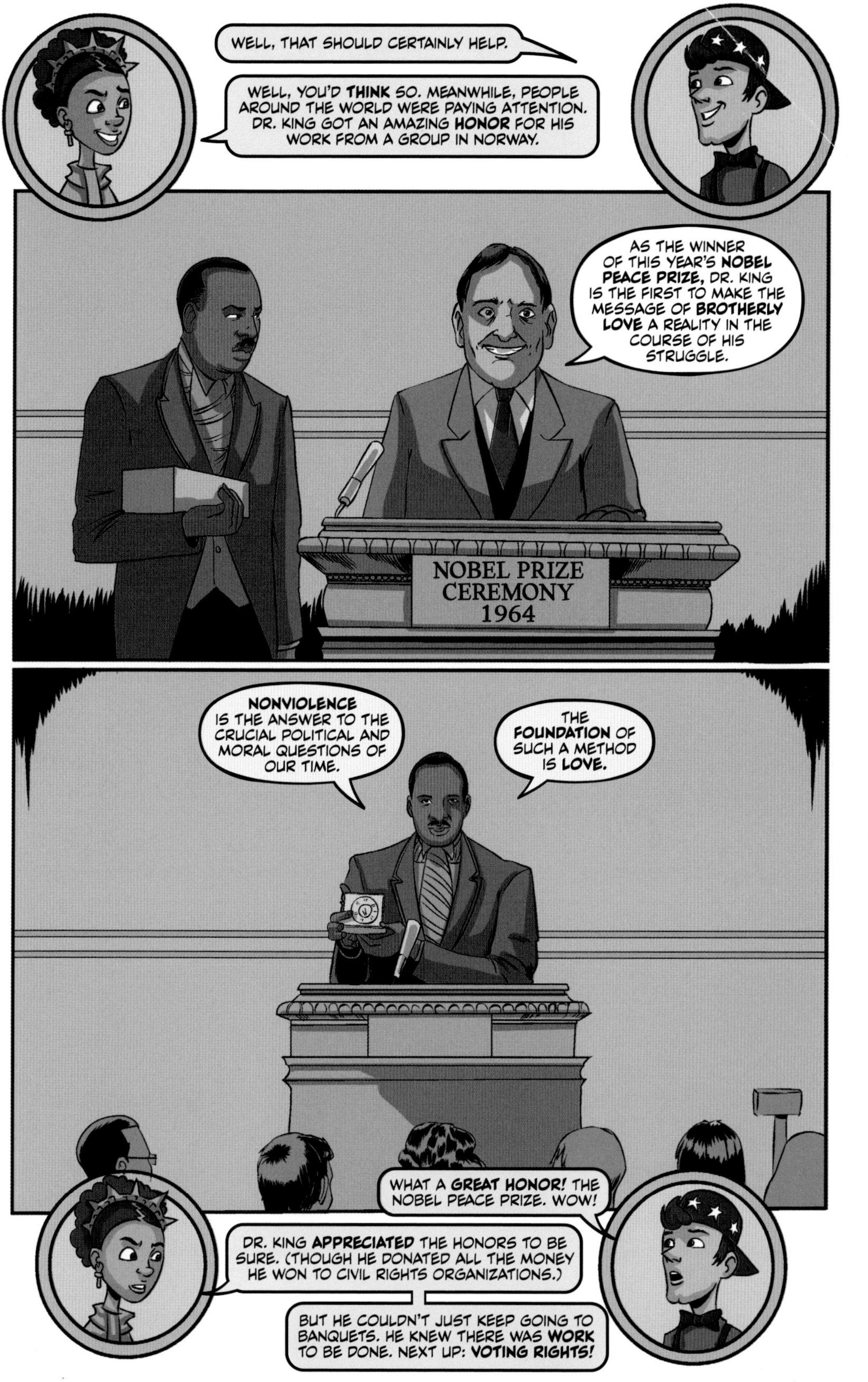
WELL, THAT SHOULD CERTAINLY HELP.
WELL, YOU'D **THINK** SO. MEANWHILE, PEOPLE AROUND THE WORLD WERE PAYING ATTENTION. DR. KING GOT AN AMAZING **HONOR** FOR HIS WORK FROM A GROUP IN NORWAY.
AS THE WINNER OF THIS YEAR'S **NOBEL PEACE PRIZE,** DR. KING IS THE FIRST TO MAKE THE MESSAGE OF **BROTHERLY LOVE** A REALITY IN THE COURSE OF HIS STRUGGLE.
NOBEL PRIZE CEREMONY 1964
NONVIOLENCE IS THE ANSWER TO THE CRUCIAL POLITICAL AND MORAL QUESTIONS OF OUR TIME.
THE **FOUNDATION** OF SUCH A METHOD IS **LOVE.**
WHAT A **GREAT HONOR!** THE NOBEL PEACE PRIZE. WOW!
DR. KING **APPRECIATED** THE HONORS TO BE SURE. (THOUGH HE DONATED ALL THE MONEY HE WON TO CIVIL RIGHTS ORGANIZATIONS.)
BUT HE COULDN'T JUST KEEP GOING TO BANQUETS. HE KNEW THERE WAS **WORK** TO BE DONE. NEXT UP: **VOTING RIGHTS!**

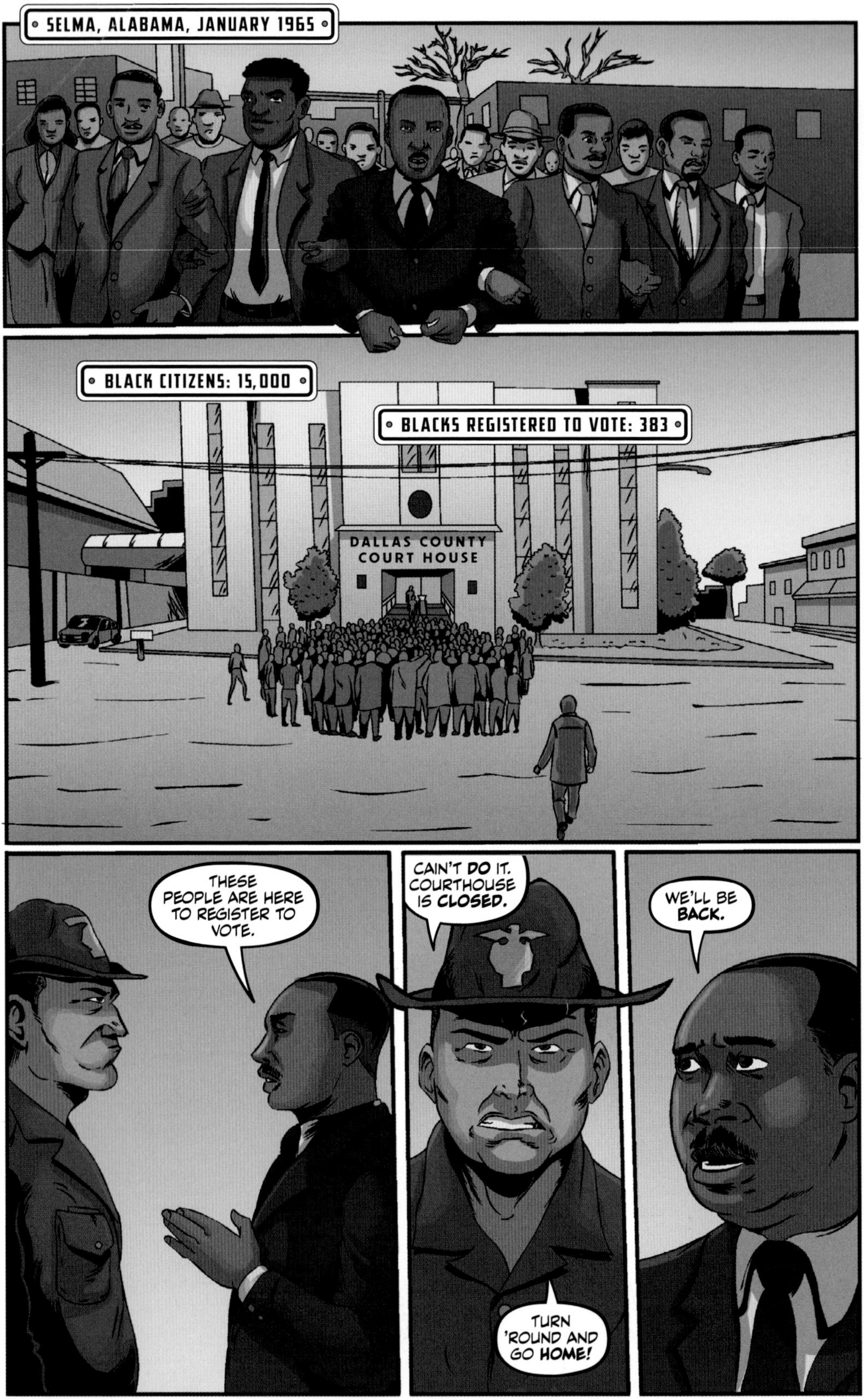
SELMA, ALABAMA, JANUARY 1965
BLACK CITIZENS: 15,000
BLACKS REGISTERED TO VOTE: 383
DALLAS COUNTY COURT HOUSE
THESE PEOPLE ARE HERE TO REGISTER TO VOTE.
CAIN'T DO IT. COURTHOUSE IS CLOSED.
TURN 'ROUND AND GO HOME!
WE'LL BE BACK.

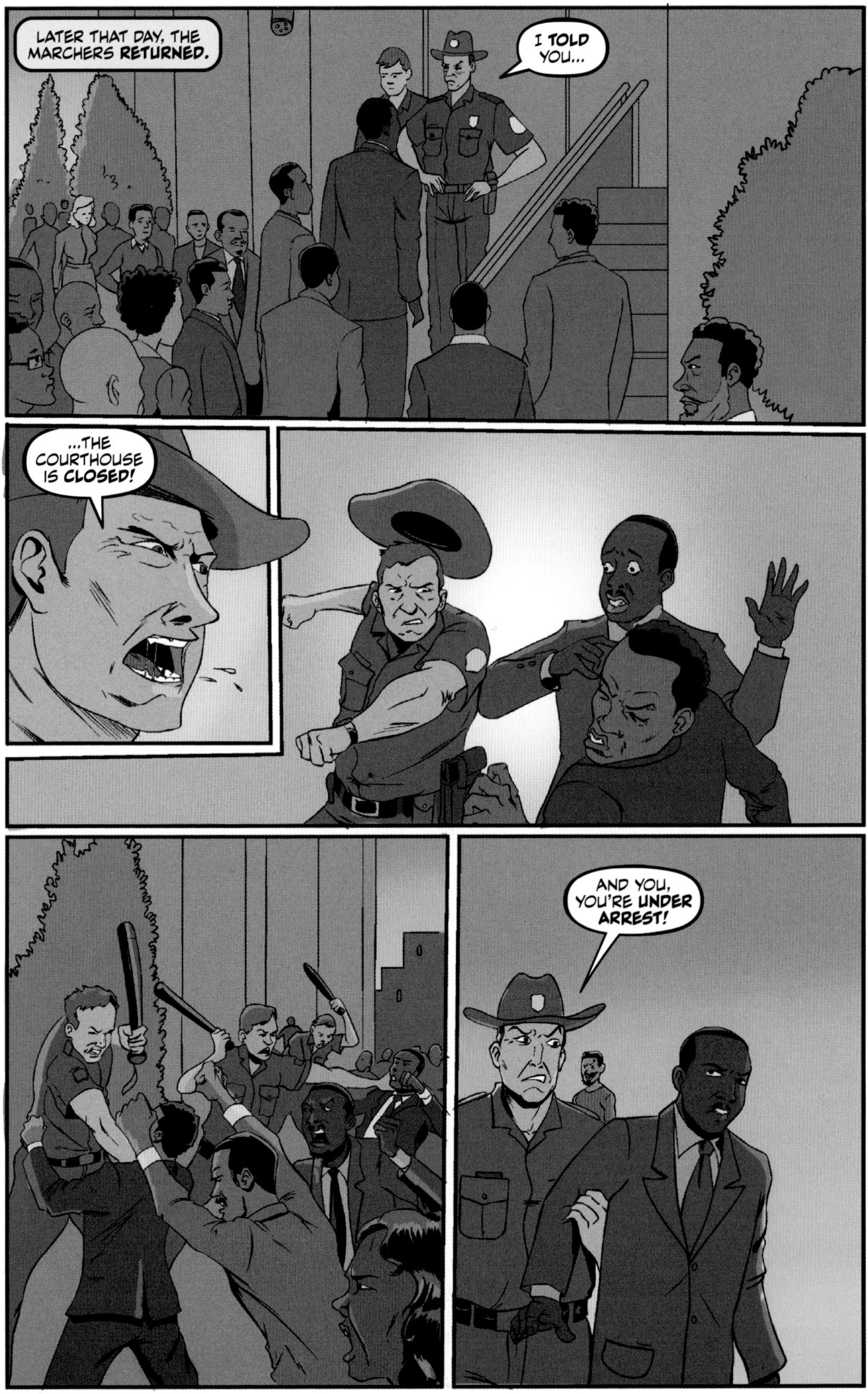
LATER THAT DAY, THE MARCHERS **RETURNED.**
I **TOLD** YOU...
...THE COURTHOUSE IS **CLOSED!**
AND YOU, YOU'RE **UNDER ARREST!**

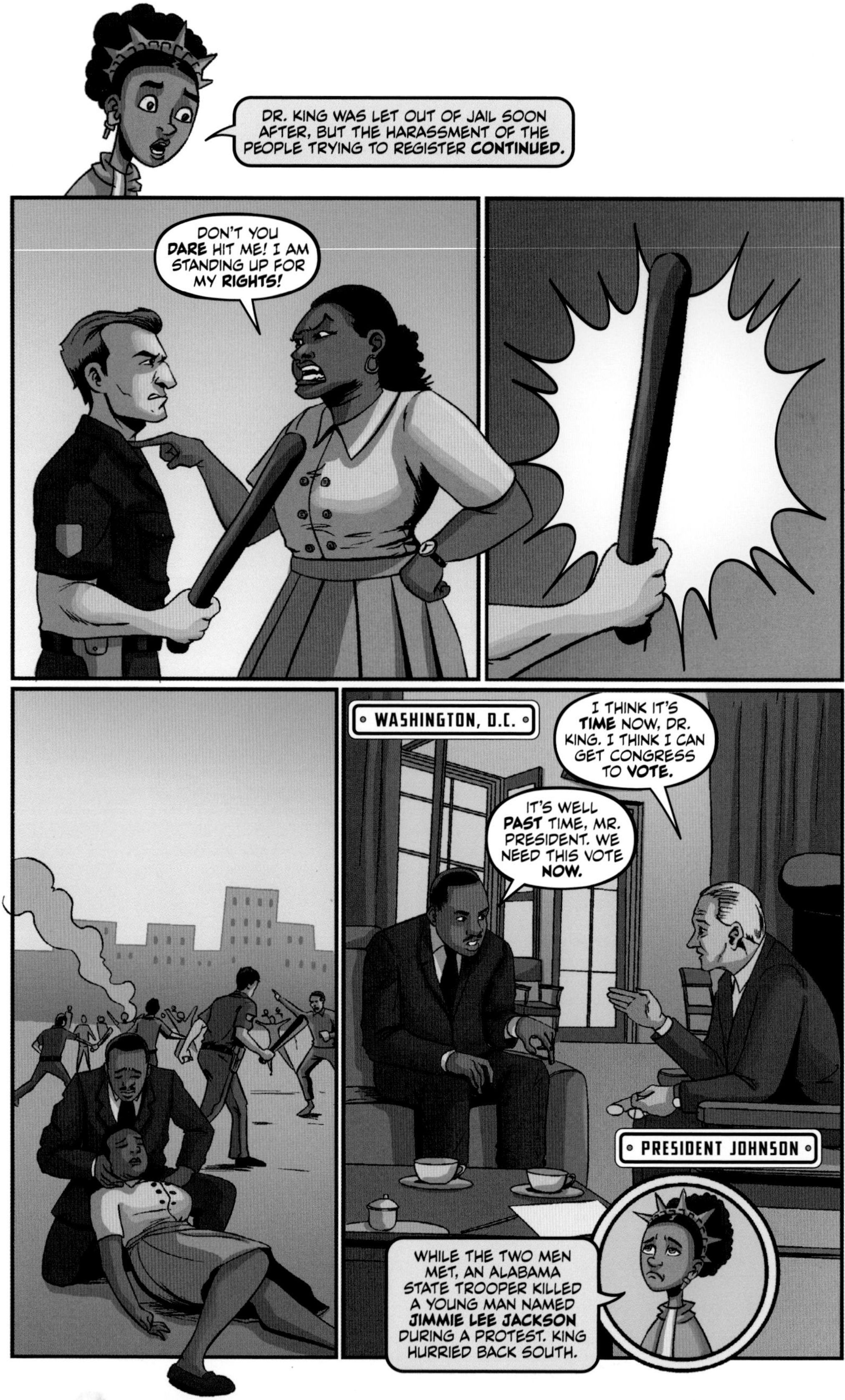

DR. KING WAS LET OUT OF JAIL SOON AFTER, BUT THE HARASSMENT OF THE PEOPLE TRYING TO REGISTER **CONTINUED.**
DON'T YOU **DARE** HIT ME! I AM STANDING UP FOR MY **RIGHTS!**
WASHINGTON, D.C.
I THINK IT'S **TIME** NOW, DR. KING. I THINK I CAN GET CONGRESS TO **VOTE.**
IT'S WELL **PAST** TIME, MR. PRESIDENT. WE NEED THIS VOTE **NOW.**
PRESIDENT JOHNSON
WHILE THE TWO MEN MET, AN ALABAMA STATE TROOPER KILLED A YOUNG MAN NAMED **JIMMIE LEE JACKSON** DURING A PROTEST. KING HURRIED BACK SOUTH.

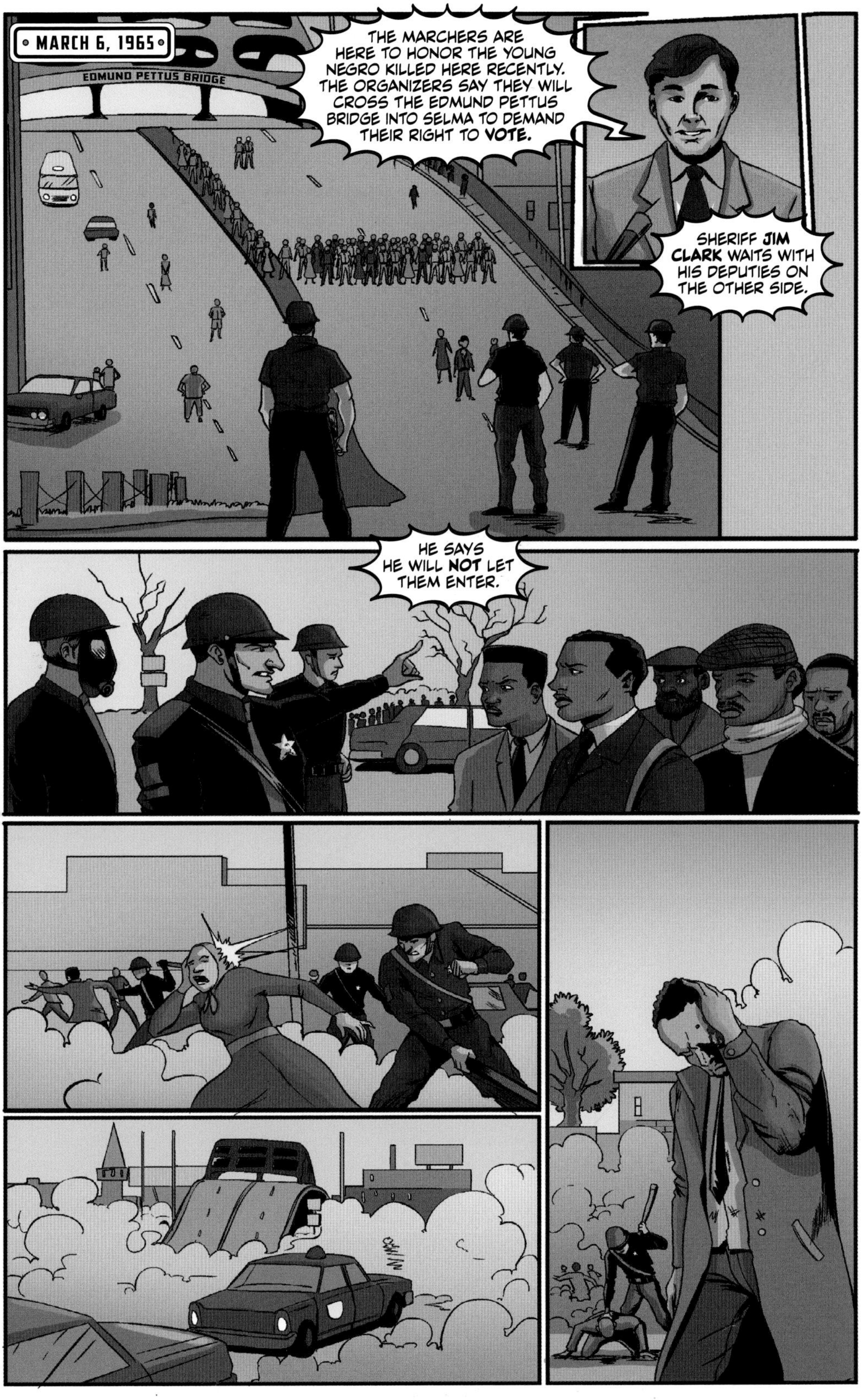

MARCH 6, 1965
EDMUND PETTUS BRIDGE
THE MARCHERS ARE HERE TO HONOR THE YOUNG NEGRO KILLED HERE RECENTLY. THE ORGANIZERS SAY THEY WILL CROSS THE EDMUND PETTUS BRIDGE INTO SELMA TO DEMAND THEIR RIGHT TO VOTE.
SHERIFF JIM CLARK WAITS WITH HIS DEPUTIES ON THE OTHER SIDE.
HE SAYS HE WILL NOT LET THEM ENTER.

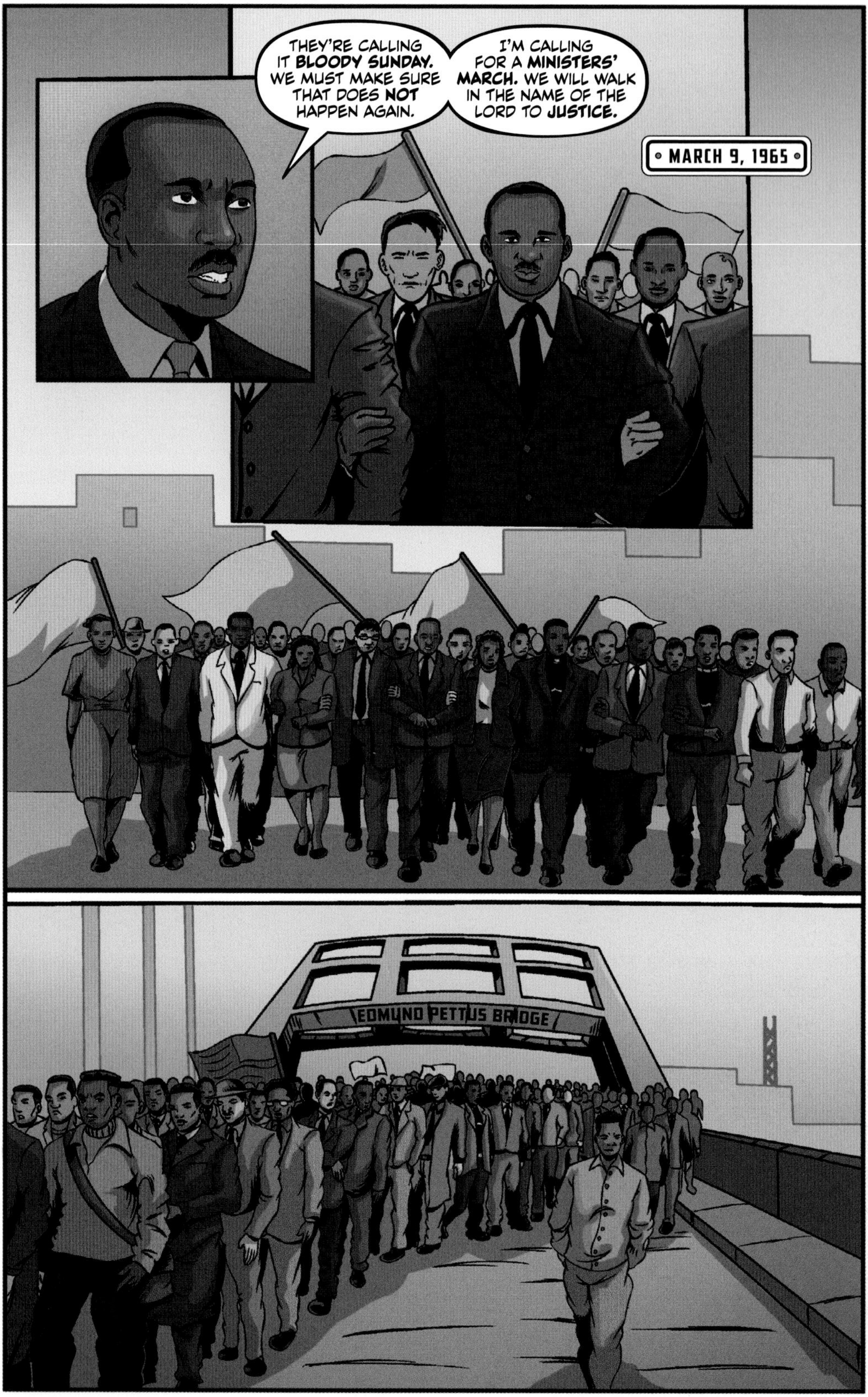
THEY'RE CALLING IT BLOODY SUNDAY. WE MUST MAKE SURE THAT DOES NOT HAPPEN AGAIN.
I'M CALLING FOR A MINISTERS' MARCH. WE WILL WALK IN THE NAME OF THE LORD TO JUSTICE.
MARCH 9, 1965
EDMUND PETTUS BRIDGE

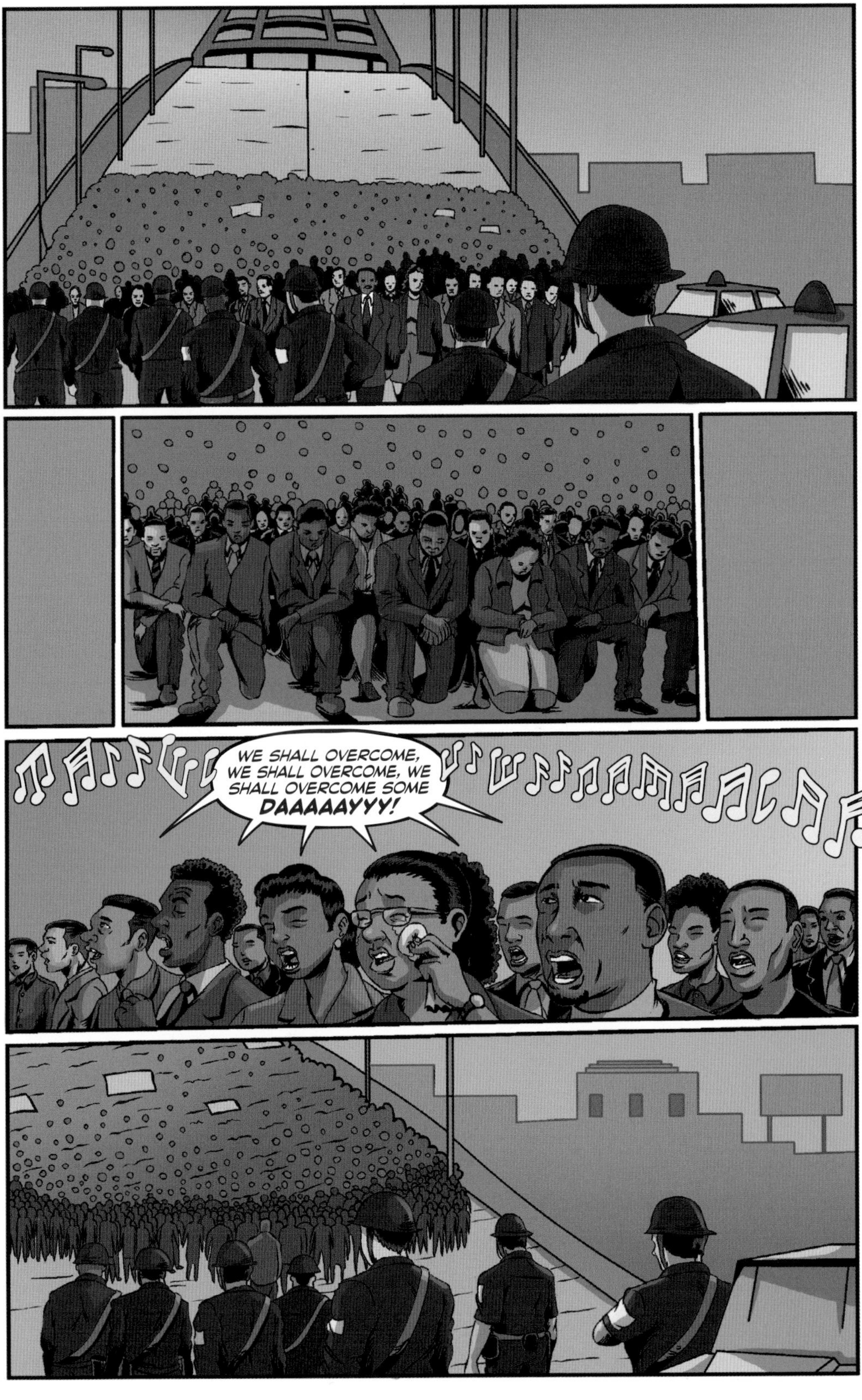
WE SHALL OVERCOME, WE SHALL OVERCOME, WE SHALL OVERCOME SOME DAAAAAYYY!

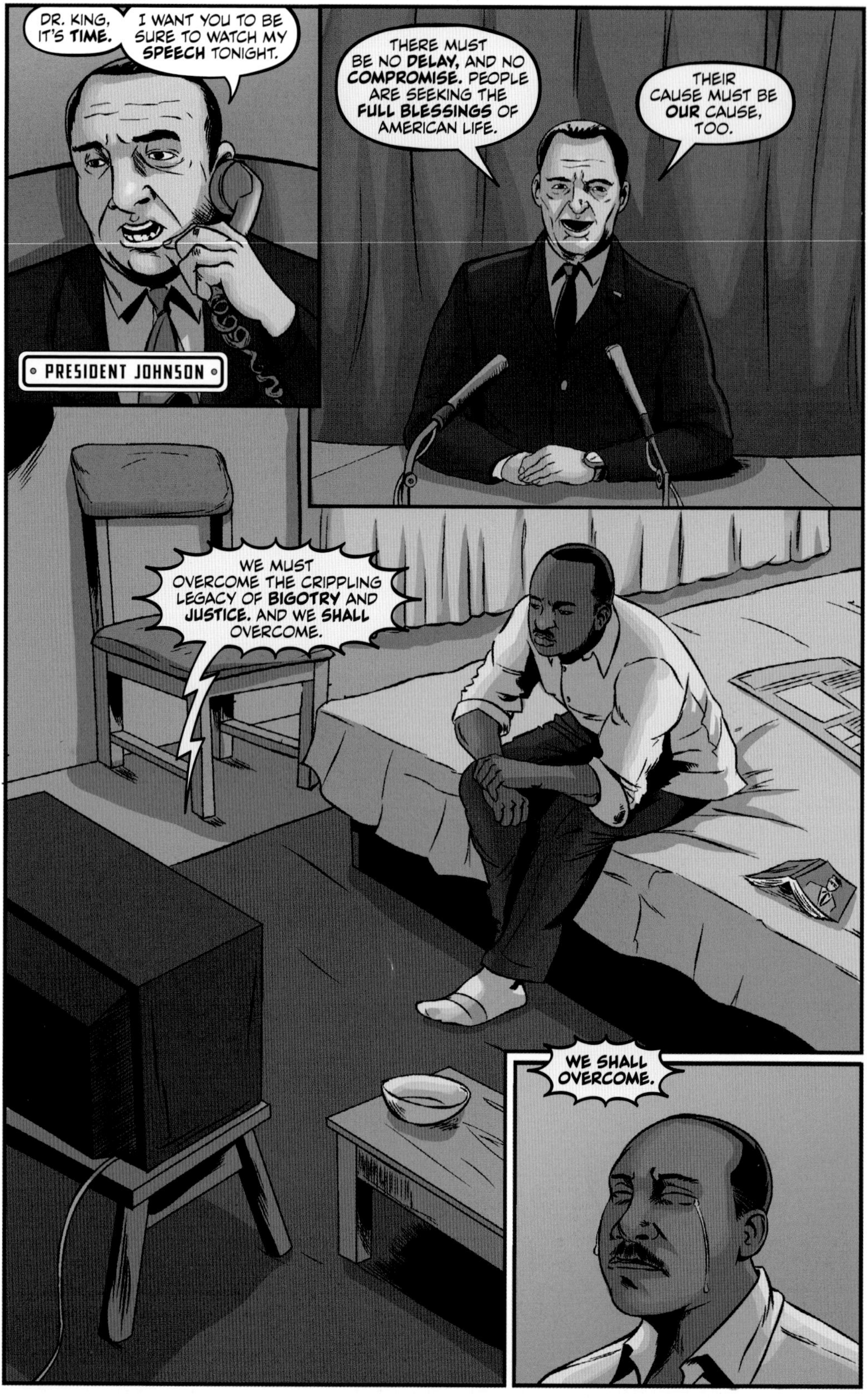
DR. KING, IT'S TIME.
I WANT YOU TO BE SURE TO WATCH MY SPEECH TONIGHT.
PRESIDENT JOHNSON
THERE MUST BE NO DELAY, AND NO COMPROMISE. PEOPLE ARE SEEKING THE FULL BLESSINGS OF AMERICAN LIFE.
THEIR CAUSE MUST BE OUR CAUSE, TOO.
WE MUST OVERCOME THE CRIPPLING LEGACY OF BIGOTRY AND JUSTICE. AND WE SHALL OVERCOME.
WE SHALL OVERCOME.

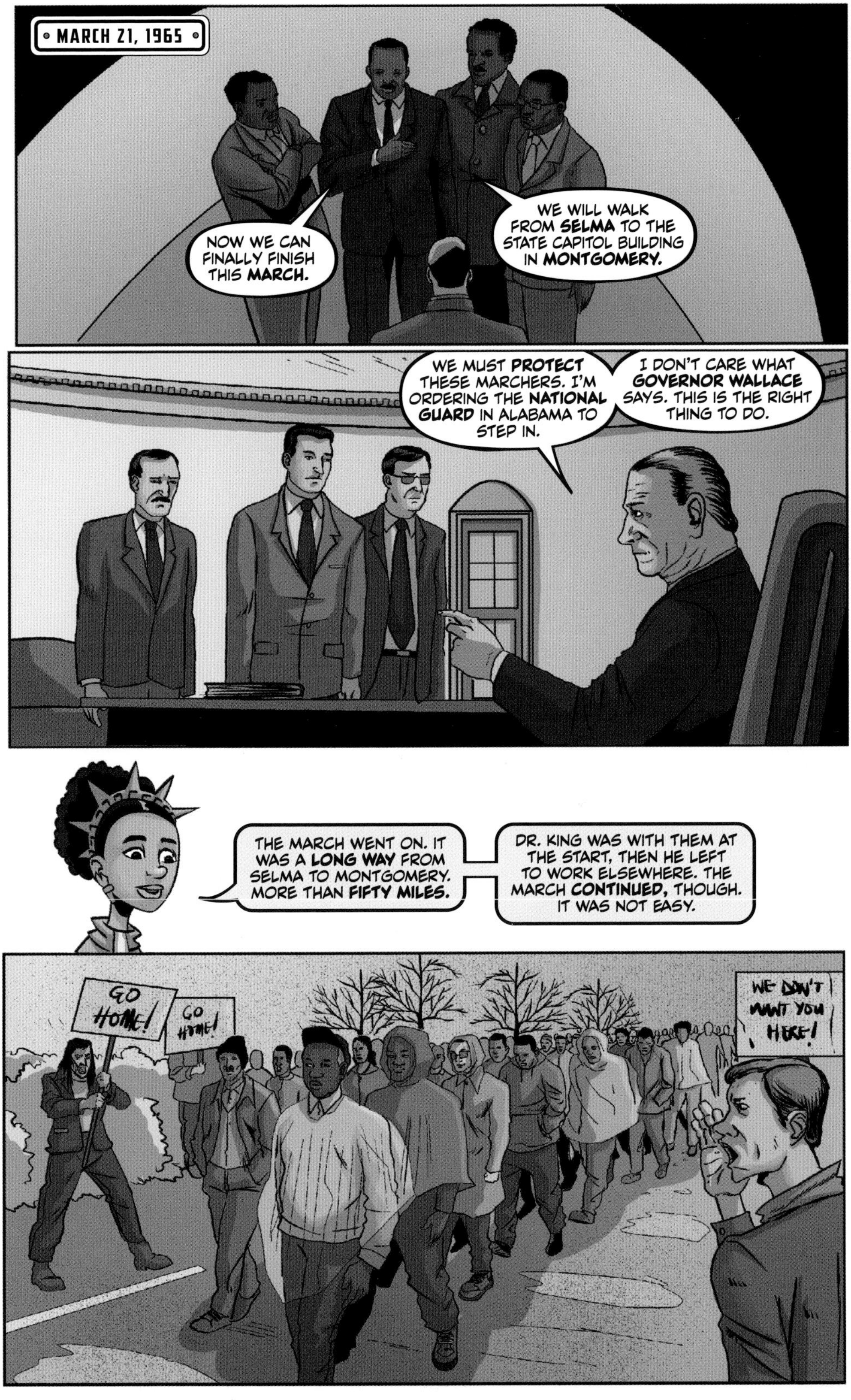
MARCH 21, 1965
NOW WE CAN FINALLY FINISH THIS MARCH.
WE WILL WALK FROM SELMA TO THE STATE CAPITOL BUILDING IN MONTGOMERY.
WE MUST PROTECT THESE MARCHERS. I'M ORDERING THE NATIONAL GUARD IN ALABAMA TO STEP IN.
I DON'T CARE WHAT GOVERNOR WALLACE SAYS. THIS IS THE RIGHT THING TO DO.
THE MARCH WENT ON. IT WAS A LONG WAY FROM SELMA TO MONTGOMERY. MORE THAN FIFTY MILES.
DR. KING WAS WITH THEM AT THE START, THEN HE LEFT TO WORK ELSEWHERE. THE MARCH CONTINUED, THOUGH. IT WAS NOT EASY.
GO HOME!
GO HOME!
WE DON'T WANT YOU HERE!

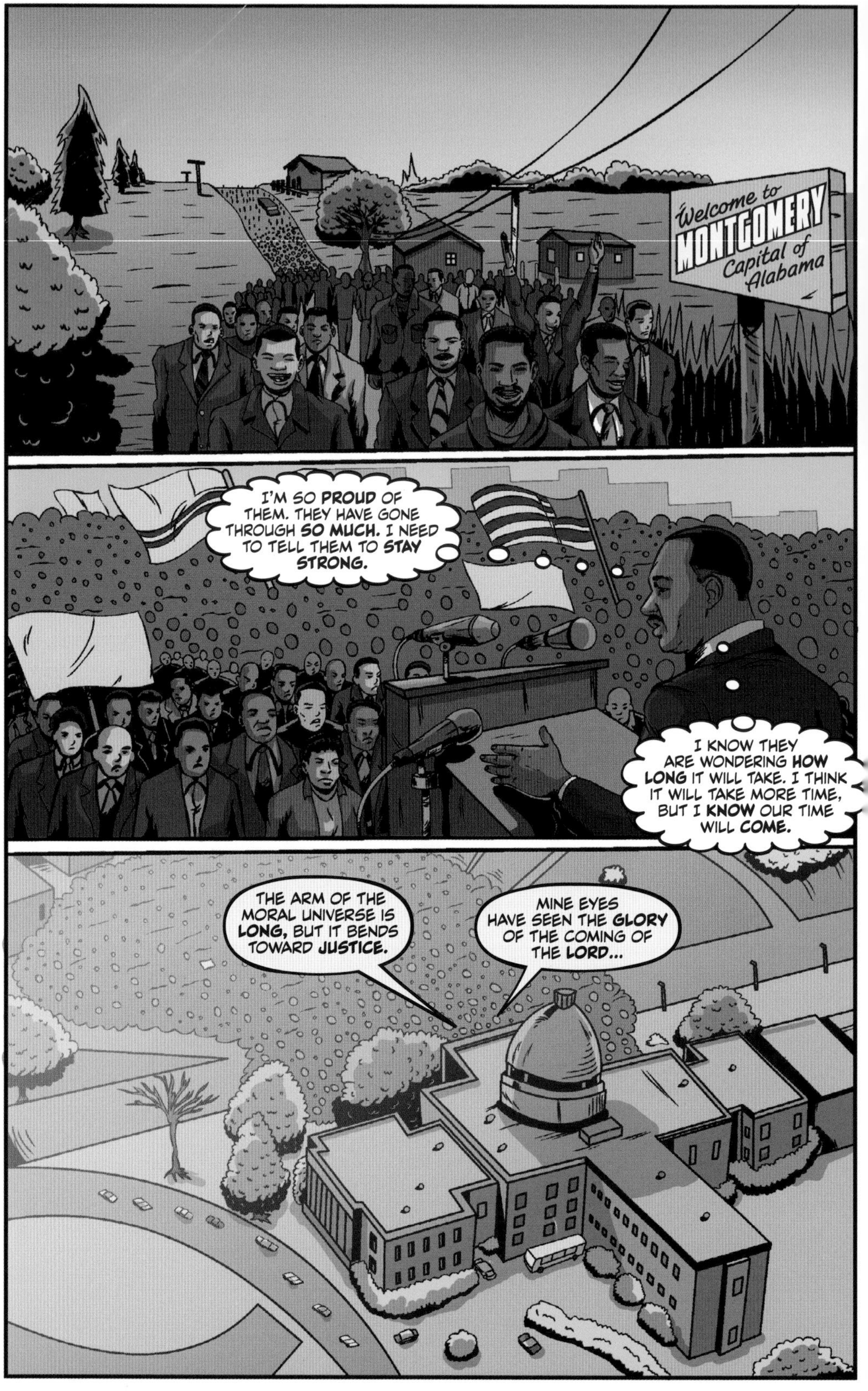
Welcome to
MONTGOMERY
Capital of Alabama
I'M SO PROUD OF THEM. THEY HAVE GONE THROUGH SO MUCH. I NEED TO TELL THEM TO STAY STRONG.
I KNOW THEY ARE WONDERING HOW LONG IT WILL TAKE. I THINK IT WILL TAKE MORE TIME, BUT I KNOW OUR TIME WILL COME.
THE ARM OF THE MORAL UNIVERSE IS LONG, BUT IT BENDS TOWARD JUSTICE.
MINE EYES HAVE SEEN THE GLORY OF THE COMING OF THE LORD...

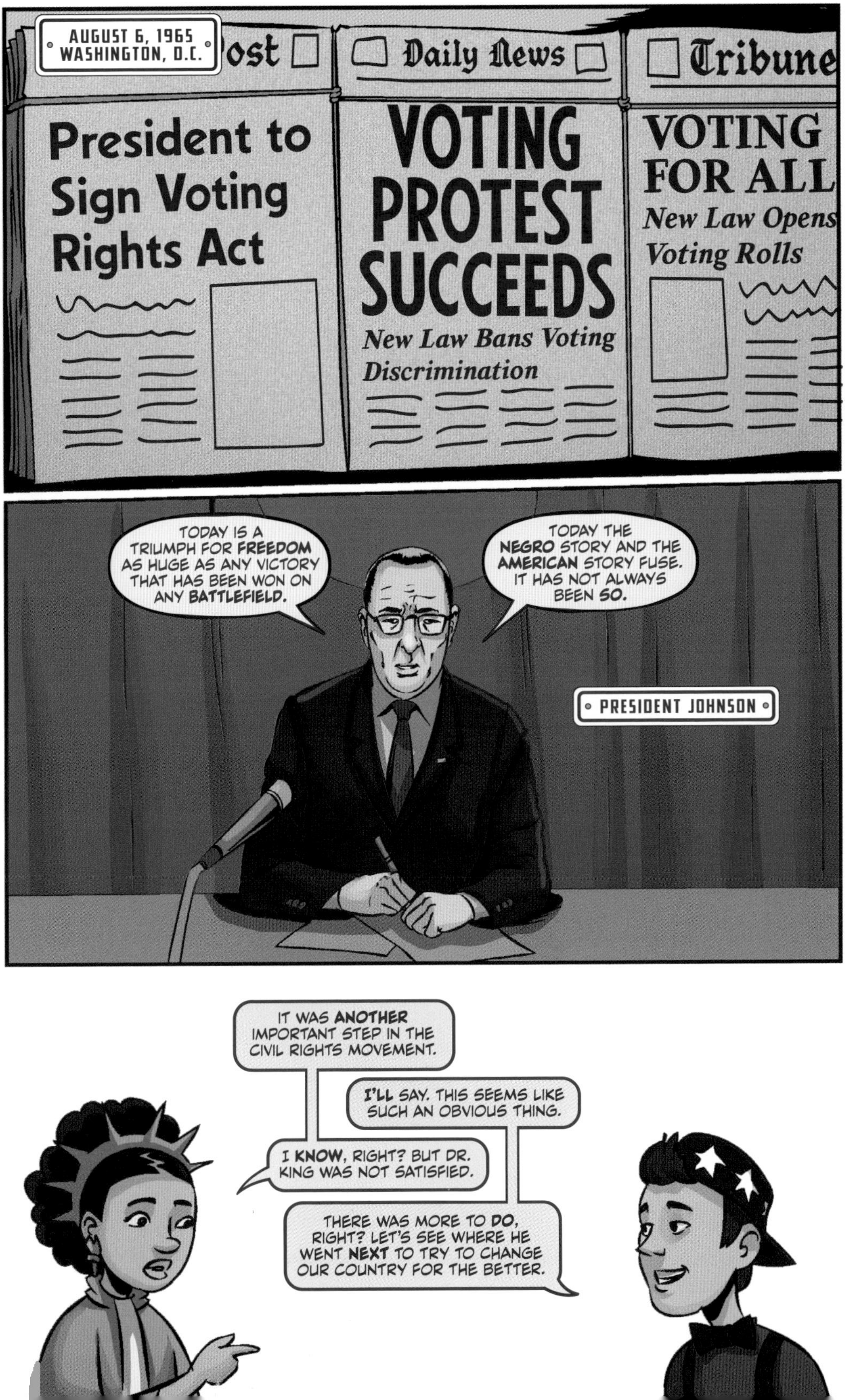
AUGUST 6, 1965 WASHINGTON, D.C.
Post
President to Sign Voting Rights Act
Daily News
VOTING PROTEST SUCCEEDS
New Law Bans Voting Discrimination
Tribune
VOTING FOR ALL
New Law Opens Voting Rolls
TODAY IS A TRIUMPH FOR FREEDOM AS HUGE AS ANY VICTORY THAT HAS BEEN WON ON ANY BATTLEFIELD.
TODAY THE NEGRO STORY AND THE AMERICAN STORY FUSE. IT HAS NOT ALWAYS BEEN SO.
PRESIDENT JOHNSON
IT WAS ANOTHER IMPORTANT STEP IN THE CIVIL RIGHTS MOVEMENT.
I'LL SAY. THIS SEEMS LIKE SUCH AN OBVIOUS THING.
I KNOW, RIGHT? BUT DR. KING WAS NOT SATISFIED.
THERE WAS MORE TO DO, RIGHT? LET'S SEE WHERE HE WENT NEXT TO TRY TO CHANGE OUR COUNTRY FOR THE BETTER.

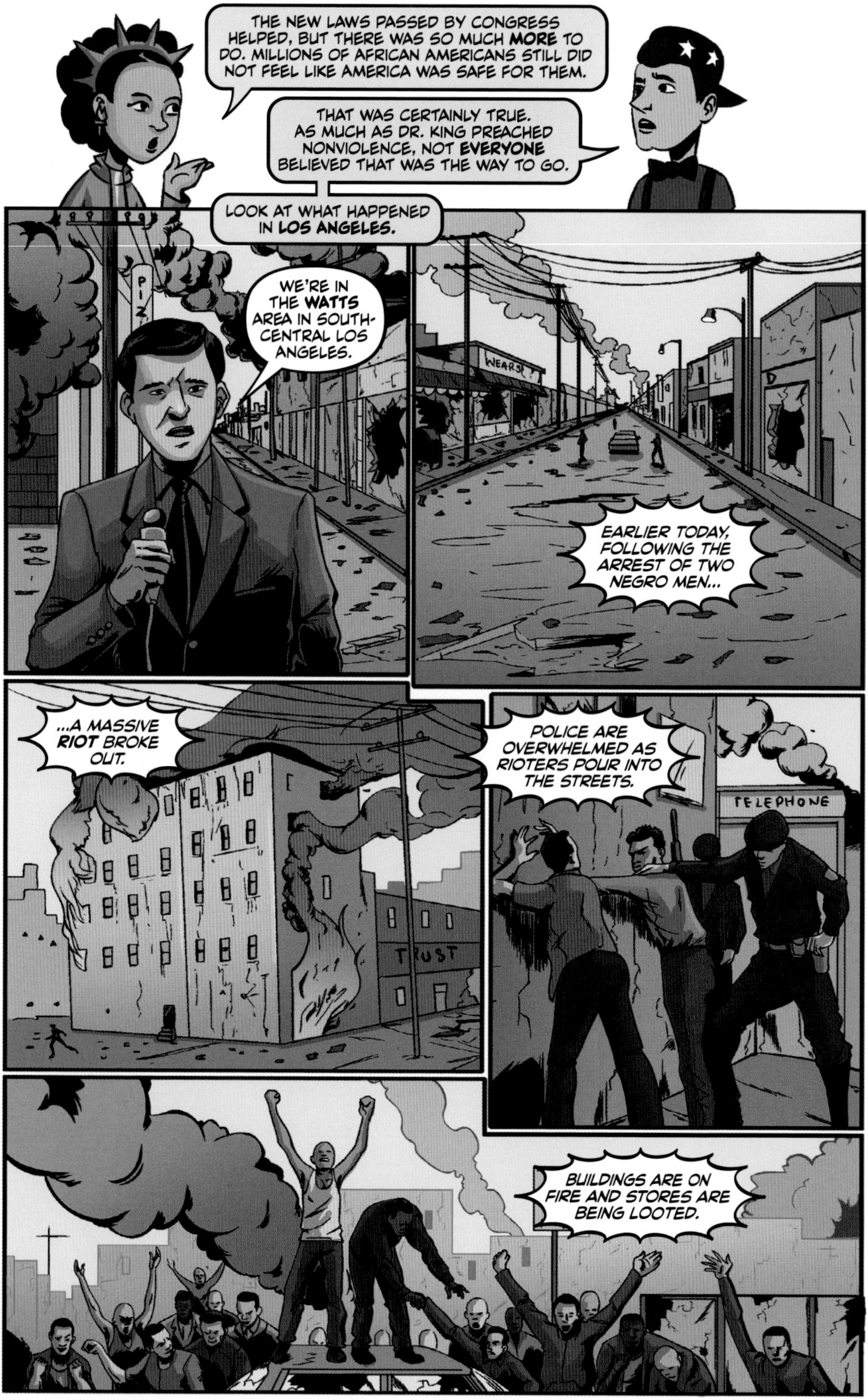
THE NEW LAWS PASSED BY CONGRESS HELPED, BUT THERE WAS SO MUCH MORE TO DO. MILLIONS OF AFRICAN AMERICANS STILL DID NOT FEEL LIKE AMERICA WAS SAFE FOR THEM.
THAT WAS CERTAINLY TRUE. AS MUCH AS DR. KING PREACHED NONVIOLENCE, NOT EVERYONE BELIEVED THAT WAS THE WAY TO GO.
LOOK AT WHAT HAPPENED IN LOS ANGELES.
WE'RE IN THE WATTS AREA IN SOUTH-CENTRAL LOS ANGELES.
WEARS
EARLIER TODAY, FOLLOWING THE ARREST OF TWO NEGRO MEN...
...A MASSIVE RIOT BROKE OUT.
TRUST
POLICE ARE OVERWHELMED AS RIOTERS POUR INTO THE STREETS.
TELEPHONE
BUILDINGS ARE ON FIRE AND STORES ARE BEING LOOTED.

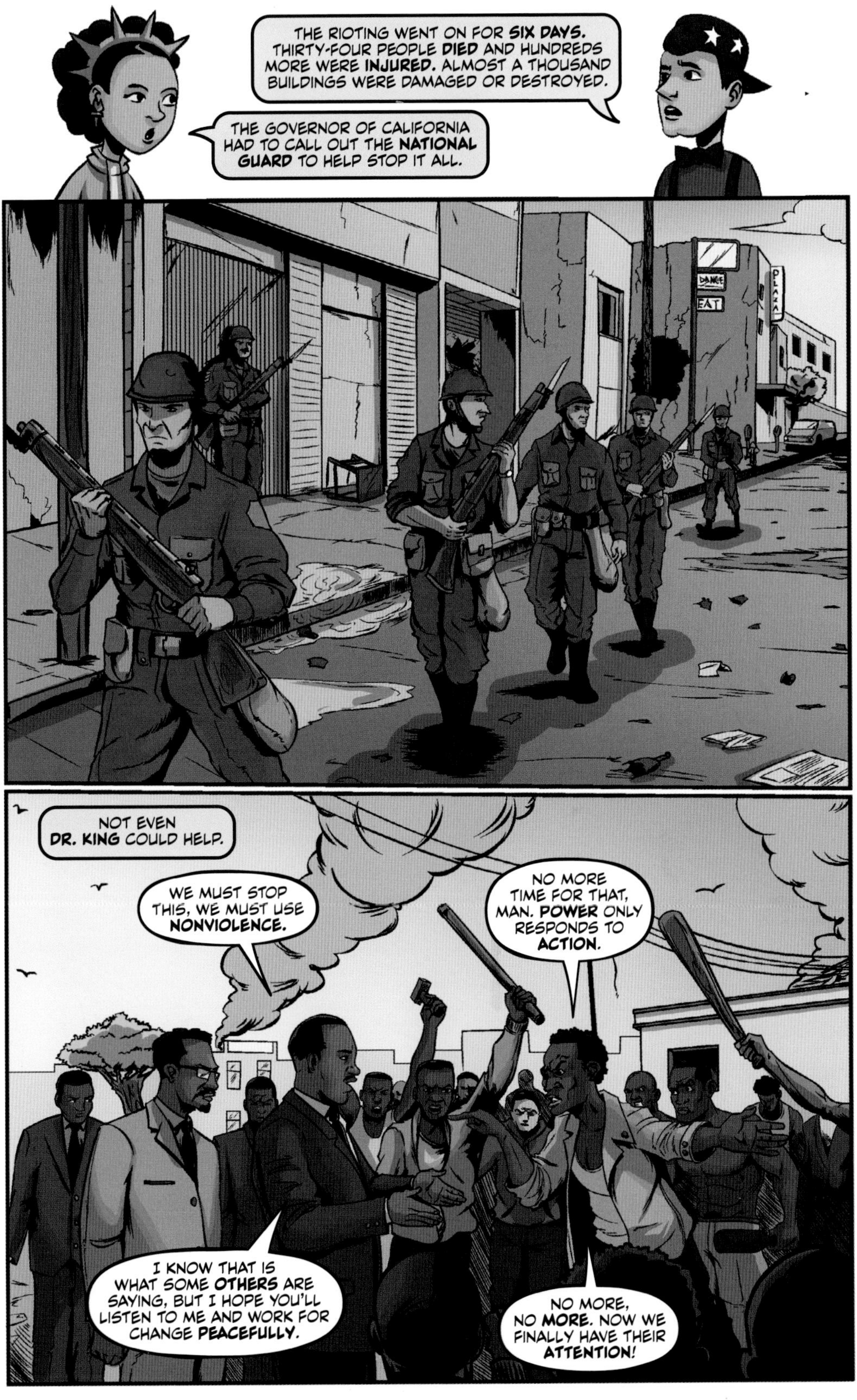
THE RIOTING WENT ON FOR **SIX DAYS.** THIRTY-FOUR PEOPLE **DIED** AND HUNDREDS MORE WERE **INJURED.** ALMOST A THOUSAND BUILDINGS WERE DAMAGED OR DESTROYED.
THE GOVERNOR OF CALIFORNIA HAD TO CALL OUT THE **NATIONAL GUARD** TO HELP STOP IT ALL.
DANCE
EAT
PLAZA
NOT EVEN **DR. KING** COULD HELP.
WE MUST STOP THIS, WE MUST USE **NONVIOLENCE.**
NO MORE TIME FOR THAT, MAN. **POWER** ONLY RESPONDS TO **ACTION**.
I KNOW THAT IS WHAT SOME **OTHERS** ARE SAYING, BUT I HOPE YOU'LL LISTEN TO ME AND WORK FOR CHANGE **PEACEFULLY**.
NO MORE, NO **MORE.** NOW WE FINALLY HAVE THEIR **ATTENTION**!

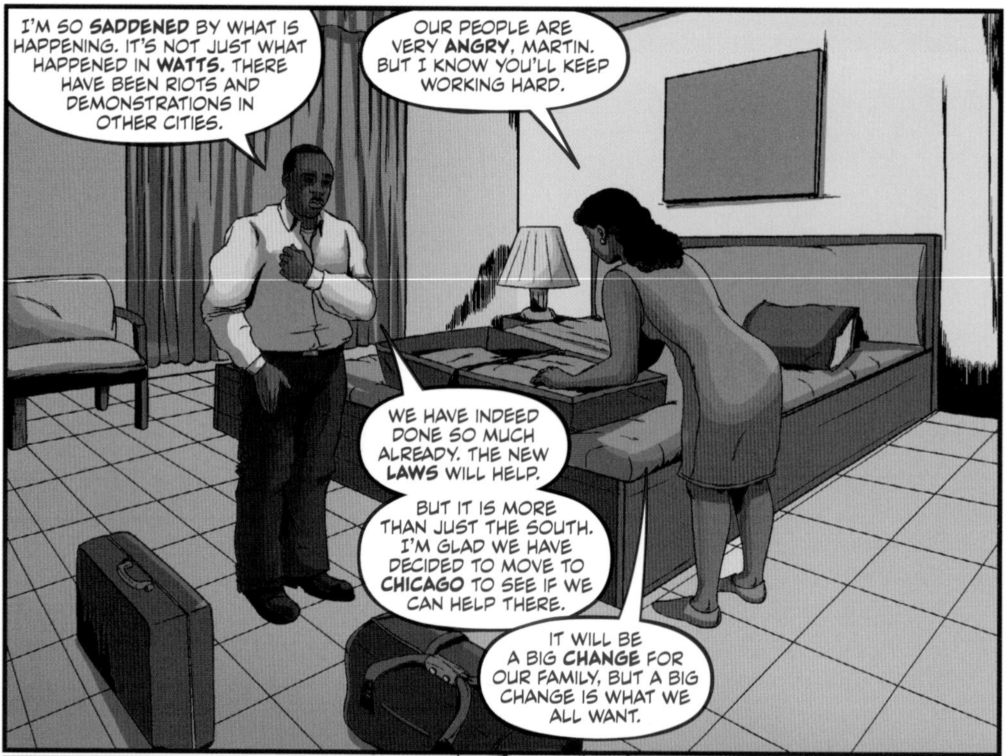
I'M SO SADDENED BY WHAT IS HAPPENING. IT'S NOT JUST WHAT HAPPENED IN WATTS. THERE HAVE BEEN RIOTS AND DEMONSTRATIONS IN OTHER CITIES.
OUR PEOPLE ARE VERY ANGRY, MARTIN. BUT I KNOW YOU'LL KEEP WORKING HARD.
WE HAVE INDEED DONE SO MUCH ALREADY. THE NEW LAWS WILL HELP.
BUT IT IS MORE THAN JUST THE SOUTH. I'M GLAD WE HAVE DECIDED TO MOVE TO CHICAGO TO SEE IF WE CAN HELP THERE.
IT WILL BE A BIG CHANGE FOR OUR FAMILY, BUT A BIG CHANGE IS WHAT WE ALL WANT.

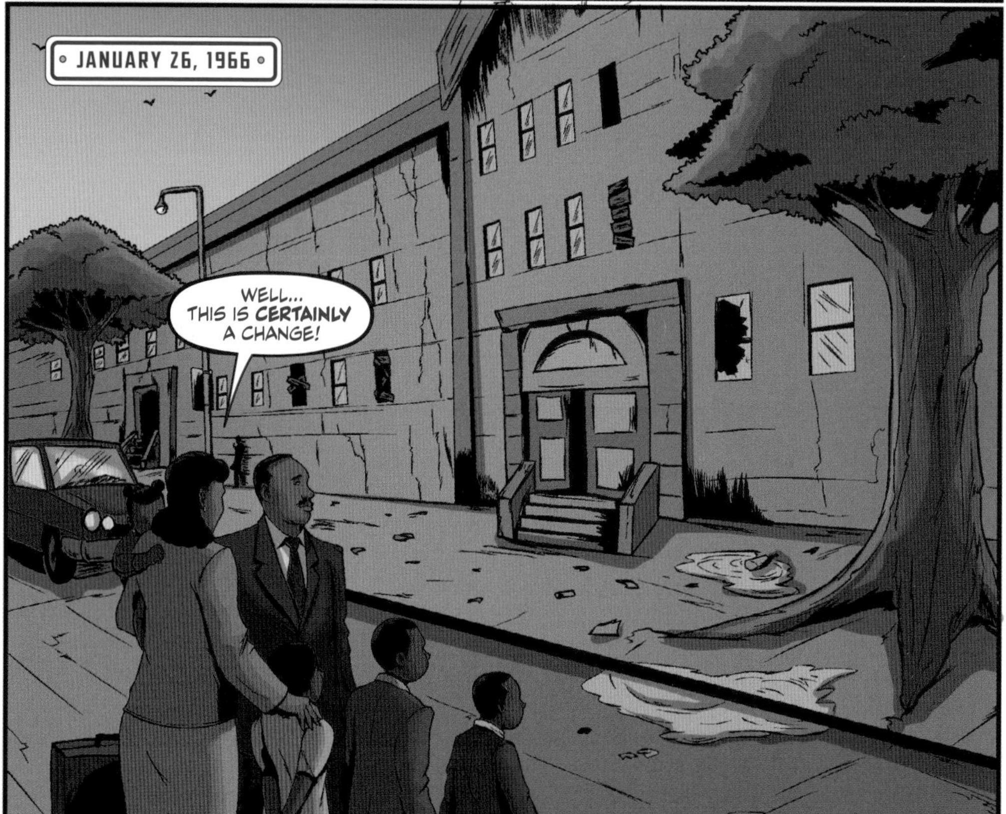
JANUARY 26, 1966
WELL... THIS IS CERTAINLY A CHANGE!

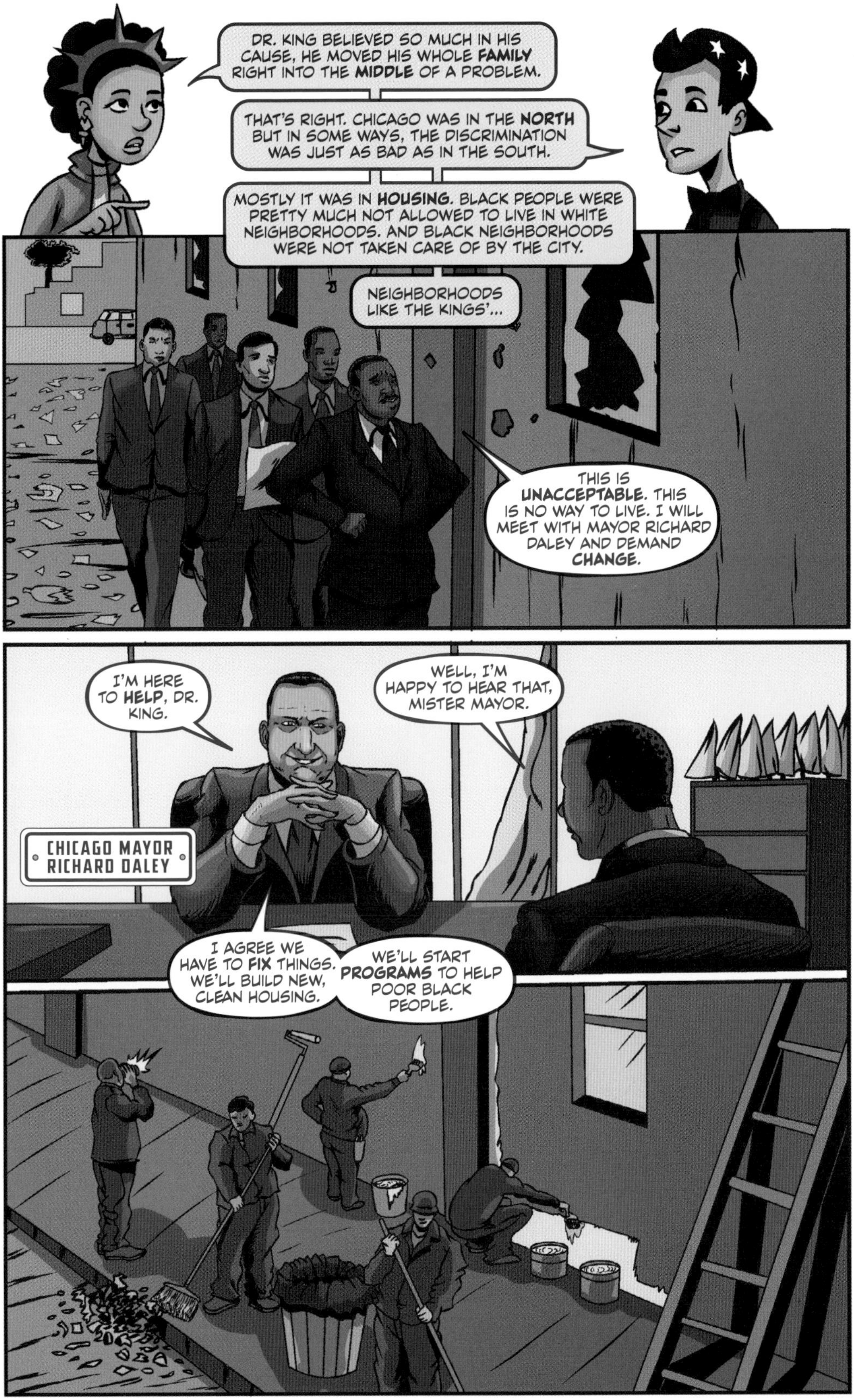
DR. KING BELIEVED SO MUCH IN HIS CAUSE, HE MOVED HIS WHOLE **FAMILY** RIGHT INTO THE **MIDDLE** OF A PROBLEM.
THAT'S RIGHT. CHICAGO WAS IN THE **NORTH** BUT IN SOME WAYS, THE DISCRIMINATION WAS JUST AS BAD AS IN THE SOUTH.
MOSTLY IT WAS IN **HOUSING**. BLACK PEOPLE WERE PRETTY MUCH NOT ALLOWED TO LIVE IN WHITE NEIGHBORHOODS. AND BLACK NEIGHBORHOODS WERE NOT TAKEN CARE OF BY THE CITY.
NEIGHBORHOODS LIKE THE KINGS'...
THIS IS **UNACCEPTABLE**. THIS IS NO WAY TO LIVE. I WILL MEET WITH MAYOR RICHARD DALEY AND DEMAND **CHANGE**.
I'M HERE TO **HELP**, DR. KING.
WELL, I'M HAPPY TO HEAR THAT, MISTER MAYOR.
CHICAGO MAYOR RICHARD DALEY
I AGREE WE HAVE TO **FIX** THINGS. WE'LL BUILD NEW, CLEAN HOUSING.
WE'LL START **PROGRAMS** TO HELP POOR BLACK PEOPLE.

IT ALL **LOOKED** PRETTY GOOD. DALEY WAS DOING ONE OR TWO OF THE MANY THINGS HE HAD PROMISED. FOR SOME IT WAS NOT ENOUGH AND NOT FAST ENOUGH.

OR ELSE THEY DIDN'T **BELIEVE** DALEY, RIGHT?

WELL, YES, THAT **TOO.** DR. KING WAS HAVING TROUBLE STOPPING OTHER LEADERS WHO WANTED TO USE MORE DIRECT ACTION. THINGS WERE **CHANGING** IN AMERICA...

...AND THINGS WERE CHANGING IN THE **CIVIL RIGHTS** MOVEMENT.

• JULY 10, 1966 • CHICAGO •

• "FREEDOM SUNDAY" •

DR. KING POSTED A LIST OF **HOUSING DEMANDS** ON THE CITY HALL DOOR. THE PROTESTORS DEMANDED:

End housing discrimination

Provide equal educational opportunities

Improve access to good jobs

Stop police brutality and unjust arrest

Honor the rights of apartment tenants

Improve the quality of life for all

HE WANTED TO MAKE SURE MAYOR DALEY GOT THE MESSAGE.

End housing discrimination
Provide equal educational opportunities
Improve access to good jobs
Stop police brutality and unjust arrest
Honor the rights of apartment tenants
Improve the quality of life for all

End housing discrimination
Provide equal educational opportunities
Improve access to good jobs
Stop police brutality and unjust arrest
Honor the rights of apartment tenants
Improve the quality of life for all

SURE, DR. KING, **SURE,** WE'LL TAKE CARE OF **ALL** OF THAT.

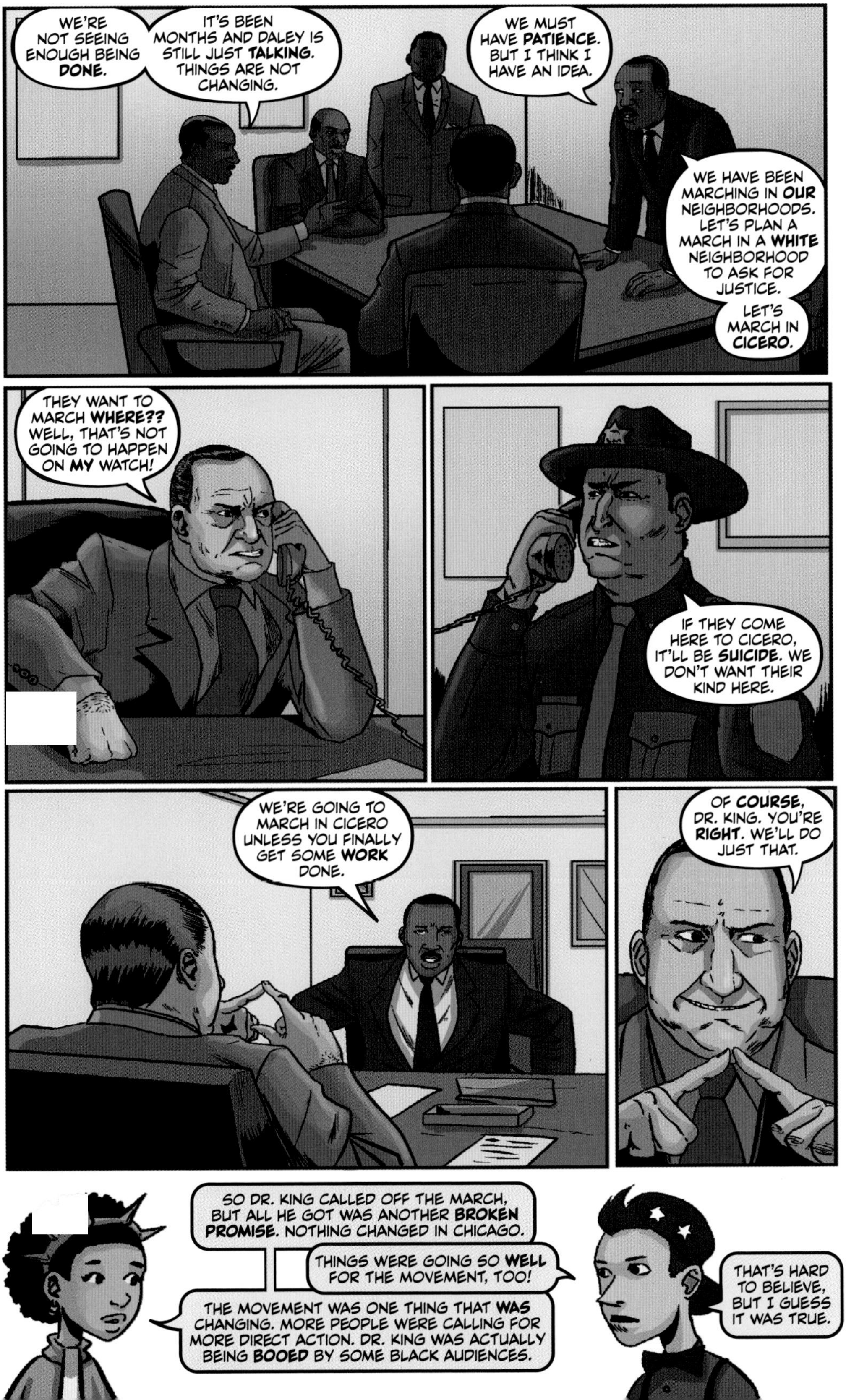
WE'RE NOT SEEING ENOUGH BEING DONE.
IT'S BEEN MONTHS AND DALEY IS STILL JUST TALKING. THINGS ARE NOT CHANGING.
WE MUST HAVE PATIENCE. BUT I THINK I HAVE AN IDEA.
WE HAVE BEEN MARCHING IN OUR NEIGHBORHOODS. LET'S PLAN A MARCH IN A WHITE NEIGHBORHOOD TO ASK FOR JUSTICE.
LET'S MARCH IN CICERO.
THEY WANT TO MARCH WHERE?? WELL, THAT'S NOT GOING TO HAPPEN ON MY WATCH!
IF THEY COME HERE TO CICERO, IT'LL BE SUICIDE. WE DON'T WANT THEIR KIND HERE.
WE'RE GOING TO MARCH IN CICERO UNLESS YOU FINALLY GET SOME WORK DONE.
OF COURSE, DR. KING. YOU'RE RIGHT. WE'LL DO JUST THAT.
SO DR. KING CALLED OFF THE MARCH, BUT ALL HE GOT WAS ANOTHER BROKEN PROMISE. NOTHING CHANGED IN CHICAGO.
THINGS WERE GOING SO WELL FOR THE MOVEMENT, TOO!
THE MOVEMENT WAS ONE THING THAT WAS CHANGING. MORE PEOPLE WERE CALLING FOR MORE DIRECT ACTION. DR. KING WAS ACTUALLY BEING BOOED BY SOME BLACK AUDIENCES.
THAT'S HARD TO BELIEVE, BUT I GUESS IT WAS TRUE.

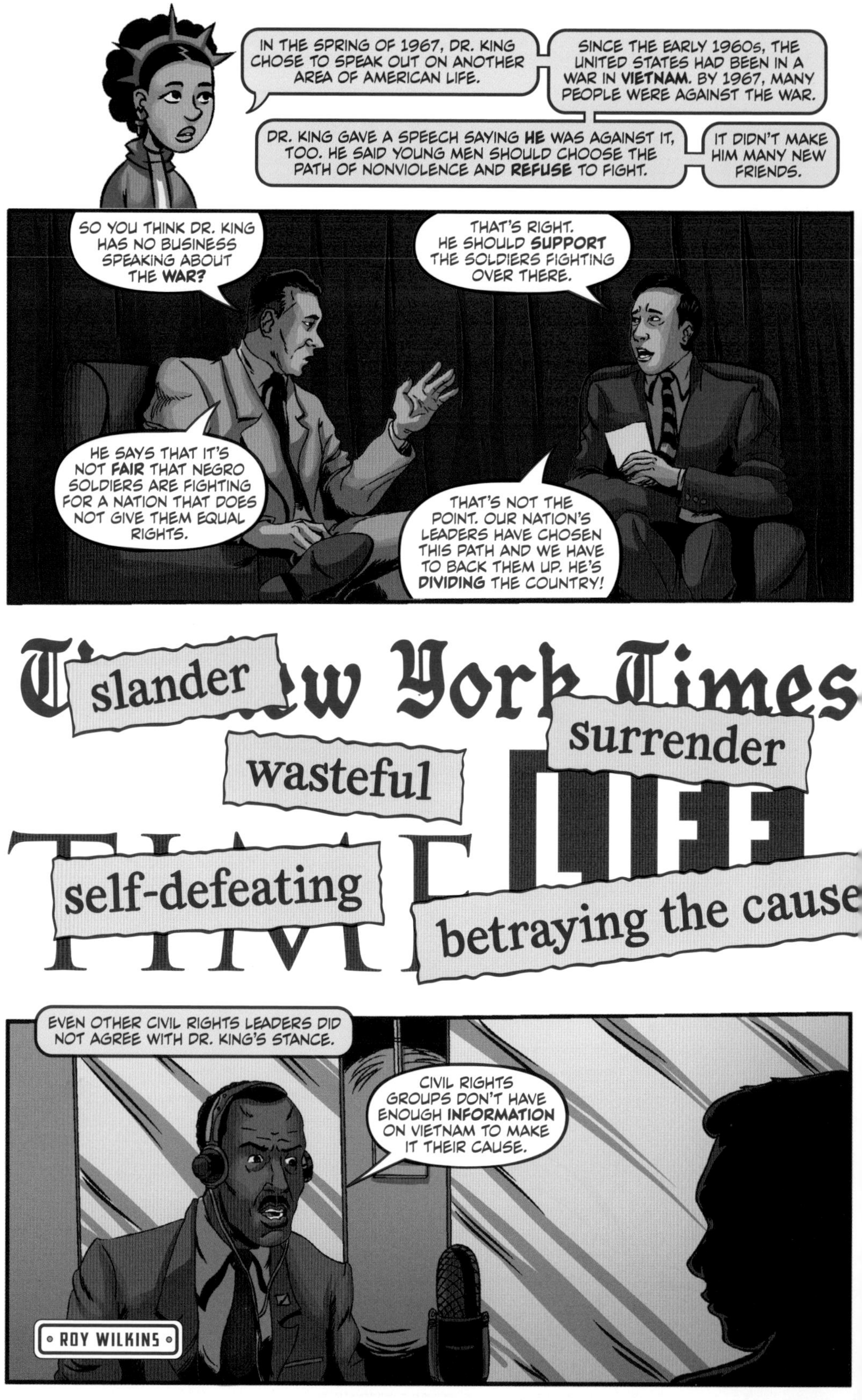
IN THE SPRING OF 1967, DR. KING CHOSE TO SPEAK OUT ON ANOTHER AREA OF AMERICAN LIFE.
SINCE THE EARLY 1960s, THE UNITED STATES HAD BEEN IN A WAR IN **VIETNAM**. BY 1967, MANY PEOPLE WERE AGAINST THE WAR.
DR. KING GAVE A SPEECH SAYING **HE** WAS AGAINST IT, TOO. HE SAID YOUNG MEN SHOULD CHOOSE THE PATH OF NONVIOLENCE AND **REFUSE** TO FIGHT.
IT DIDN'T MAKE HIM MANY NEW FRIENDS.
SO YOU THINK DR. KING HAS NO BUSINESS SPEAKING ABOUT THE **WAR?**
THAT'S RIGHT. HE SHOULD **SUPPORT** THE SOLDIERS FIGHTING OVER THERE.
HE SAYS THAT IT'S NOT **FAIR** THAT NEGRO SOLDIERS ARE FIGHTING FOR A NATION THAT DOES NOT GIVE THEM EQUAL RIGHTS.
THAT'S NOT THE POINT. OUR NATION'S LEADERS HAVE CHOSEN THIS PATH AND WE HAVE TO BACK THEM UP. HE'S **DIVIDING** THE COUNTRY!
slander
wasteful
surrender
self-defeating
betraying the cause
EVEN OTHER CIVIL RIGHTS LEADERS DID NOT AGREE WITH DR. KING'S STANCE.
CIVIL RIGHTS GROUPS DON'T HAVE ENOUGH **INFORMATION** ON VIETNAM TO MAKE IT THEIR CAUSE.
ROY WILKINS

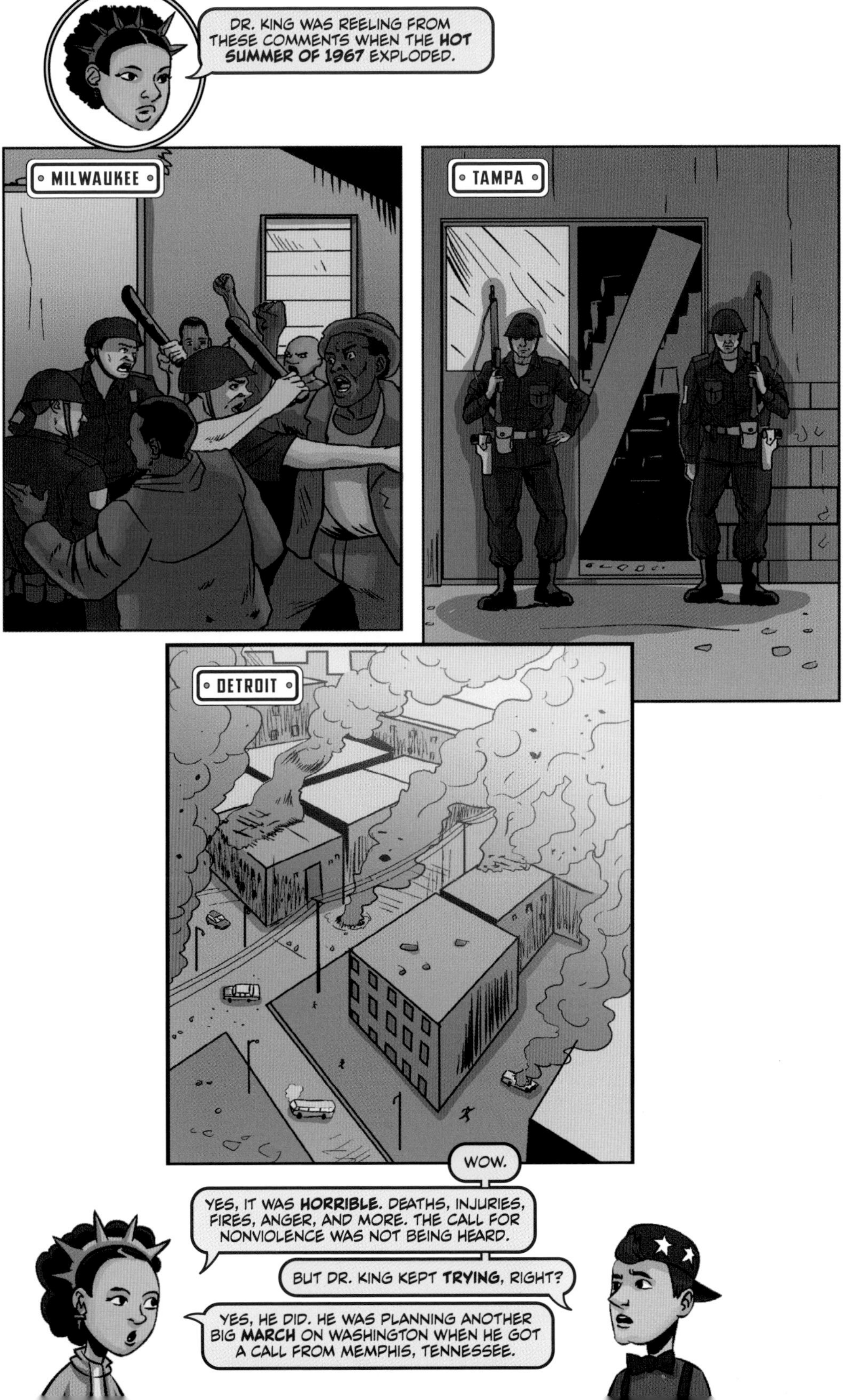
DR. KING WAS REELING FROM THESE COMMENTS WHEN THE HOT SUMMER OF 1967 EXPLODED.
MILWAUKEE
TAMPA
DETROIT
WOW.
YES, IT WAS HORRIBLE. DEATHS, INJURIES, FIRES, ANGER, AND MORE. THE CALL FOR NONVIOLENCE WAS NOT BEING HEARD.
BUT DR. KING KEPT TRYING, RIGHT?
YES, HE DID. HE WAS PLANNING ANOTHER BIG MARCH ON WASHINGTON WHEN HE GOT A CALL FROM MEMPHIS, TENNESSEE.

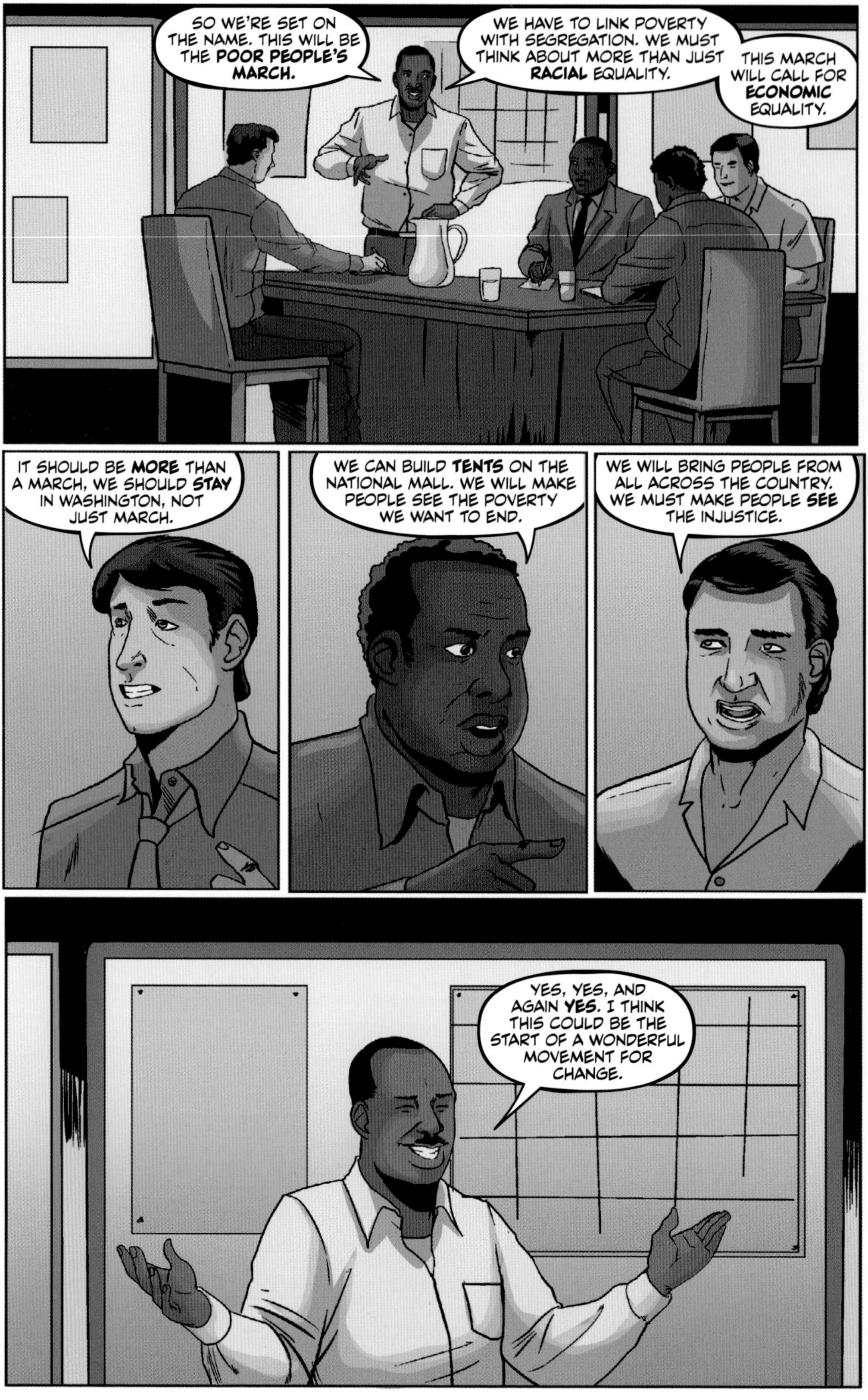
SO WE'RE SET ON THE NAME. THIS WILL BE THE **POOR PEOPLE'S MARCH.**
WE HAVE TO LINK POVERTY WITH SEGREGATION. WE MUST THINK ABOUT MORE THAN JUST **RACIAL** EQUALITY.
THIS MARCH WILL CALL FOR **ECONOMIC** EQUALITY.
IT SHOULD BE **MORE** THAN A MARCH, WE SHOULD **STAY** IN WASHINGTON, NOT JUST MARCH.
WE CAN BUILD **TENTS** ON THE NATIONAL MALL. WE WILL MAKE PEOPLE SEE THE POVERTY WE WANT TO END.
WE WILL BRING PEOPLE FROM ALL ACROSS THE COUNTRY. WE MUST MAKE PEOPLE **SEE** THE INJUSTICE.
YES, YES, AND AGAIN **YES**. I THINK THIS COULD BE THE START OF A WONDERFUL MOVEMENT FOR CHANGE.

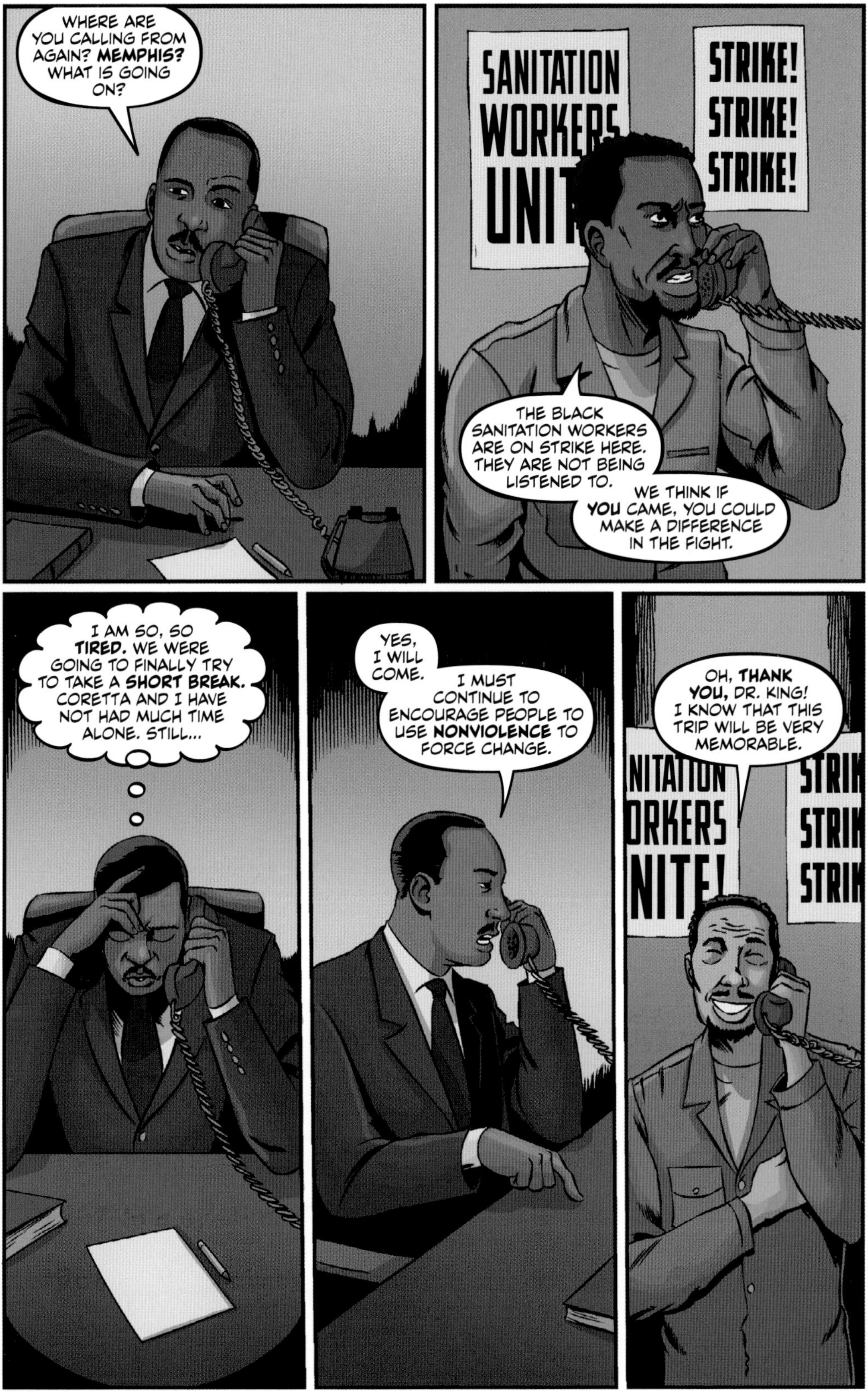

WHERE ARE YOU CALLING FROM AGAIN? **MEMPHIS?** WHAT IS GOING ON?
SANITATION WORKERS UNIT
STRIKE! STRIKE! STRIKE!
THE BLACK SANITATION WORKERS ARE ON STRIKE HERE. THEY ARE NOT BEING LISTENED TO.
WE THINK IF **YOU** CAME, YOU COULD MAKE A DIFFERENCE IN THE FIGHT.
I AM SO, SO **TIRED.** WE WERE GOING TO FINALLY TRY TO TAKE A **SHORT BREAK.** CORETTA AND I HAVE NOT HAD MUCH TIME ALONE. STILL...
YES, I WILL COME.
I MUST CONTINUE TO ENCOURAGE PEOPLE TO USE **NONVIOLENCE** TO FORCE CHANGE.
OH, **THANK YOU,** DR. KING! I KNOW THAT THIS TRIP WILL BE VERY MEMORABLE.
NITATION ORKERS NITE!
STRIK STRIK STRIK

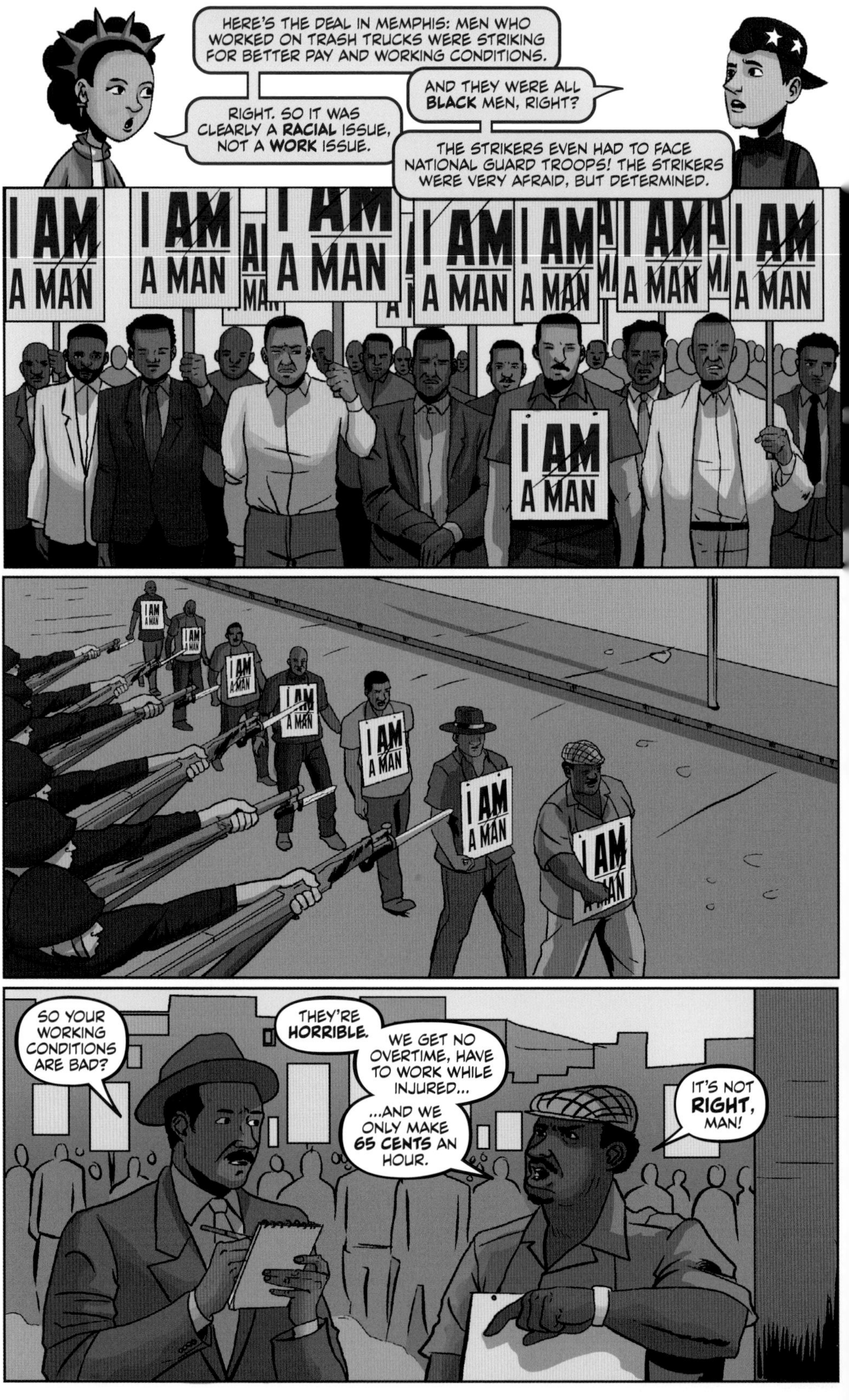
HERE'S THE DEAL IN MEMPHIS: MEN WHO WORKED ON TRASH TRUCKS WERE STRIKING FOR BETTER PAY AND WORKING CONDITIONS.
RIGHT. SO IT WAS CLEARLY A **RACIAL** ISSUE, NOT A **WORK** ISSUE.
AND THEY WERE ALL **BLACK** MEN, RIGHT?
THE STRIKERS EVEN HAD TO FACE NATIONAL GUARD TROOPS! THE STRIKERS WERE VERY AFRAID, BUT DETERMINED.
I AM A MAN
SO YOUR WORKING CONDITIONS ARE BAD?
THEY'RE **HORRIBLE.**
WE GET NO OVERTIME, HAVE TO WORK WHILE INJURED...
...AND WE ONLY MAKE **65 CENTS** AN HOUR.
IT'S NOT **RIGHT**, MAN!

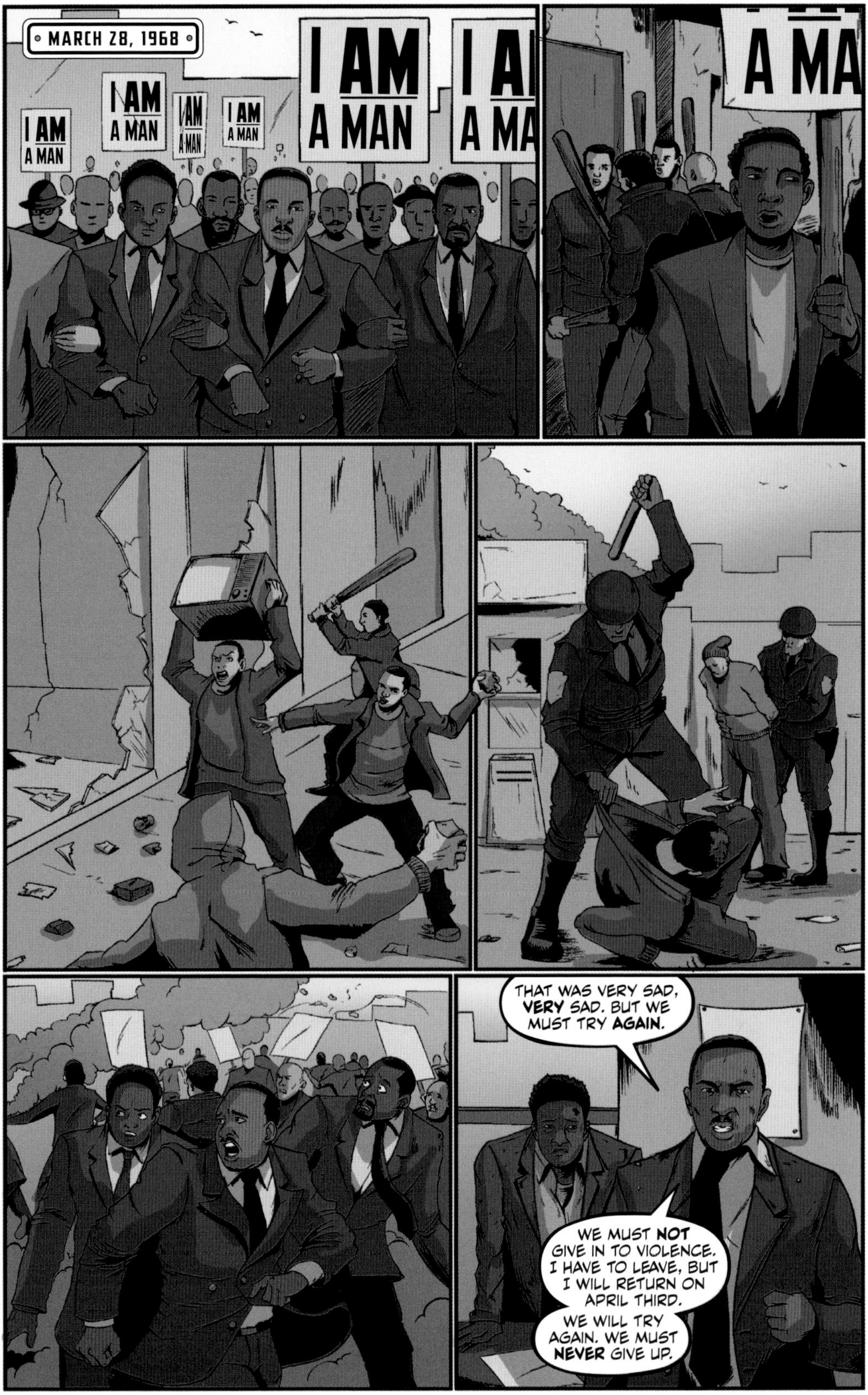
MARCH 28, 1968
I AM A MAN
I AM A MAN
I AM A MAN
I AM A MAN
I AM A MAN
I A A MA
A MA
THAT WAS VERY SAD, **VERY** SAD. BUT WE MUST TRY **AGAIN.**
WE MUST **NOT** GIVE IN TO VIOLENCE. I HAVE TO LEAVE, BUT I WILL RETURN ON APRIL THIRD.
WE WILL TRY AGAIN. WE MUST **NEVER** GIVE UP.

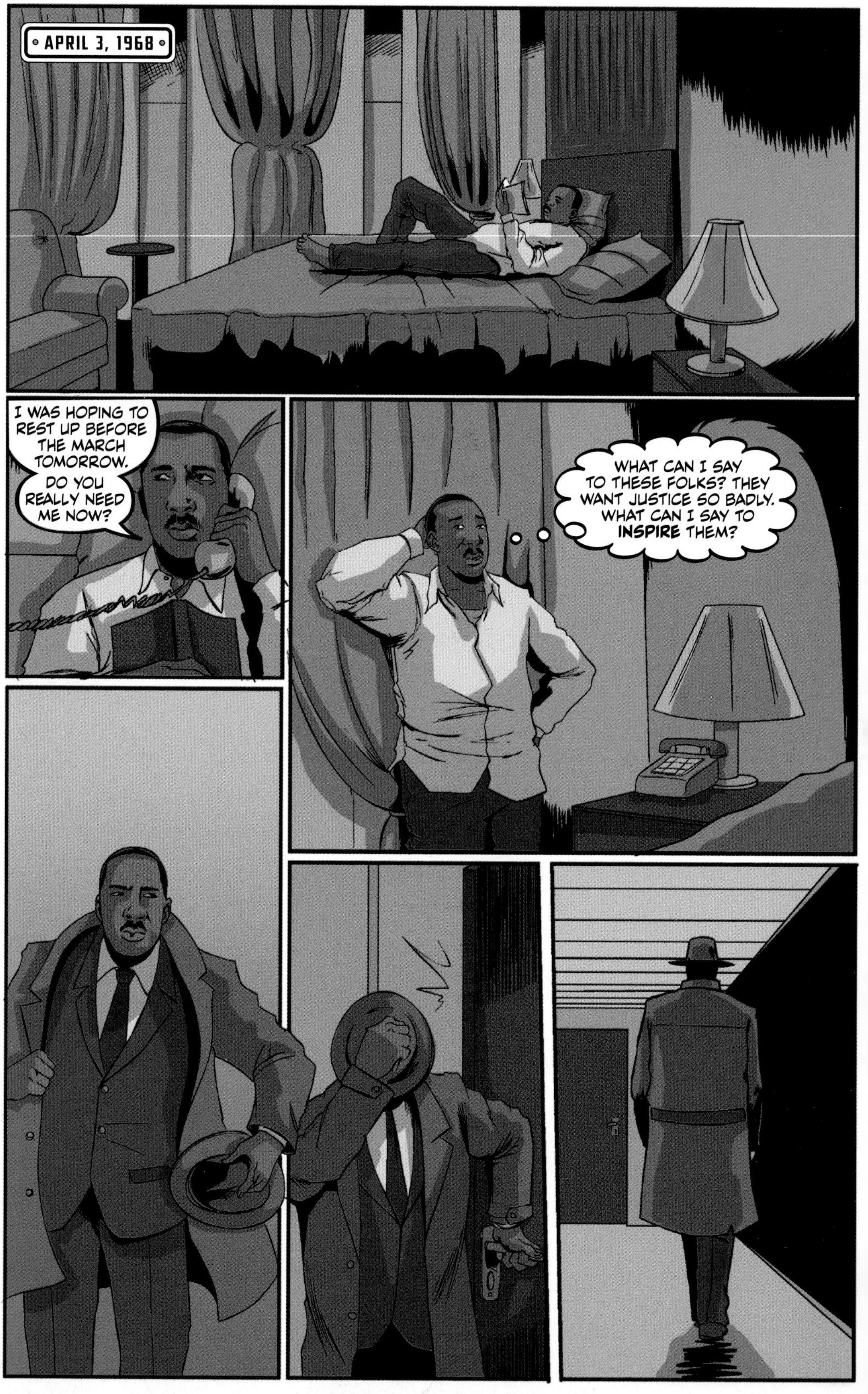
APRIL 3, 1968
I WAS HOPING TO REST UP BEFORE THE MARCH TOMORROW.
DO YOU REALLY NEED ME NOW?
WHAT CAN I SAY TO THESE FOLKS? THEY WANT JUSTICE SO BADLY. WHAT CAN I SAY TO **INSPIRE** THEM?

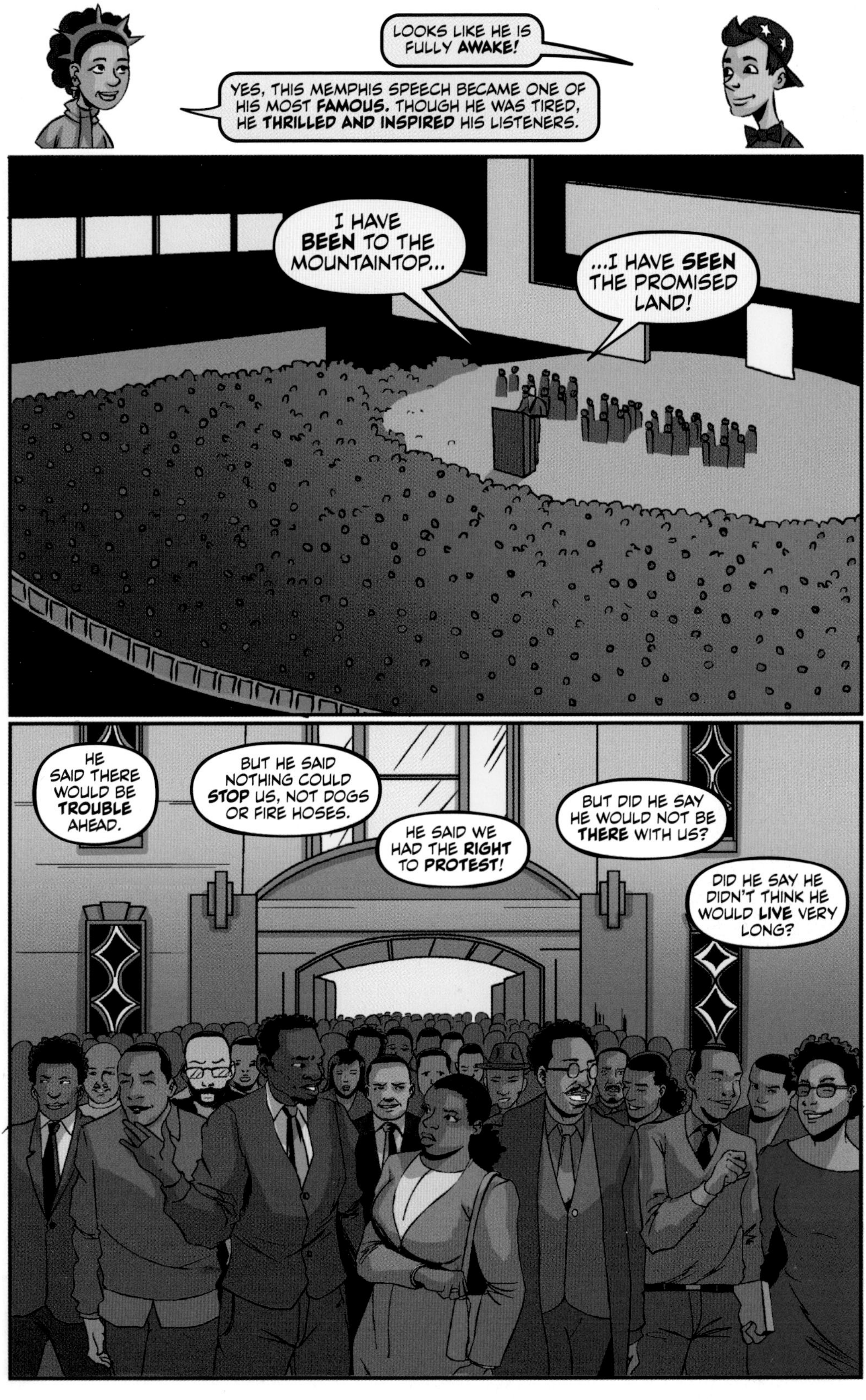
LOOKS LIKE HE IS FULLY AWAKE!
YES, THIS MEMPHIS SPEECH BECAME ONE OF HIS MOST FAMOUS. THOUGH HE WAS TIRED, HE THRILLED AND INSPIRED HIS LISTENERS.
I HAVE BEEN TO THE MOUNTAINTOP...
...I HAVE SEEN THE PROMISED LAND!
HE SAID THERE WOULD BE TROUBLE AHEAD.
BUT HE SAID NOTHING COULD STOP US, NOT DOGS OR FIRE HOSES.
HE SAID WE HAD THE RIGHT TO PROTEST!
BUT DID HE SAY HE WOULD NOT BE THERE WITH US?
DID HE SAY HE DIDN'T THINK HE WOULD LIVE VERY LONG?

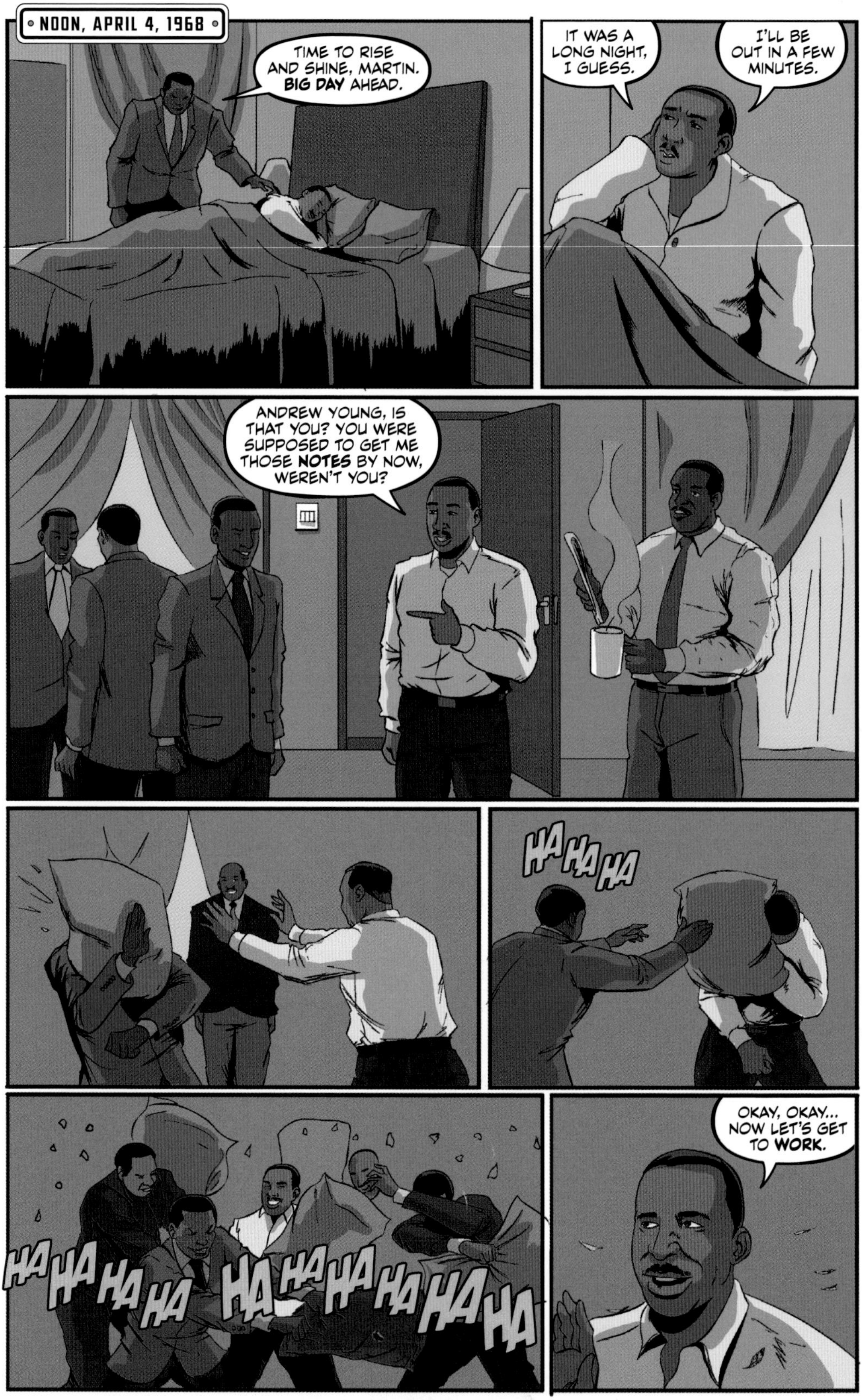
NOON, APRIL 4, 1968
TIME TO RISE AND SHINE, MARTIN. BIG DAY AHEAD.
IT WAS A LONG NIGHT, I GUESS.
I'LL BE OUT IN A FEW MINUTES.
ANDREW YOUNG, IS THAT YOU? YOU WERE SUPPOSED TO GET ME THOSE NOTES BY NOW, WEREN'T YOU?
HA HA HA
HA HA HA HA HA HA HA HA HA HA HA
OKAY, OKAY... NOW LET'S GET TO WORK.

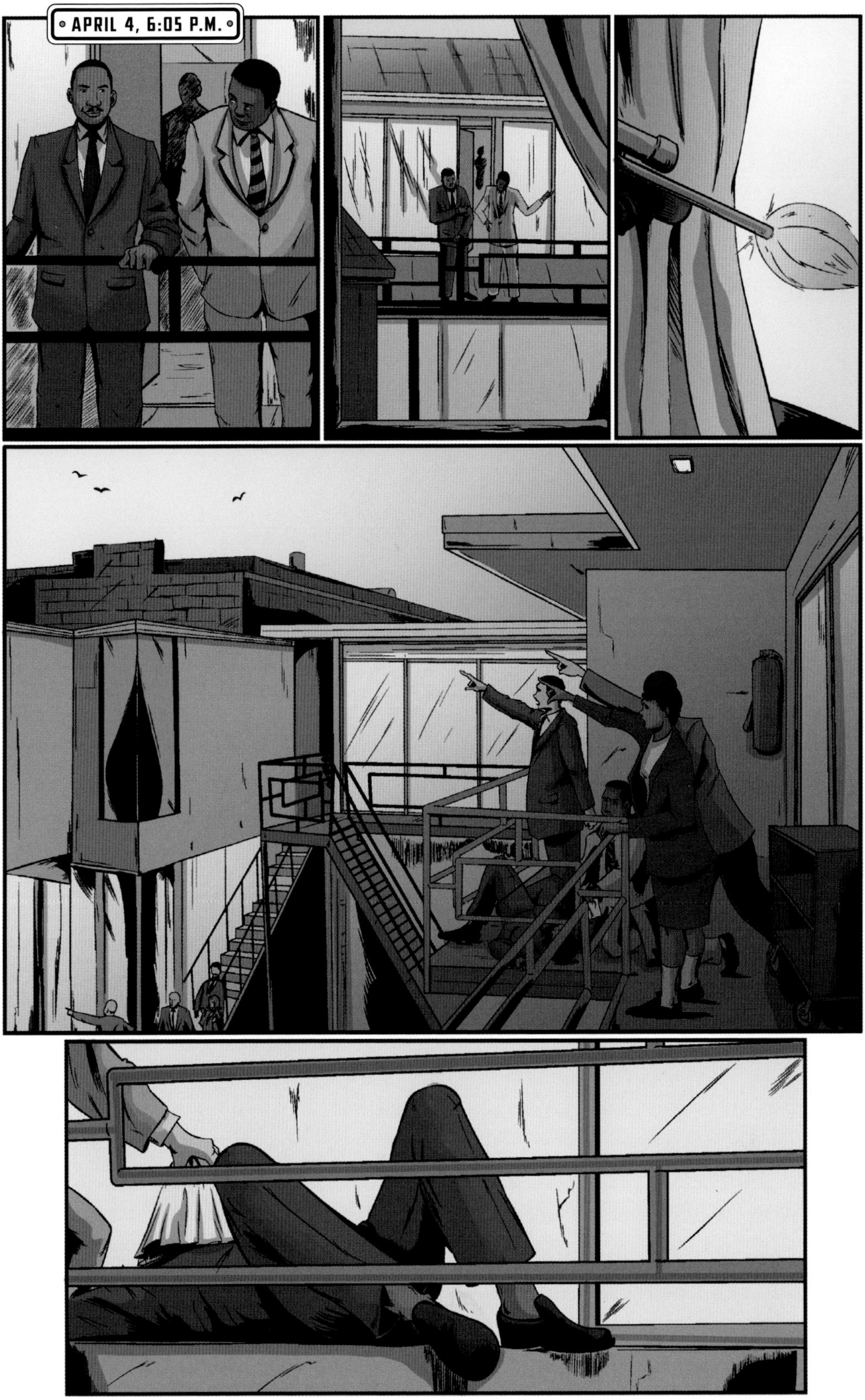
APRIL 4, 6:05 P.M.

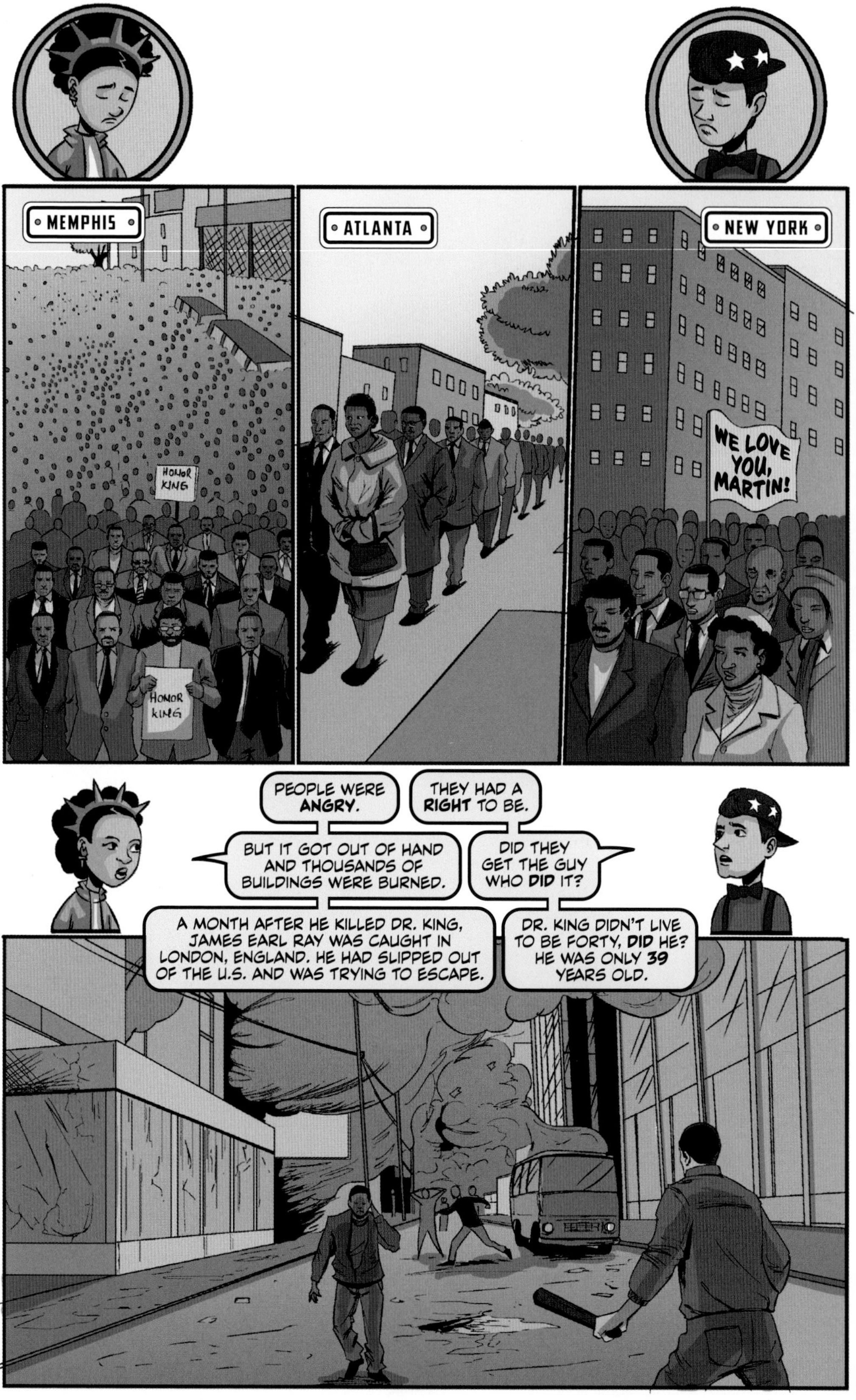
MEMPHIS
HONOR KING
HONOR KING
ATLANTA
NEW YORK
WE LOVE YOU, MARTIN!
PEOPLE WERE **ANGRY**.
THEY HAD A **RIGHT** TO BE.
BUT IT GOT OUT OF HAND AND THOUSANDS OF BUILDINGS WERE BURNED.
DID THEY GET THE GUY WHO **DID** IT?
A MONTH AFTER HE KILLED DR. KING, JAMES EARL RAY WAS CAUGHT IN LONDON, ENGLAND. HE HAD SLIPPED OUT OF THE U.S. AND WAS TRYING TO ESCAPE.
DR. KING DIDN'T LIVE TO BE FORTY, **DID** HE? HE WAS ONLY **39** YEARS OLD.

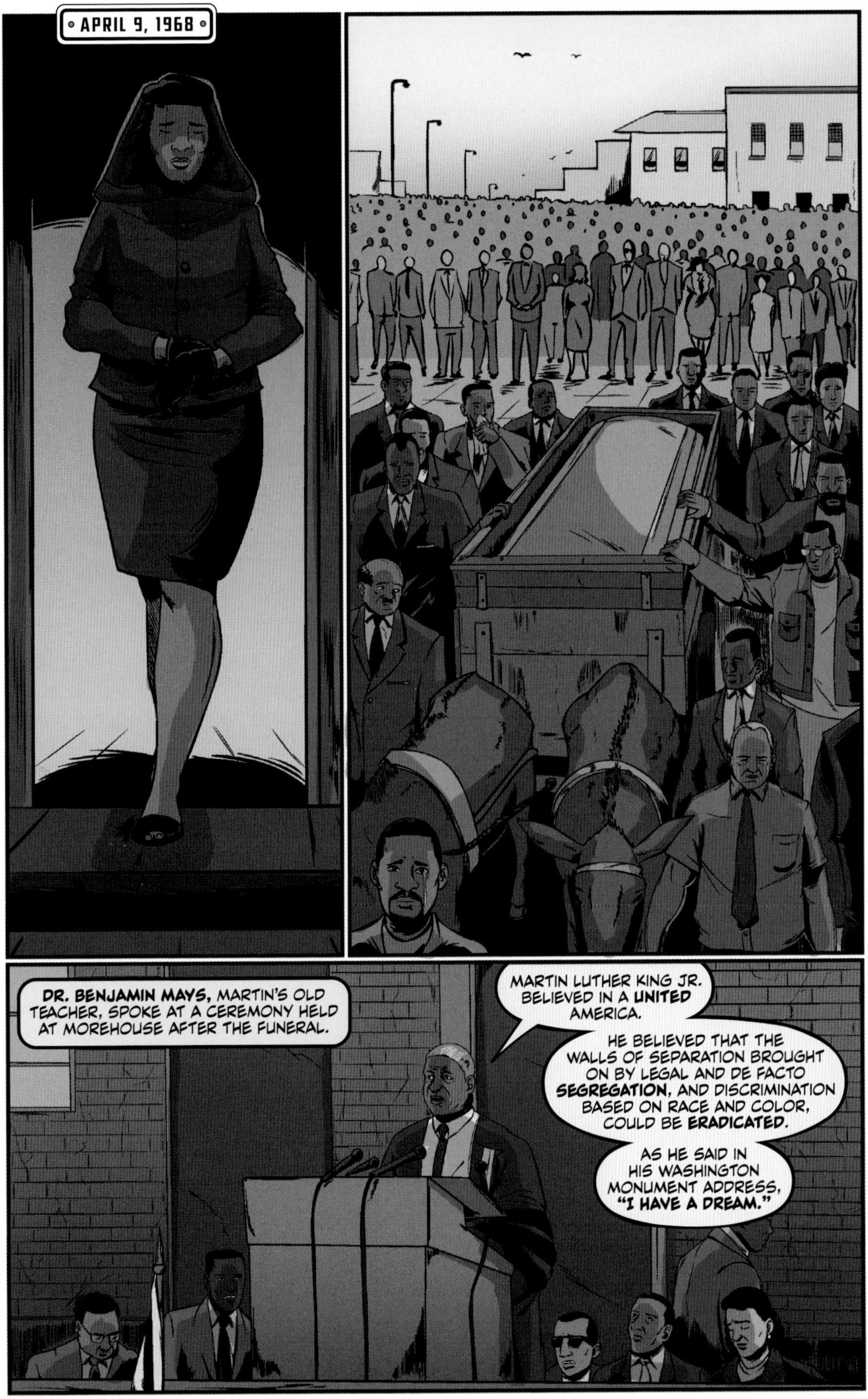
APRIL 9, 1968
DR. BENJAMIN MAYS, MARTIN'S OLD TEACHER, SPOKE AT A CEREMONY HELD AT MOREHOUSE AFTER THE FUNERAL.
MARTIN LUTHER KING JR. BELIEVED IN A UNITED AMERICA.
HE BELIEVED THAT THE WALLS OF SEPARATION BROUGHT ON BY LEGAL AND DE FACTO SEGREGATION, AND DISCRIMINATION BASED ON RACE AND COLOR, COULD BE ERADICATED.
AS HE SAID IN HIS WASHINGTON MONUMENT ADDRESS, "I HAVE A DREAM."

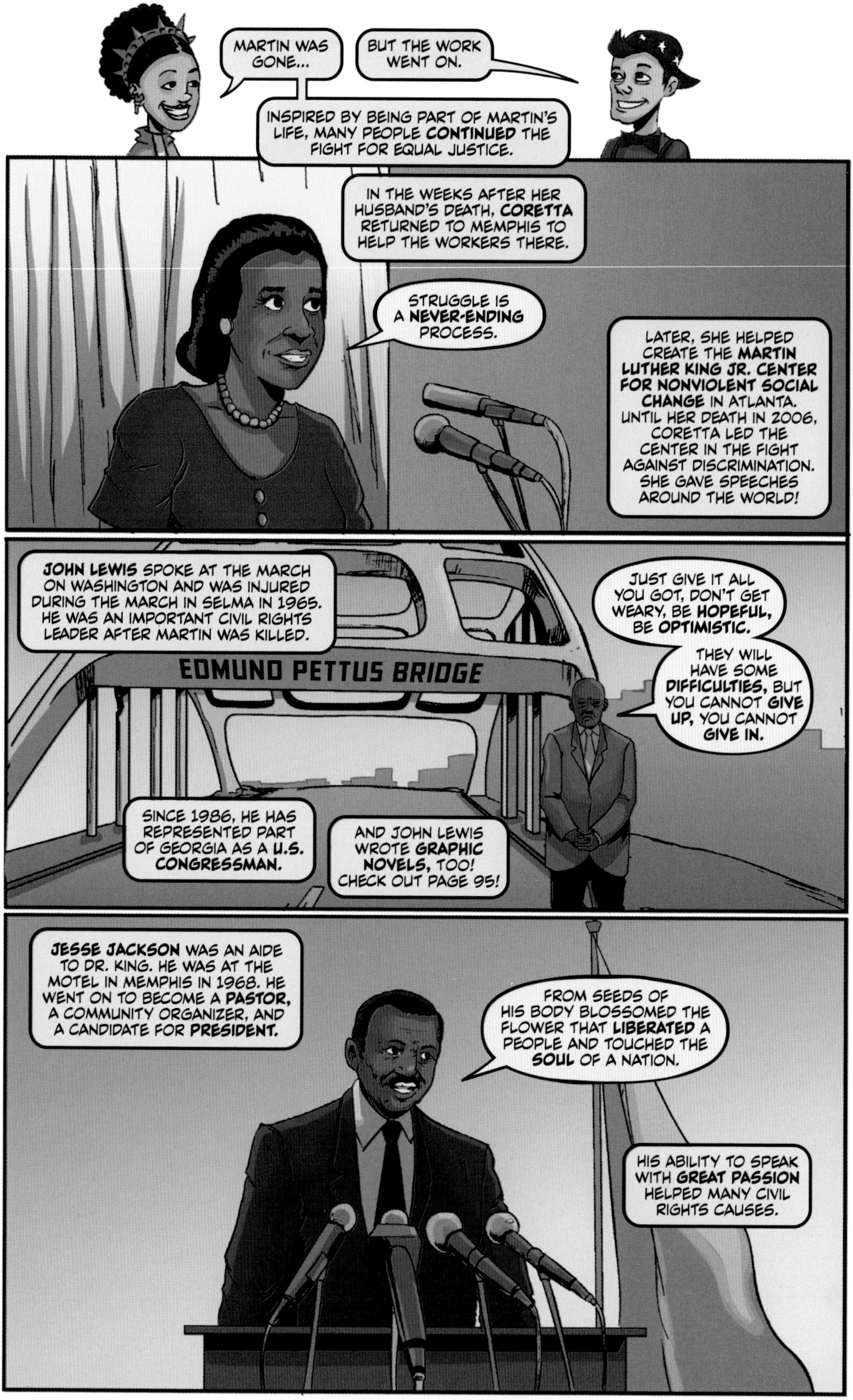

MARTIN WAS GONE...
BUT THE WORK WENT ON.
INSPIRED BY BEING PART OF MARTIN'S LIFE, MANY PEOPLE **CONTINUED** THE FIGHT FOR EQUAL JUSTICE.
IN THE WEEKS AFTER HER HUSBAND'S DEATH, **CORETTA** RETURNED TO MEMPHIS TO HELP THE WORKERS THERE.
STRUGGLE IS A **NEVER-ENDING** PROCESS.
LATER, SHE HELPED CREATE THE **MARTIN LUTHER KING JR. CENTER FOR NONVIOLENT SOCIAL CHANGE** IN ATLANTA. UNTIL HER DEATH IN 2006, CORETTA LED THE CENTER IN THE FIGHT AGAINST DISCRIMINATION. SHE GAVE SPEECHES AROUND THE WORLD!
JOHN LEWIS SPOKE AT THE MARCH ON WASHINGTON AND WAS INJURED DURING THE MARCH IN SELMA IN 1965. HE WAS AN IMPORTANT CIVIL RIGHTS LEADER AFTER MARTIN WAS KILLED.
EDMUND PETTUS BRIDGE
JUST GIVE IT ALL YOU GOT, DON'T GET WEARY, BE **HOPEFUL,** BE **OPTIMISTIC.**
THEY WILL HAVE SOME **DIFFICULTIES,** BUT YOU CANNOT **GIVE UP,** YOU CANNOT **GIVE IN.**
SINCE 1986, HE HAS REPRESENTED PART OF GEORGIA AS A **U.S. CONGRESSMAN.**
AND JOHN LEWIS WROTE **GRAPHIC NOVELS,** TOO! CHECK OUT PAGE 95!
JESSE JACKSON WAS AN AIDE TO DR. KING. HE WAS AT THE MOTEL IN MEMPHIS IN 1968. HE WENT ON TO BECOME A **PASTOR,** A COMMUNITY ORGANIZER, AND A CANDIDATE FOR **PRESIDENT.**
FROM SEEDS OF HIS BODY BLOSSOMED THE FLOWER THAT **LIBERATED** A PEOPLE AND TOUCHED THE **SOUL** OF A NATION.
HIS ABILITY TO SPEAK WITH **GREAT PASSION** HELPED MANY CIVIL RIGHTS CAUSES.

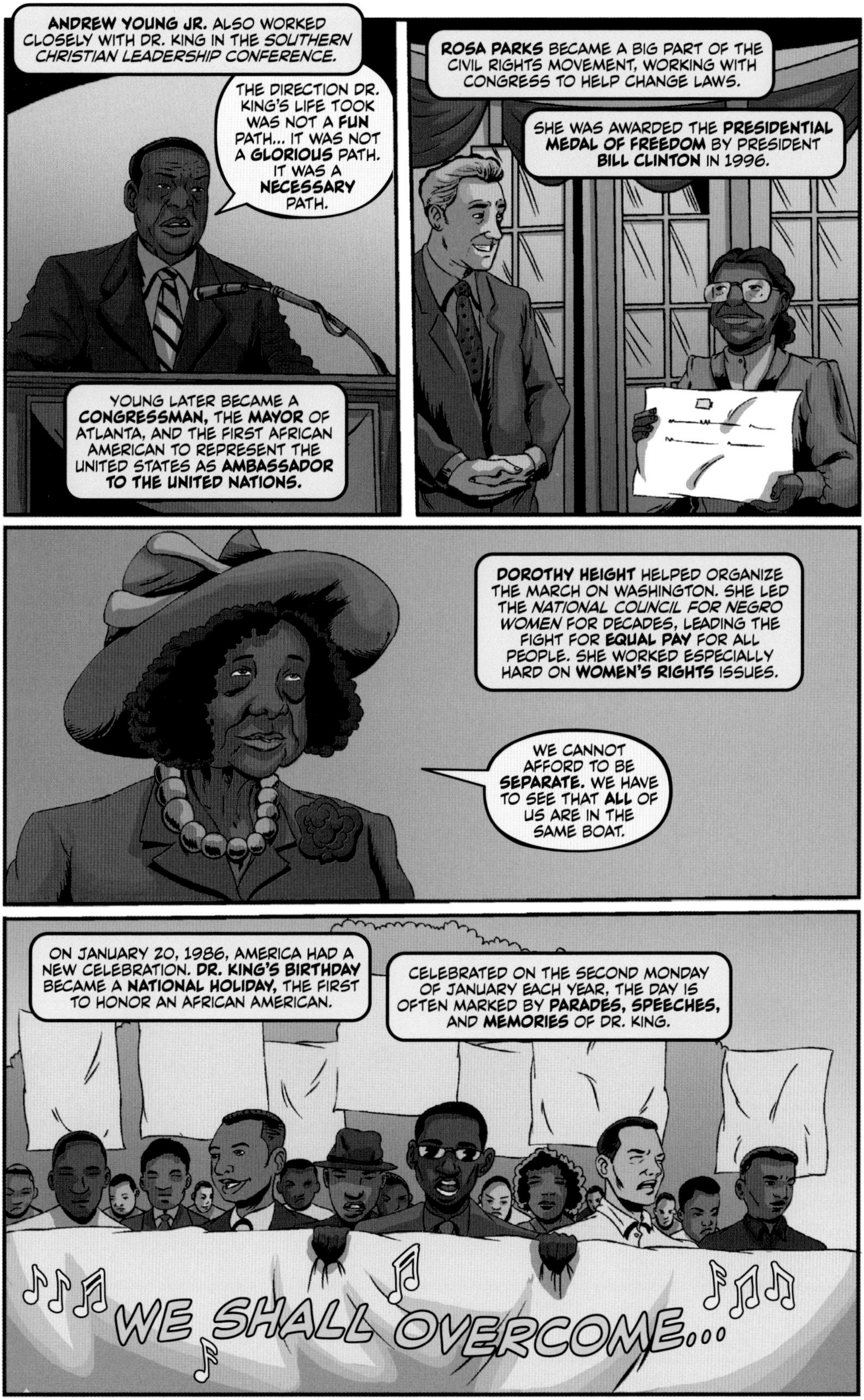

ANDREW YOUNG JR. ALSO WORKED CLOSELY WITH DR. KING IN THE SOUTHERN CHRISTIAN LEADERSHIP CONFERENCE.
THE DIRECTION DR. KING'S LIFE TOOK WAS NOT A FUN PATH... IT WAS NOT A GLORIOUS PATH. IT WAS A NECESSARY PATH.
YOUNG LATER BECAME A CONGRESSMAN, THE MAYOR OF ATLANTA, AND THE FIRST AFRICAN AMERICAN TO REPRESENT THE UNITED STATES AS AMBASSADOR TO THE UNITED NATIONS.
ROSA PARKS BECAME A BIG PART OF THE CIVIL RIGHTS MOVEMENT, WORKING WITH CONGRESS TO HELP CHANGE LAWS.
SHE WAS AWARDED THE PRESIDENTIAL MEDAL OF FREEDOM BY PRESIDENT BILL CLINTON IN 1996.
DOROTHY HEIGHT HELPED ORGANIZE THE MARCH ON WASHINGTON. SHE LED THE NATIONAL COUNCIL FOR NEGRO WOMEN FOR DECADES, LEADING THE FIGHT FOR EQUAL PAY FOR ALL PEOPLE. SHE WORKED ESPECIALLY HARD ON WOMEN'S RIGHTS ISSUES.
WE CANNOT AFFORD TO BE SEPARATE. WE HAVE TO SEE THAT ALL OF US ARE IN THE SAME BOAT.
ON JANUARY 20, 1986, AMERICA HAD A NEW CELEBRATION. DR. KING'S BIRTHDAY BECAME A NATIONAL HOLIDAY, THE FIRST TO HONOR AN AFRICAN AMERICAN.
CELEBRATED ON THE SECOND MONDAY OF JANUARY EACH YEAR, THE DAY IS OFTEN MARKED BY PARADES, SPEECHES, AND MEMORIES OF DR. KING.
WE SHALL OVERCOME...

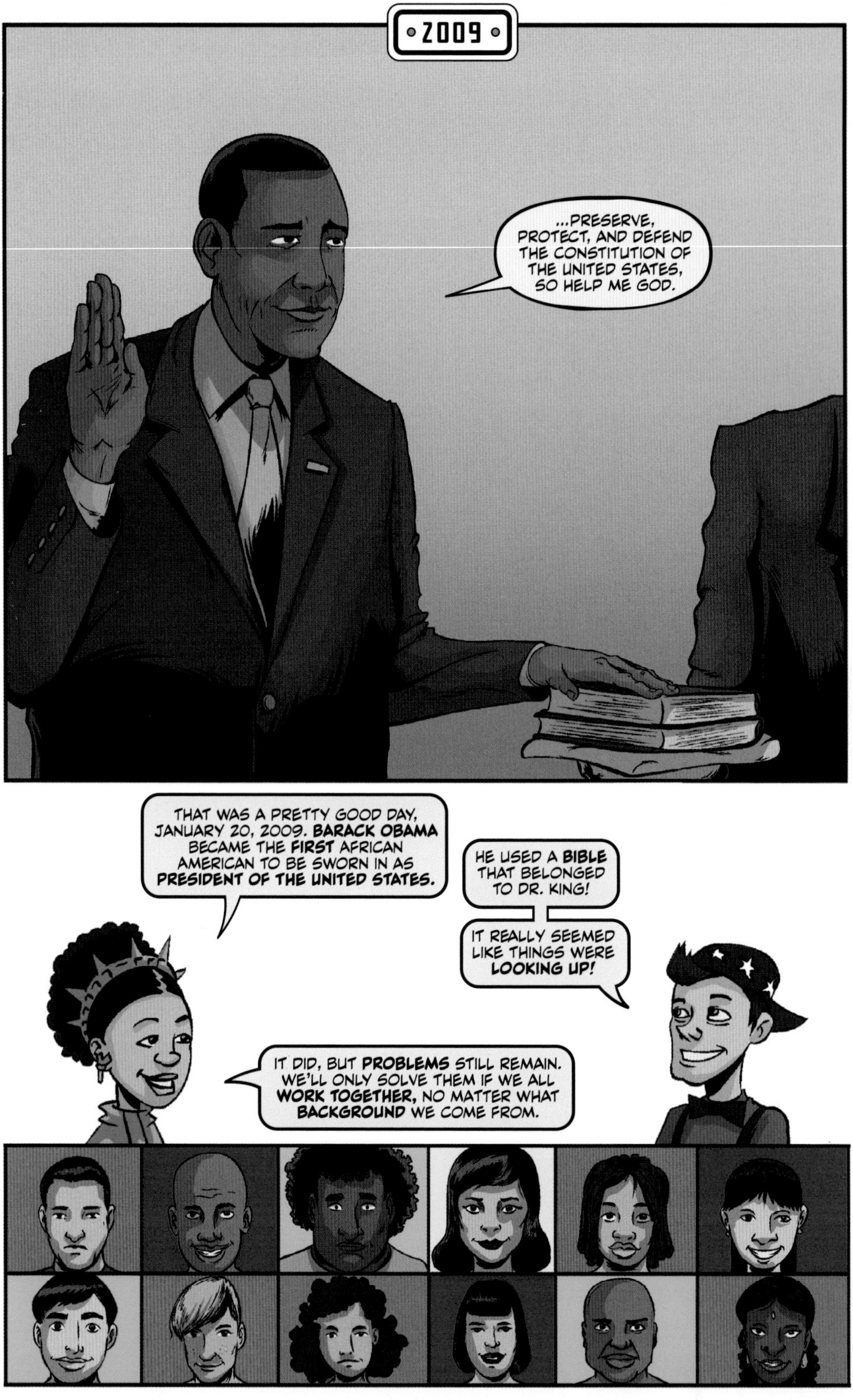
2009
...PRESERVE, PROTECT, AND DEFEND THE CONSTITUTION OF THE UNITED STATES, SO HELP ME GOD.
THAT WAS A PRETTY GOOD DAY, JANUARY 20, 2009. **BARACK OBAMA** BECAME THE **FIRST** AFRICAN AMERICAN TO BE SWORN IN AS **PRESIDENT OF THE UNITED STATES.**
HE USED A **BIBLE** THAT BELONGED TO DR. KING!
IT REALLY SEEMED LIKE THINGS WERE **LOOKING UP!**
IT DID, BUT **PROBLEMS** STILL REMAIN. WE'LL ONLY SOLVE THEM IF WE ALL **WORK TOGETHER,** NO MATTER WHAT **BACKGROUND** WE COME FROM.

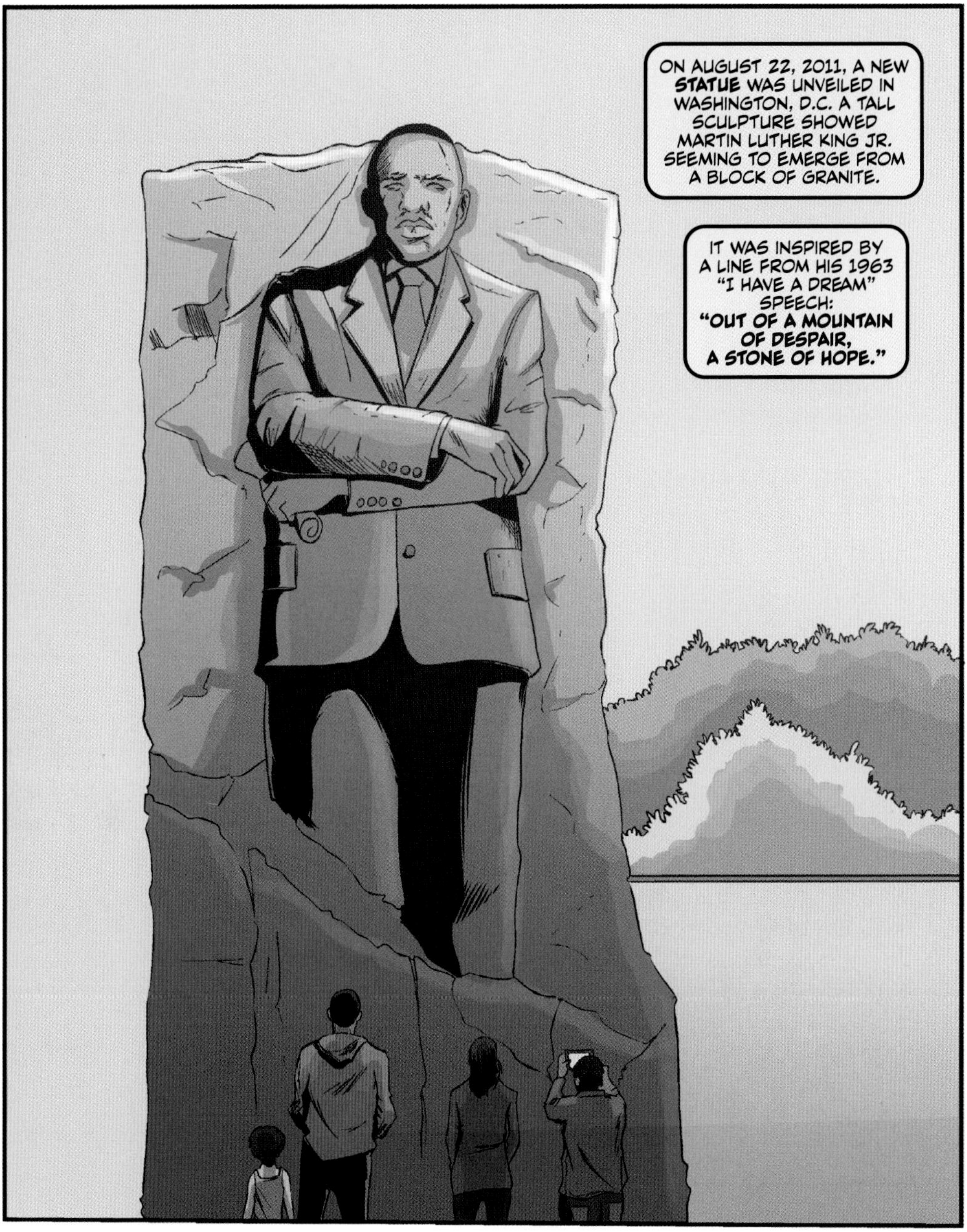
ON AUGUST 22, 2011, A NEW STATUE WAS UNVEILED IN WASHINGTON, D.C. A TALL SCULPTURE SHOWED MARTIN LUTHER KING JR. SEEMING TO EMERGE FROM A BLOCK OF GRANITE.
IT WAS INSPIRED BY A LINE FROM HIS 1963 "I HAVE A DREAM" SPEECH: "OUT OF A MOUNTAIN OF DESPAIR, A STONE OF HOPE."

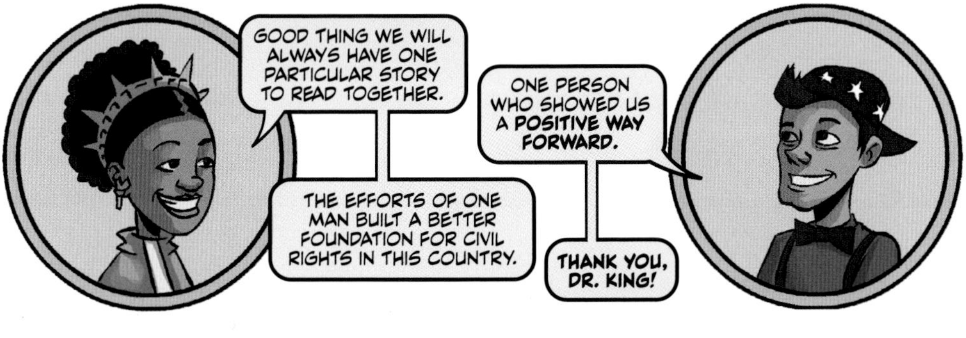
GOOD THING WE WILL ALWAYS HAVE ONE PARTICULAR STORY TO READ TOGETHER.
THE EFFORTS OF ONE MAN BUILT A BETTER FOUNDATION FOR CIVIL RIGHTS IN THIS COUNTRY.
ONE PERSON WHO SHOWED US A POSITIVE WAY FORWARD.
THANK YOU, DR. KING!

OTHER CIVIL RIGHTS HEROES

SUSAN B. ANTHONY (1820-1906): She was the leader of the women's suffrage movement that led to women obtaining the right to vote in 1920.

CESAR CHAVEZ (1927-1993): A union leader who exposed the problems of Mexican and Mexican American migrant farm workers to the eyes of the world.

DOROTHY HEIGHT (1912-2010): She ran the *National Council for Negro Women* for 40 years and was part of the 1960s civil rights movement leadership.

JOHN LEWIS (1940-): A hero of the Selma march, Rep. Lewis has represented Georgia in the House of Representatives since 1987.

ROY WILKINS (1901-1981): The longtime leader of the *NAACP*, who helped get important civil rights laws passed.

ANDREW YOUNG JR. (1932-): An aide to Dr. King, he was later a congressman, mayor of Atlanta, and U.S. ambassador to the United Nations.

WHITNEY YOUNG (1932-): Leader of the *National Urban League*, he also became an advisor to President Johnson.

THE WORK OF MARTIN LUTHER KING JR. CARRIED ON THROUGH THE COURAGE AND HARD WORK OF PEOPLE LIKE THESE... AND MANY MORE.

MARTIN LUTHER KING JR. TIMELINE

1929 Martin Luther King Jr. (birthname: Michael King Jr.) is born on January 15.

1948 Martin graduates from Morehouse College.

1953 Martin marries Coretta Scott.

1954 Martin becomes pastor at Dexter Avenue Baptist Church in Montgomery, Alabama.

1955 After earning a doctorate in theology from Boston University, Martin helps organize the Montgomery bus boycott later that year.

1957 After helping to form the *Southern Christian Leadership Conference,* Martin travels to Ghana.

1959 With Coretta, Martin travels to India.

1963 On April 13, Martin writes the famous "Letter From a Birmingham Jail" after his arrest at a protest. On August 28, he gives the "I Have a Dream" speech in Washington, D.C.

1964 On July 2, Martin attends a White House ceremony to witness the signing of Civil Rights Act of 1964. On December 10, he accepts the Nobel Peace Prize.

1965 Martin leads marches in Selma, Alabama.

1967 In a speech, he opposes the Vietnam War.

1968 While in Memphis to help striking workers, Martin is killed by assassin James Earl Ray.

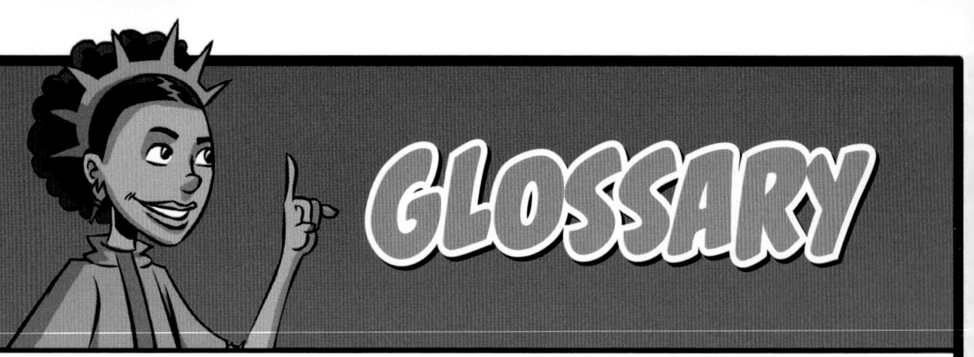

GLOSSARY

ADVOCATE: To urge positive change.

BENEDICTION: A prayer, a blessing.

BOYCOTT: When people refuse to do something or take part in something to protest injustice and promote change.

DEBATE: A formal discussion of opposing views in a public forum.

DISCRIMINATION: Laws and rules that favor one group of people over another.

GENTILE: A name for people who are not Jewish.

HAMLET: A very small town or settlement.

JIM CROW LAWS: The laws in Southern states that discriminated against African Americans.

OPPRESSION: The state of holding a people or a group down through force or laws.

PASTOR: A spiritual advisor or leader of a church.

PREJUDICE: Choosing to believe something without knowing all the facts.

SEGREGATION: Separating or isolating a race, class, or ethnic group.

SHAM: A fake, a pretender.

SIT-IN: An organized protest in which people simply refuse to move from their seats.

UNION: An organization of working people, usually with similar jobs.

VESTIGES: The last parts of something.

FIND OUT MORE

BOOKS

Bader, Boonie. *Who Was Martin Luther King, Jr.* New York: Penguin Books for Young Readers, 2008.

Calkhoven, Laurie. *DK Life Stories: Martin Luther King, Jr.* New York: DK Books, 2019.

Clayton, Ed. *Martin Luther King: The Peaceful Warrior.* Boston: Candlewick, 2017.

Duncan, Alice Faye. *Memphis, Martin, and the Mountaintop: The Sanitation Strike of 1968.* Honesdale, PA: Calkins Creek, 2018.

Jakoubek, Robert: *Martin Luther King Jr.: Civil Rights Leader (Black Americans of Achievement).* New York: Checkmark Books, 2005.

King, Martin Luther, Jr. *A Testament of Hope: The Essential Writings of Martin Luther King, Jr.* New York: HarperCollins, 1986.

Lewis, John and Andrew Aydin. *March: Book One (March Trilogy).* Marietta, GA: Top Shelf Productions, 2013.

Pastan, Amy. *Martin Luther King Jr. (DK Biography).* New York: DK Books, 2004.

Teitelbaum, Michael and Lewis Helfand. *Martin Luther King Jr.: Let Freedom Ring (Campfire Graphic Novels).* Delhi: Kalyani Navyug Media, 2012.

WEBSITES

Martin Luther King Jr. Papers Project, Stanford University.
https://kinginstitute.stanford.edu/king-kids

National Geographic for Kids: Martin Luther King, Jr.
https://kids.nationalgeographic.com/explore/history/martin-luther-king-jr/

Social Studies for Kids: Martin Luther King, Jr.
http://www.socialstudiesforkids.com/articles/ushistory/martinlutherking1.htm

VIDEO

Martin Luther King: Road to Memphis (American Experience Series). PBS, 2010.

SHOW ME HISTORY!

COLLECT EVERY BOOK IN THE SERIES AND FIND THE *STORY* IN HISTORY!

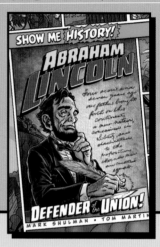

PARENTS AND TEACHERS: VISIT OUR WEBSITE FOR MORE *SHOW ME HISTORY!* FUN:

PORTABLEPRESS.COM

Enjoy a video about the series.

Learn more about the authors and illustrators.

Download a free preview of each book.

Sign up for our email newsletter.

Access our *Show Me History!* Reading Guide, perfect for teachers, librarians, homeschoolers, and parents.

FOLLOW US ON SOCIAL MEDIA:

 www.facebook.com/ portablepress

 www.pinterest.com/ portablepress

 @portablepress

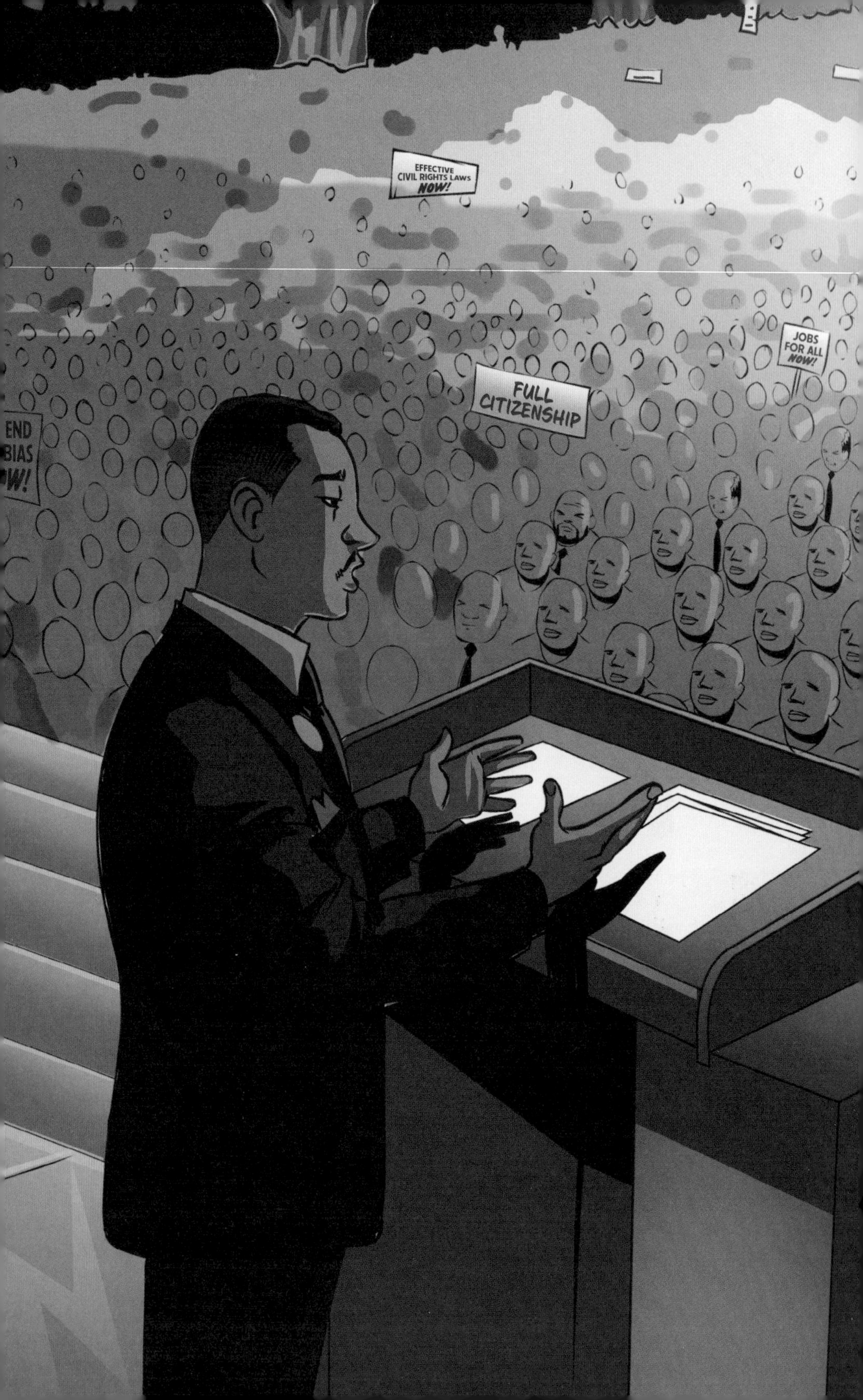
EFFECTIVE CIVIL RIGHTS LAWS NOW!
JOBS FOR ALL NOW!
FULL CITIZENSHIP
END BIAS